WOMEN'S WRITING

WOMEN'S WRITING

Text and Context

(Revised and Enlarged)

THIRD EDITION

Edited by
JASBIR JAIN

RAWAT PUBLICATIONS
Jaipur • New Delhi • Bangalore • Hyderabad • Guwahati • Ko'

ISBN 978-81-316-0636-0 (HB)
ISBN 978-81-316-0637-7 (PB)

First published, 1996
Second Edition, 1999
Third Edition, 2014

Published by
Prem Rawat for **Rawat Publications**
Satyam Apts, Sector 3, Jawahar Nagar, Jaipur 302 004 (India)
Phone: 0141 265 1748 / 7006 Fax: 0141 265 1748
E-mail: info@rawatbooks.com
Website: www.rawatbooks.com

New Delhi Office
4858/24, Ansari Road, Daryaganj, New Delhi 110 002
Phone: 011 2326 3290

Also at *Bangalore, Hyderabad, Guwahati* and *Kolkata*

Typeset by Rawat Computers, Jaipur
Printed at Nice Printing Press, New Delhi

For all of us in the department
and to our shared experience

Contents

9 The World of Cranford: A S

Preface

This volume brings together papers related to the history and development of feminist thought and interpretations and responses to individual texts, together they explore the "text"—the individual literary text, the socio-cultural text and the framed narrative—and the "context" of the socio-cultural text and the framed narrative—and the "context" of the socio-cultural situations, the historical phases and the dimensions of protest. The attempt has been to make a journey through the continuities and discontinuities, across cultural and generic boundaries.

In August 1995, we at the department of English, University of Rajasthan organised a four-day workshop on Women's Writing. Most of the papers included here are either presentations made at the workshop or are based on the presentations made. With the objective of reaching out to other perspectives and strengthening connections some papers were solicited and have been specially written for this volume. Professor Viney Kirpal, Dr. Vijayshree and Dr. Savita Goel have been good enough to find time for sharing their work with us. Dr. Sarla Palkar has contributed a paper on feminist theory which had earlier been published in *Critical Practice*. Amongst those papers which have been published elsewhere are Dr. Ranjana Harish's and Dr. Iqbal Kaur's papers on Kamala Das's *My Story* and Professor Jasbir Jain's "Questioning Purdah". Dr. Fatima Sugarwala and Dr. Surendran have contributed revised versions of the papers they presented at a seminar on "Contemporary British Writings" organised by the Department of English, Saurashtra University, Rajkot in March 1996.

We organised the workshop on women's writing with three main objectives: first, to share our reading and interpretations of women's writing and feminist aesthetics, second, to discuss at length the texts we have put together for a course at the post-graduate level, to contextualise their origins, influences and impacts and third, to generate our own material to support the course. The workshop was successful in achieving these objectives in fair measure. The measure of success was the enthusiasm that it generated and the work and reading which went into the workshop. For several months prior to the workshop there was an air of excitement, we had several interactive sessions and a spirit of camaraderie prevailed. Almost all of us contributed to the workshop—from the young research scholar to the seniormost professor. Several of our colleagues and scholars from other places supported their own participation. The funding was generated by the group. Books were borrowed and loaned and there was on open-mindedness about learning. When the workshop was in progress, the sessions were alive with interest, inquiry and curiosity, They were participative and stimulating.

This volume completes the third objective of the workshop by bringing together the papers which trace the history of the intellectual responses and bring it right to our times in the work of Sahgal, Dharker and Das, it brings us not only to our times but also our contemporariness from Rousseau's *Emile*, moving through the work of Mary Wollstonecraft, Mary Shelly, J.S. Mill, Virginia Woolf, and Simone de Beauvoir—writers whose work continues to surface in contemporary theoretical formulations—, it moves to the texts which reveal the wide range of women's writing from comedy to serious polemics, from confessional autobiography to generational conflicts, from power structures to colonized realities and personal struggles (like those of Aurora Leigh), the papers travel through a wide range of human experience.

A book of this nature owes debts which spread far and wide; it is collaborative in nature and hence demands a kind of effort which is different from the one claimed by single author works. A number of people through their advice, support, discussion, criticism, patience, and even silence have helped me along the way. I thank all of them. All those who have contributed to this volume have placed me in their debt. I am grateful to them for contributing to a common cause.

Jasbir Jain

Acknowledgements

The editor and the publishers gratefully acknowledge the permission given by the following for the articles specified—Mr. Singh for the use of part of Dr Iqbal Kaur's paper "Protest Against Sexual Colonialism: Margaret Atwood's *Surfacing* and Kamala Das's *My Story*" (*Gender and Literature* ed. Iqbal Kaur. Delhi: B.R. Cooperation, 1992); Dr. Sarla Palkar for "Feminist Literary Theory: Creating New Maps" (*Critical Practice* II. 1. January 1995, ed. A.K. Singh); Dr. Ranjana Harish for "*My Story*" (*Indian Women's Autobiographies*. New Delhi: Arnold Publishers, 1993); Dr. Veena Singh for "The World of *Cranford:* A Structural Approach", and Dr. Sarojini for "Better Deal for the Better Half", both papers first published in a special issue of *Rajasthan University Studies in English* on Victorian Literature: Professor Jasbir Jain for "Erasing the Margins: Questioning Purdah", (*Margins of Erasure*. New Delhi: Sterling, 1994).

Introduction

Eighteen years have passed since this work was first published in 1996. This is the third edition and as enough time has passed between the first and the third, it is legitimate to raise questions regarding its relevance and the legitimacy of a categorisation in literature based on gender. Has the scenario changed either in the literary canon or the world outside? What new developments have taken place in the intervening years? Has a new phase begun where writing by women is concerned?

The legitimacy for the term 'women's writing' exists in the fact of its different perspective both in creative and critical writing. Located in different social structures and familial roles, women have so far only marginally succeeded in altering or achieving freedom from these constraints. Women write differently, yet they too need to aspire to visibility and recognition in the literary and political world, and for their work to be read across gender divisions.

When we foreground writing, three things are of importance—first, their subject matter/theme—what are they writing about? Self, society, political reality, history or are they creating an imaginative world? Second, their perspective? Is it gender-based or does it locate itself in a wider economic world—as we see in Elizabeth Gaskell's *Crawford* and *Mary Barton*? This year Alice Munro has been awarded the Nobel Prize which should make us sit up and recognise the significance of what women say. The third aspect which adds further meaning to women's writing is the extent to which communication takes place between the writing and its readers. In this, part of the responsibility has been shifted to the reader, no matter of which sex. How do we approach it, read and interpret it and locate it?—all those issues are of importance. Keeping this in mind, we have an essay on new interpretative strategies based on an essay by Annette Kolodny, "Dancing Through the Minefield". As Elaine Showalter has observed in her essay "What do Feminist Literary Critics Want?" do we read Thomas Hardy's *Mayor of Casterbridge* from Henchard's point of view or from his wife Susan's point of view? Which perspective unravels the social structure in its reality? How do we read a text?

Incidentally, in order to understand a novel, a short story or any other genre of writing, even an autobiography, one needs to turn it round and round, follow the various clues dropped all over, and often go outside it and beyond it. Gaskell's *Mary Barton* deserves such a multifold reading. "Whose story is Mary Barton?" opens out the discourse in several directions placing women and women's writing in a larger socio-economic world of politics and power, of moral values and emotional conflicts, of sensitive mends at work as it comments on the shafts in urban settings. It is an irony of history that though Jane Austen's and the Bronte novels found an early entry into the literary canon, Gaskell attained recognition only by the mid-twentieth century.

Manjula Padmanabhan's play *Harvest* also moves beyond the woman character and works both with moral and immoral uses of technology and the ease with which the third world allows itself to be sucked in by capitalistic exploitation as well as the inhuman exploitation of a brutalised material organisation. Where is the human being? The play debates the idea of power as well as the idea of progress. Amidst this is the myopic vision of the victims who will themselves to be exploited. Urmil Talwar draws your attention to these aspects in her analysis of the play in the essay "Spare Parts in a Human Garage."

It is obvious that women's writing has mistakenly been confined to victimisation narratives. It reflects concern with almost everything that is of significance to human life. And this is not a new happening, earlier writers had also turned to politics, revolutions and morals. If we *read* them correctly, Jane Austen takes note of the presence of imperialism as well as of gender ghettoisation. Jane Austen's predecessors such as Fanny Burney, Mary Hay, Mary Wollstonecraft and Maria Edgeworth they comment an education and politics. In fact Wollstonecraft's *Vindication of the Rights of Woman* is a political and philosophical debate. The suffragette movement owes its origins to this. Wollstonecraft's stay in France during the revolution and her confrontation with political terror and the consequent instability made a substantial contribution to her writing.

If we choose to pause for a moment, we can trace the arguments for rights, freedom, visibility all along the history of the last two centuries. Of course, there are regressions when patriarchal morality has successfully used women writers such as Hannah Moore as its propagandist. Several Victorian writers, taken in by phrase 'angel in the house', equivalent to the 'Sita-Savitri' syndrome in our culture, have painted sentimental situations and created stereotypes as Mrs Henry Wood has done in *East Lynne*. Adultery condemns the woman to a life of slavery and guilt. But suppose we try and read the novel differently, can we rescue it from its sentimentality? This is a question worth pondering on.

Throughout the nineteenth century all over Europe and in the late nineteenth century in India as well, women authors and activists have moved ahead struggling for equality, freedom and greater political participation. Women's writing courses in universities contributed to the 'second wave' feminism begun in the postwar world. Betty Friedman's *The Feminine Mystique* (1961) was both a deconstruction of accepted role models and a statement of the resultant psychological conflicts in their lives, brought about by their passive acceptance of the roles thrust on them. Feminism closely related to women's wring, has fed and has been nourished by it. Identity for women has also included a gender-free social identity. Their notion of subjectivity has aspired to acquire an agency. Acquiring an 'agency' would signify the right to choose, to decide, to act and would include such simple things as wanting to play games, having access to higher education, choice in marriage and a political voice—in fact an abandonment of passive submission.

Each culture, because of its own traditional constructs has to find ways and means of addressing the problems related to gender. Some of this is reflected in this volume. Women's writing has served this purpose more than any other. Not only does it project the observations, situations, responses and struggles of half of humanity, it also reflects a consciousness constructed by gender, the *being* which is defined traditionally by frameworks of kinship, marriage and procreation. At another level it questions values and structures hitherto considered axiomatic. It focuses attention on the definition of freedom and creativity. Women's writing throws up all kinds of queries related to oppression and colonisation. It has helped to build and express the idea of a female "self", and dismantle the concept of the all-inclusive male "I".

Working through radical movements and silent changes, through legal and political battles and psychological barriers, women are learning to know and discover themselves. True, all women's writing is not feminist; equally true that even when gender identifications cross cultures, cultural constructs also help to differentiate feminist positions. Yet it needs to be recognised that feminist interpretations can emerge even through absence and negation, they do not necessarily have to be through identification and equation. Many women writers, for fear of being ghettoised and of being marginalised, are tentative about their feminist affiliations even today. For the feminist is not juxtaposed with the masculine, but with the universal and as such is treated as a sub-culture. It is pushed into the language and category of the victim and the oppressed; patriarchal viewpoints are not very generous in conceding it space or equality.

In India the disbelief and disdain towards feminist writing is rooted in the disapproval of the victim syndrome. Several critics and writers are dismissive of its aesthetics. Jaidev in a 1992 article "Problematizing Feminism" (*Gender and Literature* ed. Iqbal Kaur) advises feminist scholarship to stay within "the range of sanity and possibility" Dipankar Gupta in a equally myopic article "Feminification of Theory" (*EPW* March 25, 1995) laments the postmodern denigration of theory and the partisan encouragement it offers feminist scholarship. He is critical of its self-imposed boundaries. Feminist studies have, he is of the opinion, shut themselves in and have disrupted intersubjective communication and interpretation. They, he pronounces, "will typically ignore those areas where women interface with men" and are largely about "how women give life, about childbirth, about menstruation" (620). Criticism of this nature tends to ignore the gendered reality of human existence and the cultural constraints which focus on a woman's body. It does not realise the difficulty of growing out of subordinate structures and the 'male' habit of thought. Women have had to discard their passivity, rebel against their merger into a permanent 'other', and to realise the nature of desire.

Feminism begins with the self which may not necessarily be the intellectual self. Most cultures define women's roles through their bodily behaviour, menstruation and puberty, chastity and marriage, procreative ability and power. Most societies have fostered their own variety of conduct books. Majority of these have been written by men whether it be *Manu-Smriti* or *Perfecting Women,* or Rousseau's *Émile.*

Barbara Daly Metcalf in her introduction to the English translation of Maulana Ashraf Ali Thanawi's *Bihishti Zewar* (translated as *Perfecting Women,* OUP, 1992), writes that the book written in the early years of this century became a bestseller in its own time and became "a classic gift for Muslim brides" who entered their husband's home "with the Holy Qur'an in one hand and the *Bihishti Zewar* in the the other". These books, like J.S. Mill's *Liberty,* talked of equality but defined it on their own terms.

Women's writing is engaged in changing the terms of these definitions. With all its variety, timidity and marginality it has been moving through self-expression and self-questioning toward self-assertion and redefinitions. It has projected alternative structures and meanings, and transformed disorder and chaos into enabling structures. It has attempted to dissolve polarities and move towards pluralistic meanings. Amongst some of the questionings which have helped relocations of meaning are the works of Mary Wollstonecraft, Browning's *Aurora Leigh,* Virginia Woolf's *A Room of One's Own* and de Beauvoir's *The Second Sex.* (There are several others but these invariably resurface in some way or the other). In Indian writing the names which find an equal importance are Pundita Ramabai's *The High Caste Hindu Woman* (1888) which is engaged in a questioning of Manu's Laws, Tarabai Shinde's *Istri Purush Tulna* (1882) translated as *A Comparison Between Women and Men* (1994) which addresses itself to social prejudicies and inherent character values and *Simantni Updesh* (1882) which while attacking the practice of dowry and women's love for jewellery, aims at dismantling women's view of themselves as the "other".

The essays in the present volume set themselves the task of (a) textual analysis, (b) tracing the development of theoretical perspectives and (c) contextualising these in social and political change. In the selection of texts, poetry, drama, fiction and non-fiction including autobiography all find a place. Creative writing itself generates critical perspectives and critical writing acquires a creative fictional framework. Elizabeth Barrett Browning's *Aurora Leigh* belongs to the first category while Virginia Woolf's *A Room of One's Own* to the second. Mary Shelley's radical novel *Frankenstein* turns the concept of creativity inside out and works at several parallel levels.

Jain's "Reading Women's Writing" asserts the validity of women's writing as a category. Providing a historical perspective about its neglect and the bias against it, Jain goes on to develop the areas of difference. It is necessary to look at the history of education and the changing concepts of freedom. Rousseau's *Émile* was a major negative influence on the eighteenth century. There is an attempt to see in the women's movement a distancing from the French Revolution. No major radical movement ever takes care of subsidiary movements.

"Feminist Literary Theory: Creating New Maps" provides an overview of the beginnings of feminist literary theory. Sarla Palkar identifies three major texts which have provided a base to the American feminist theory. Katherine M. Rogers, Mary Ellman and Kate Millett's work adopted positions which helped overcome the early feminist indifference to literary theory and defined new directions of approach to patriarchal structures. Critiquing their work, Palkar goes on to examine the contribution of Elaine Showalter and her contemporaries, connects her work with that of Frantz Fanon (has been done by other critics like Susie Tharu and K. Lalita) and underlines the essential connections between the oppressed of any category. French Feminist theory is mainly represented by Julia Kristeva's questioning of Freudian concepts. A major contribution of Palkar's essay is the emphasis on the emergence of an Indian perspective through the work of Susie Tharu, K. Lalita and Rajeshwari Sunder Rajan.

Creativity and creation are regarded highly and viewed as god given gifts. Mary Shelley's gothic tale *Frankenstein* explores its multi-dimensional meanings. Preeti Kapoor in her essay contextualises it in the feminist context. Relating it to

Biblical origins, it critiques the male usurpation of the act and the destruction which is let loose because of this patchwork inhuman creation. Creativity arises out of a totality, a wholeness, here it is a put-together job. The monster's need for companionship, the human experience of loneliness, the ultimate sacrifice, the negative relationship between the creator and the created, the independence which the monster claims—all are acts which question the unleashed growth of science, *Frankenstein* is recognised as a classic statement at the heart of the controversy between nature and science. Kapoor draws attention to its feminist aspects.

Neelam Raisinghani in "The Rights of Women in the Nineteenth Century" focuses her attention on the legal provisions related to marriage, children and divorce. This is the period which forms the background to the work of the major writers of the nineteenth century. Raisinghani's discussion not only draws attention to the legal situation but also to the building of rebellion against its constrains and the gradual change as embodied in the Married Women's Property Act, 1870 and the provisions related to divorce. Power was concentrated in male hands. Krishna Rathore's "Inching Toward Freedom: Women in Victorian England" supplements Raisinghani's paper. It concentrates on the role of education, on conduct books, on the process of urbanisation dislocating and infringing upon women's freedom. The two together help raise social issues and link them with the concept of personal freedom.

J.S. Mill's *The Subjection of Women* is a classic which should not be ignored. The realisation on part of men that concentration of power is self-destructive is an important part of the women's movement. Sarojini works through the relationship of J.S. Mill and Harriet Taylor, connects the level of civilization with civil freedom and civil disabilities, draws attention to the need for enfranchisement, and the emerging attitude towards family as an institution of shared responsibility where the wife and children are not merely the property of men, but are co-sharers. This is the argument which runs counter to the dominant patriarchal ideology, and maintains that women are equals not inferior.

Elizabeth Barrett Browning's *Aurora Leigh,* a long narrative poem, has often been neglected specially in the Indian context. It awaits to be discovered by this generation. *Aurora Leigh* raises questions which are still valid for Charlotte Keatley's women characters, the conflict between personal aspirations and social compulsions, between individual freedom and the institution of marriage. Santosh Gupta focusing on Book II of the poem discusses its major conflicts, its narrative and dramatic qualities and its relevance for feminist theory.

One of the important texts considered in this collection is *Cranford*. It highlights three significant things (i) women can write comedy, and a comedy which is not bogged down by narrow concerns, there is a female comic tradition traceable from Burney, Jane Austen, Charlotte Bronte to Gaskell; (ii) comedy can be a means of subversion and criticism. Social and patriarchal structures, class-divisions, snobbery, fashion can all be criticised. Gaskell as a contemporary of Dickens does exactly what he does, but from a woman's point of view. (iii) The use of feminist space is important in this novel. Veena Singh's two articles on *Cranford* are a study of Gaskell's feminist thought. While one critiques family patterns, the other examines structure and narrative strategy.

Savita Goel and Surendran's essays on Virginia Woolf provide a comprehensive analysis of a *A Room of One's Own, Killing the Angel in the House* and *Three Guineas.* Goel concentrates on the *Room,* reflects upon the gender inequality and the exclusion of women from several spheres of life, contextualises it in critical theory and dwells upon its narrative framework. Surendran relates Woolf's work to the work of her contemporaries like Arnold Bennett and Samuel Butler and projects her concern with women outside the intellectual world. Together they bring out Woolf's sensitivity to the issues, her concern with the women's movement as well the limits she defined for herself. Woolf's arguments are a response to the unfavourable intellectual climate of her times.

The colonial connections begin to emerge in the consideration of *Wide Sargasso Sea,* Jean Rhys's mid-twentieth century novel. Veena Jain explores its historical perspectives, the colonial past of West Indies, projects it as a prologue to Bronte's *Jane Eyre* while C. Vijayshree looks at the narratorial voices. Vijayshree places it in the context of postcolonalism and feminist theory and with great sensitivity explores the subtextual aspects of the novel.

Santosh Gupta's "The Epistemology of Inequality: A Look at the Second Sex" and Madhuri Chatterjee's "Simone de Beauvoir's *Memoirs of A Dutiful Daughter*" provide complementary perspectives on Simone de Beauvoir. While Chatterjee examines the autobiographical dimensions, the parent-child relationship, the conflictual process of growing-up, Gupta concentrates on the epistemological framework and Beauvoir's questioning of the 'given'. It explores the philosophical dimensions of the construction of knowledge which is never and cannot ever be neutral. Gupta also proceeds to examine Beauvoir's handling of Freudian psychoanalysis.

Nayantara Sahgal's novel *Rich Like Us* has been taken as a representative postcolonial text. Viney Kirpal's incisive essay "*Rich Like Us:* Text, Context and Subtext", concerns itself with the relationship of gender and social reality, and with the novel as a feminist text. She provides a continued tradition of gender and social reality and foregrounds the work of male writers who have supported feminist causes. Kirpal locates Sahgal's work against this background. Kirpal traces the archetypal and mythical patterns which surface in *Rich Like Us* and explores the metaphor of birthing. Power structures are also the subject of study of Mini Nanda's article on "Power Structure in Nayantara Sahgal's *Rich Like Us*". Nanda focuses on spatial metaphors and perceptively analysis the paintings and physical symbols presented in the novel to build up her argument.

Sudha Rai's focus is on the political and the feminist discourse and Sahgal's contribution to the growth of the political novel in India. Rai places *Rich Like Us* in the context of her other works, foregrounds the postcolonial aspects and projects the feminist parallels. She relates this to the theoretical framework which surfaces in *Rich Like Us.*

"Mythologising History: Indo-British Experience" extends the study of myth and history to a comparative framework. Jasbir Jain looks at the two sides of the Indo-British encounter by juxtaposing Paul Scott's *The Jewel in the Crown* with Nayantara Sahgal's *Rich Like Us.* Tracing the parallels and the difference, Jain works out the postcoloniality of Scott's novel and centralises the double discourse of the rape metaphor which is part of the colonial discourse.

Working with theory, poetry and fiction, the move is to encompass the whole gamut of literary genres. Sarojini's essay "Autobiography: A Literary Genre" introduces autobiography as a genre and attempts to distinguish it from memories, diaries, journals and the like. Autobiography is a story of the self-in-making. Social contexts are secondary concerns, the primary focus is on the individual. The narrative strategies and the rhetoric devices which autobiography uses are often very close to fiction. Fact or fiction remains a central question in the next three papers which concern themselves with Kamala Das's controversial autobiography *My Story.* Das's recantation twenty years after its publication has added an additional aura of vagueness and uncertainty. Ranjana Harish treats it as an autobiography and reads it as an account of Kamala Das's conflict between the rôle of the "Angel in the House" and her own erotic sensibility. It is also representative of the gap between her romantic imagination and the crude, physical reality of a sexual encounter. Harish considers her poetic creativity a part of her creation of a woman's text, and her autobiography as a description of this journey.

Iqbal Kaur's "Protest Against Sexual Colonialism: Kamala Das's *My Story*" locates her defiance of conventional moral and social structures in her desire to deconstruct the ideal woman subordinated and created by male power structures. A woman's life is bound from all sides and parental and personal relationships are indissolubly linked together. The possibility of a new self lies in the process of decolonisation. Building on a similar argument Rama Rani Lall locates Kamala Das's "celebration of the self" within the framework of rebellion. The separation between the physical and the emotional is perceived as an act of mimicry of male attitudes—if men see woman as a body, women can hit back by treating it a body. The alternative present in society of a religious escape is also embraced by Kamala Das like Mira and Radha before her in Lall's article "Rebellion and Escape".

Cultural constructs are important where feminists positions are defined. As a prelude to Dharker's "Purdah" Jain in "Erasing the Margins: Questioning Purdah" delineates the details of the origins and practice of purdah and its psychological and social constraints. She points out that purdah as a demarcation between the two sexes is a strategy of exclusion and confinement and governs the assignment of duties and defines gender-roles. As it confines the woman, it privileges the man. It has social and ideological dimensions more than those of religion. It also governs attitudes to the female body. Jain also posits the idea that at times purdah cultures enable an observer's role which open cultures may not.

Both Ashok Tiwari and Rashmi Chaturvedi critique Dharker's purdah poems. While Chaturvedi adopts a Bakhtian stance and explores the interstitial space which women occupy and the way they use it to create a heterotopia, Tiwari in "Discreet Rebellion" emphasise the stylistic devices employed by Dharkar to project cultural frameworks and the individual's rebellion against them. He meticulously builds up the pattern as it moves from anonymity and loneliness to a sense of the self which stands outside it. Chaturvedi's essay opens out the gender roles and reaches out to the references to other cultures.

The next three papers in this collection are concerned with feminist drama. While Jasbir Jain's essay is about feminist drama and the politics of self, Tanuja Mathur proceeds to work in depth or Charlotte Keatley's play *My Mother Said I Never Should*. Mathur applies the various categories of space and works out the connections between the different generations. She also studies the repetitive pattern of the spatial metaphors to establish the feminist thrust of the play.

Fatima Sugarwala's study of *My Mother Said I Never Should* complements Tanuja Mathur's paper by focusing on the thematic aspects and the significance of the child-scenes. Sugarwala's interpretation draws upon the play's structure and very subtly links the child-scenes with the main play. She also build up an interesting interpretation of the mother-daughter relationship.

Subsequently to the above essays in the first edition, two more were added in the second edition. Supriya Agarwal wrote on Marianne Moore's poetry and N.K. Jain on perceptive analysis of *A Room of One's Own*. And for the present, the third edition, three more papers have been added, each catering to a different genre. Santosh Gupta's essay through her study of Kolodny's highlights the advantages of a feminist perspective as an interpretative strategy. A new approach unravels the hidden nuances and the underlying weanings of a text. We learn to read it differently. And Urmil Talwar's discussion of Manjula Padmanabhan's play, *Harvest* expands on the capitalistic exploitation of the human body. It also emphasises the point that women when they write, do not always write about women. They too live in a wider world.

It is pleasure to be able to mark the shifts in women's writing at the different stages of recognition and awareness. This collection of essays intended as an introduction to feminist studies for the initiate, does not limit itself to remaining an introduction. It goes beyond that to establish connections and interconnections and to indicate new directions of explorations. It also comes to grips with individual texts and cultural formations to enable cross-cultural approaches. One is surprised by the depth and scope of feminist thought and the issues it raised, and the multiple ways in which women's writing can be read.

1

Reading Women's Writing

Jasbir Jain

"Imaginatively she is of the highest importance; practically she is completely insignificant, she pervades poetry from cover to cover; she is all but absent from history"

(Woolf, *A Room of One's Own*)

I

I begin with this quotation from Virginia Woolf's *A Room of One's Own* for it expresses the ironical paradox of a woman's life. Men need her, love her, worship her and write about her but they do so in relation to their ownselves. The desires and aspects of a woman's life which do not relate to them ordinarily do not interest them. Women's writing struggling against internalization of role models thrust on women has learnt to express the untold narrative of being a woman. Women's writing is important, today more than ever before. Literature is a cultural construct and provides us with valuable insights into the development of societies, it helps psychological understanding, and reformulations of epistemological constructs. Literature in itself is a rich source material for interpreting the past. Women's writing focuses attention on both the manifestation of a female sensibility, a feminine reality, and on its significance as a means of bringing about an awareness of this reality. Gender, like other categories such as race and class, it has become abundantly clear, is a significant category of social and political reality.

Women's writing has been slow to come into its own for several reasons. There were not enough women writers and not enough access to education to make their writing possible; history has ignored and submerged their contribution, their work has been dismissed as concerned with a limited world of experience as they were confined to domestic life. Women's writing has also been dismissed as hardly of any consequence because religious and political thought had assigned them a place of subordination and labelled them as beings less rational and intellectual than the male of the species. George Eliot, herself a well-known writer, in an essay in 1856, "Silly Novels By Lady Novelists", found fault with their formula plot, unrealistic setting and their escape into a make-belief world. Labelling these novels as the "mind-and-millinery" species, she comments on their recipe for solving even the knottiest problems, "Take a woman's head, stuff it with a smattering of philosophy and literature chopped small, and with false notions of society baked hard, let it hang over a desk for a few hours every day, and serve it hot in feeble English, when not required" (Eliot 149). These writers, she observes, make little use of their education which remains an acquisition and does not get integrated into culture (155). Surprisingly, she admits, the degree of critical enthusiasm has no logical relation to the quality of the work. When women show talent, "critical enthusiasm drops to the freezing point" (161). Thus, apparently, popularity is related to the level of mediocrity. Two years earlier in 1854, in an essay "Woman in France: Madame de Sable", Eliot had made another observation which deserves to be remembered. Pointing out that the French women had contributed more to literature, she attributed this to three things—(a) the superiority of the Gallic race to the Teutonic race, (b) the institution of the salons where men and women mixed freely and (c) "laxity of opinion and practice with regard to the marriage-tie" (11). The third point should not be taken as a plea for lax morality, but is a statement which refers to the narrow and negative confines of Rousseau-like conservatism and isolation.[1]

Virginia Woolf similarly refers to Aphra Behn, a woman forced by circumstances to earn her own living and work "on equal terms with men". And "here begins the freedom of the mind, or rather the possibility that in course of time the mind will be free to write what it likes" (Woolf 61).

Freedom thus is perhaps the first requirement, for 'taboos' and inhibitions do not allow the pursuit of experience. And freedom means to breathe freely, to meet people, to have an openness of experience. But women have been kept in kitchens and parlours, in purdah and in luxury but deprived freedom. Virginia Woolf in her two lectures on "Women and Fiction" (1928) later developed into *A Room of One's Own* (1929) develops this at length. The narrative begins with the young woman being shooed off the lawn and being denied entrance to the library, both acts of exclusion. She is treated as a trespasser and must needs have a chaperon. Her freedom is curtailed and made dependent on other people.

Other causes which have kept women tied to their chains were the needs of society, child-marriages, child-bearing and child-rearing. It was not possible in one lifetime to bear thirteen children and still contribute to intellectual thought. Women's lives had been split into two—the physical and the intellectual—and the latter had been left underdeveloped by the artificial constructs of society. Romance thrived on this underdevelopment and romantic notions served to keep women happy, longing for their demon lover. Paradoxically, while on the one hand women have been placed outside culture, outside history, outside time on the other they have been treated as the custodians of culture, preserving it and continuing it through procreation, tradition, rituals and conservatism. Surprisingly their own relationships and values are referred to as a subculture even when families are extended, boundaries are crossed and kinship founded through them. Veena Das in *Critical Events* while referring to the partition of India and the political moral dilemma of whether or not to bring the abducted women back home comments that the female body in such cases becomes the site for mediating other social forces (Das 56)[2].

Receiving its impetus from the feminist movements, a process of self-discovery and of recovery of a female tradition has been set in motion. It is a journey of questioning of the form of epistemological formulations and of personal awareness. The process has also necessitated a reworking of strategies in order to break through power structures and to render status and relationships more equal for inequality had been created through exclusion. Denial of access to learning, to languages and to ideas was only one form of this exclusion. Most cultures kept women outside the universities and the Gurukuls, refused them access to learning and priestly tasks and made virtue dependent on female self-control. And for this female self-control it appeared necessary to keep them ignorant and cloistered.[3]

Women's education has been a subject of controversy and debate: should women have access to learning, if so what should be the role and nature of this learning? Rousseau in *Emile* while setting forth his ideas on education, outlined a different kind of education for women. He begins Book V by making a statement which is rendered irrelevant by the very next page, "But for her sex, a woman is a man. . . the difference is only in degree" (Rousseau 321). The difference is a difference of roles, for while "the man should be strong and active; the woman should be weak and passive; the one must have both the power and the will; it is enough that the other should offer little resistance" (322). Rousseau proceeds to set up a system of morality, virtue, marriage and kinship—even citizenship—resting on the docility, submission and fidelity of a woman. Woman, designed for the delight of man, is both his plaything and prisoner.

Of one of the earliest women to question attitudes of this kind, was Mary Astell who in 1696—more than half a century before the writing of *Emile*–had drawn attention to the need for an equal education and pointed out that the "incapacity, if there be any, is acquired not natural" (Jones 98). Other women writers also—both in their writing of conduct books and their critiquing of them—protested against the discrimination in educational practices. Mary Wollstonecraft in *Vindication of the Rights of Woman* (1792) was critical of Rousseau's theory of education and argued in favour of giving women the same kind of education which was being imparted to men.[4] Catherine Macaulay was another radical writer of the same period.[5] In fiction this continued to be reflected even in the mid-nineteenth century novel. It is not only the heroines of Fanny Burney's, Jane Austen's and Charlotte Bronte's novels who are ill-equipped to meet the challenges of the male world, but the heroines of George Eliot also stand outside this male preserve and while Maggie (*The Mill on the Floss*) indulges in shadow learning, Dorothea (*Middlemarch*) seeks intellectual satisfaction through a proxy.

Women's writing also questioned other patriarchal constructs like marriage and family. The development of the novel is in itself a testimony to this questioning. As the prose narrative moved from religious and political allegory to middle class bourgeois existence, it began to concern itself with issues of marriage and respectability. Defoe's *Moll Flanders* (1722) selects a petty thief for its protagonist primarily because morality is not an issue, but a few years later Richardson's choice of heroines in the mid-forties is guided by middle-class value structures. No longer is the subject of the novels love and romance; instead it is sex and respectability. Women are seen and presented from the male point of view and from the view of social morality. *Clarissa* raises a host of questions–the justification of parental control on the life of their children, Clarissa's freedom or lack of freedom to choose a husband, the mistaken premises of her trust (highlighting the inadequacy of her judgment), her vulnerability and seduction, and the resulting conflict which ends in her death.

Respectability was another constraint on women, for the rights and wrongs were decided by male consent. In Oliver

Goldsmith's *The Vicar of Wakefield* (1766) it is not the seduction which is of concern but whether the facade of respectability has been maintained or not. But *The Vicar of Wakefield*, as Vineta Colby observes is also the font of the novels of domestic realism, "The idyll is home-based and family-centered". Later generations of writers have grown up on it, "It is unlikely that a single major Victorian novelist did not know the book and probably, at least in his youth, love it" (Colby 8). This idyll was transformed in the hands of writers like Jane Austen, Maria Edgeworth and Charlotte Bronte, who wrote anti-romances, and in a manner, as Marilyn Butler remarks, they also wrote anti-novels.[6] The father-figure is marginalised in many of their novels. Both Mr. Bennet (*Pride and Prejudice*) and Mr. Woodhouse (*Emma*) are marginalised figures and Sir Thomas (*Mansfield Park*) though a strong, ruling patriarch finds his values being challenged by Fanny Price, even though ever so mildly. Charlotte Bronte's novels either do not have the father-figure, or they make fun of it, or they distant it. Even mothers are very often absent. Jane (*Jane Eyre*) is an orphan, as are Shirley (*Shirley*) and Lucy (*Villette*) like the heroines of Fanny Burney's novels. Thus through these projections parental control and family structures are questioned or abandoned. Marriage is also deromanticised, husbands and wives do not get along, are non-communicative or worlds apart. George Eliot goes a step further when she recognizes the nature of passion in *The Mill on The Floss*.

In recent years a great deal of research has been done on women's writing. Amongst some of the pioneers are Elizabeth Showalter, Sandra Gilbert and Susan Gubar, Patricia Meyer Spacks and Ellen Moers. A great deal of theoretical work has also been done. Janet Todd has written *Feminist Literary History*. Bibliographies have been compiled and texts which were not available have been reprinted. Mothers of The Novel series has brought out a large number of titles. Women's Presses have come into being and have provided space for women writers. All this literary and intellectual activity has generated a whole lot of new perspectives. What has happened in the last three decades has not been an isolated development: it is the result of the efforts of hundreds of women across cultures and languages who have resisted domination. The accessibility to education, the right to economic earning and right to property, right to vote, which have been won slowly and gradually, are the result of a socio-political struggles. Women asked for male positions in order to step outside their confines and accepted the challenges of performing jobs associated with male competence in order to claim equality. It is only later that the specificity of being women and yet being worthy of equality has become an issue.[7] Gender differences are acknowledged but they do not make women inferior in any way. It is this which has led to an introspective analysis of the female self and the right to pride and dignity within it. To achieve this the barriers of thought created by scientists like Darwin and psychologists like Freud have had to be overcome. For them woman was an incomplete man, and the female body a mutilated one. It is only when this has been transcended that a 'self' can come into being.[8]

II

Women's writing cannot be treated as a monolithic structure and all women's writing is not necessarily feminist. But women when they write "think back through their mothers" (Woolf 93) and their writing has its own characteristics and qualities. George Eliot in her essay "Woman in France: Madame de Sable" (1854) observed:

> We think it an immense mistake to maintain there is no sex in literature. Science has no sex: the mere knowing and reasoning faculties, if they act correctly, must go through the same process, and arrive at the same result. But in art and literature, which imply the action of the entire being, in which every fiber of the nature is engaged, in which every peculiar modification of the individual makes itself felt, woman has something specific to contribute (8).

More than seven decades later, Virginia Woolf in *A Room of One's Own* sketches "a plan of the soul" where "in each of us two powers preside, one male, one female; and in the man's brain the man predominates over the woman, and in the woman's brain the woman predominates over the man" (Woolf 93-94). She goes on to state that "if this theory of the two sides of the mind holds good, . . .men . . . are now writing only with the male side of their brains" (96). Virginia Woolf explores the emotional attitudes which may be one of equanimity or anger. Charlotte Bronte wrote in rage while Jane Austen did not. The writer's attitude affects narrative strategies and/or linguistic and stylistic aspects. Women's writing had been called flowery and, in contrast, Jane Austen turned to short, terse sentences (77) whereas Bronte wrote in discontinuities and jerks (66-67) and her work has an undercurrent of disagreement with the prevailing code of values - but an undercurrent which is imperfectly expressed (71). Women, in their writing, were learning to handle language which had developed through masculine constructs. The sentence prevalent at the beginning of the nineteenth century was "a man's sentence" (73) and women writers stumbled against it. Further the form of the book also "has somehow to be adapted to the body" (74). Women's writing is different in more than one way. Woolf goes on to observe "It would be a thousand pities if women wrote like men, or lived like men". Yet the ideal for Woolf is androgynous writing!

At another level women's writing is the literature of silence. Its meaning lies enclosed and camouflaged. It is also the literature of silence for it seeks to express that which has been submerged and suppressed. Writing in itself, has always been an act of courage. And women have often resorted to different strategies to say what they wished to get across. In many of the women's novels, walking is used as a narrative strategy, illness becomes another, and dreams and hallucinations reveal hidden desires. The role of the listener is heightened. Many of these novels fall into the category of the *bildungsroman*. Elizabeth Abel in *The Voyage In: Novels of Female Development* (1983) and Rita Felski in *Beyond Feminist Aesthetics* (1989) have explored the development of the genre at length. Felski observes that the heroine of the female *bildungsroman* is not necessarily the young adolescent but very often the woman who has experienced sexual relationships, marriage and even motherhood (Felski 136-138).

The work of women writers reflects an engagement with social and political issues, with theoretical perspectives and moves outside cultural and disciplinary boundaries. The act of writing has enabled them to move outside the narrow role of man's helpmeet, outside the role of the seductress, the angel or the witch. It helps problematize the areas of conflict and facilitates a search for alternative models. Women as they deconstruct literary forms and politico-social constructs continue to struggle with the ghosts of their fathers and the inheritance of their mothers. And they invite the reader to do the same.

Notes

1. Mary Wollstonecraft was also critical of Rousseau's theory of education and of the discriminatory attitude which was aimed at subjugating women to male desire. Arguing against Rousseau's view of educating women through fear and through isolation, she points out the need both for bodily exercise and intellectual freedom if human virtue was to survive. Wollstonecraft writes, "I, therefore, will venture to assert that till women are more rationally educated, the progress of human virtue and improvement in knowledge must receive continual checks" (*Vindication* 45).

   Rousseau's theory influenced several 18th century thinkers. A friend of Maria Edgeworth's father, Thomas Day, actually tried the experiment of bringing up two orphan girls and educating them with a view to choosing a wife from one of them. But while he was waiting for them to grow up, he fell in love with two other women, both of whom rejected him. Recording this in his *Memoirs* (*Memoirs of Richard Lovell Edgeworth* (1820) Shannon: Irish University Press, I 214,340), Edgeworth observed that he would never behave in such a manner and the whole idea was absurd. Rousseau's theory sought to emphasize the role which men played as bestowers of female identity. Maria Edgeworth fictionalized Day's experiment in her novel *Belinda* and highlighted its limitations.

2. Veena Das writes, "... the political programme of creating the two nations of India and Pakistan was inscribed upon the bodies of women. The sexual and reproductive violence to which they were subjected cannot be understood as belonging only to the discourse of family; it has to be understood as doubly articulated in the domains of kinship and politics" (56).
3. There are parallel or somewhat similar situations in almost all cultures but for the purpose of continuity the examples are primarily from the social conditions prevalent in England and reflected in the literature of England. Taboos regarding menstruation and religious ceremonies exist in the early phases of most cultures.
4. Mary Wollstonecraft's concern with education was an on-going one. Earlier in 1787 she had written, *Thoughts on the Education of Daughters* which was also concerned with the same subject.
5. Catherine Macaulay in *Letters on Education* (1790), had pleaded for an opening out of the educational curriculum so that both men and women could enjoy its benefits: "Be no longer niggards then, O ye parents, in bestowing on your offspring, every blessing which nature and fortune renders them capable of enjoying! Confine not the education of your daughters to what is regarded as the ornamental part of it, nor deny the graces to your son" (Jones 113-114). Also see 192-243 for reference to other eighteenth century female protests against male hegemony.
6. A constant effort was made to show that life was different from literature and had to be faced with feet firmly on the ground and not with the head up in the clouds. Many of these novels were courtship novels and tried to educate girls how to choose their future husbands wisely. Many of the heroines reject offers of marriage unless they are able to get these offers on their own terms. Thus marriage is not seen as the main purpose of a woman's life.
7. See Hester Eisenstein and Alice Jardine ed. *The Future of Difference* (1985).
8. The parallels between oppressed categories have been worked out at several levels. Marxist criticism has similarities with feminist

criticism. Discrimination whether based on gender, class or caste leads to similar problems.

References

Abel, Elizabeth, Hirsch, Marianne and Langland, Elizabeth. *The Voyage In: The Novel of Female Development*, University Press of New England. 1983.

Colby, Vineta. *Yesterday's Woman: Domestic Realism in the English Novel*, Princeton: Princeton University Press. 1974.

Das, Veena. *Critical Events: An Anthropological Perspective on Contemporary India*, Delhi: Oxford University Press. 1995.

Eliot, George. *Selected Essays, Poems and Other Writings*, ed. A.S. Byatt and Nicholas Warran. London: Penguin Books, 1990.

Felski, Rita. *Beyond Feminist Aesthetics*, Harvard University Press, 1989.

Rousseau, Jean Jacques. *Emile* (1762), trans Barbara Foxley, Introduction by P.D. Jimack (1974). London: Everyman (1911) 1986.

Wollstonecraft, Mary. *A Vindication of the Rights of Woman*, in *A Vindication of the Rights of Woman and The Subjection of Women* by Mary Wollstonecraft and John Stuart Mill. London: J.M. Dent and Co. (1929) 1989.

2

Feminist Literary Theory: Creating New Maps

Sarla Palkar

Feminist theory, as Rajeswari Sunder Rajan reminds us, is by no means a single or homogeneous body of speculation and argument (103). If one discerns a common strand in the great diversity of the feminist scholarship it is its critique of the patriarchal modes of thinking and its political approach to literature and literary criticism. Feminist literary theory has evolved according to the needs and demands of the international women's movement. This women's liberation movement was initiated in the 1960s by women who were politically committed—women who were active participants in the civil rights movements or in the protest actions against the war in Vietnam or those who belonged to the various progressive or Marxist groups. It was their bitter experience of the blatantly sexist attitudes that were evinced by their male associates in these politically progressive movements that finally led women to form their own groups and associations. For instance, in America Betty Friedan, the author of *The Feminine Mystique*, founded National Organization of Women popularly known as NOW, so that women could voice their grievances and fight for their own rights. By the late 60s and 70s feminism had emerged as an important political force in the Western world.

As the early feminists were mainly concerned with social and political change, little attention was paid to literature and literary criticism at the initial stage of the women's movement. But soon enough their political action was extended to the cultural field as it is here that gender differences are created and naturalized. The feminists who worked in academic institutions became convinced that literature and literary criticism were powerful cultural weapons in the hands of male hegemony to perpetuate its sexual politics in the name of universality, objectivity and neutrality. Opposed to these claims made by the humanist discourse is the central tenet of feminist criticism that no account, whether creative, critical or theoretical, can be neutral. A work of literature invariably reflects the personal or cultural bias of its author. The first task before the feminists, therefore, was to lay bare the patriarchal practices in literary discourse as they had done it in other walks of life. That is why, as Elaine Showalter observes, "In its earliest years, feminist criticism concentrated on exposing the misogyny of literary practice: the stereotyped images of women in literature as angels or monsters, the literary abuse or textual harassments of women in classic and popular male literature and the exclusion of women from literary history' (*The New Feminist Criticism* 5). Three crucial and influential works deserve special mention in this respect; (1) Katharine M. Roger's *The Troublesome Helpmate* (1966), (2) Mary Ellmann's *Thinking About Women* (1968), and (3) Kate Millett's *Sexual Politics* (1969). These texts form the solid basis for the later developments in Anglo-American Feminist Criticism.

Katharine M. Rogers's book is a study of sexism in literature. In her work on male misogyny, Rogers claims that patriarchal feeling or the desire to keep women subject to men is the "most important cause of misogyny, because the most widely and firmly entrenched in society" (Rogers 272). Mary Ellmann's brilliant, witty work has a direct appeal for feminists with literary interests as she is interested in the phenomenon of "women as words" (Ellmann xv). The main thesis of *Thinking About Women* is that the Western culture at all levels is permeated by a phenomenon that Ellmann labels as "thought by sexual analogy" (Ellmann 6). Ellmann, in the words of Toril Moi, "manages to demonstrate first that the very concepts of masculinity and femininity are social constructs which refer to no real essence in the world, and second that the feminine stereotypes she describes invariably deconstruct themselves" (Moi 36).

Though these two books are excellent examples of feminist criticism, they do not enjoy the immense popularity and explosive effect of Kate Millett's *Sexual Politics*. Kate Millett defines sexual politics as the process whereby the ruling sex seeks to maintain and extend its power over the subordinate sex. In the first place, she emphasizes the need to study social and cultural contexts if a work of art is to be properly understood. In this respect she is as opposed to the ahistoricism of the New Critical canon as are the rest of the feminists. Together they all refuse to look upon a literary text as a "verbal icon", divorced from or independent of social and historical reality. Millett, through her analysis of the novels of male writers like Norman Mailer and Henry Miller, exposes their patriarchal bias and their sexual/textual harassment of women. She considers their work as part of their sexual politics. She also challenges the author's authority and insists on the reader's right to express her own viewpoint. This view is in direct opposition to the concepts pronounced by New Criticism. As Toril Moi observes, "Her approach destroys the prevailing image of the reader/critic as passive/feminine recipient of authoritarian discourse, and as a such is exactly suited to feminism's political purposes" (Moi 25). This method has come to be known as "reading against the grain", which the feminist critics have used to great profit in their critique of the patriarchal discourse and ideology.

It is easy at this juncture of the feminist scholarship to see the gaps and weaknesses in Millett's writings and this is what feminists like Toril Moi have done. For example, it is pointed out that

Millett pays no attention to literary strategies and formal structures. Also, she does not acknowledge her female precursors, particularly Simone de Beauvoir, who had already written about women's existential otherness in *The Second Sex*. Another flaw in Millett's work is that she looks upon patriarchy as something monolithic and conscious and therefore does not recognize the fact that patriarchy may be fraught with contradictions and inconsistencies and very often patriarchal attitudes, including misogyny, are unconscious and are also shared by women. Another troubling aspect of Millett's thesis is her fierce critique of Sigmund Freud as a great supporter and perpetuator of patriarchal conspiracy against women. But here, as Catharine R. Stimpson points out, Millett does reflect an ambivalence about psychoanalysis that haunts feminist criticism (Stimpson 265). Feminists like Luce Irigaray, the French feminist, have carried out a critique of the patriarchal figures in psychoanalysis, especially Freud and Lacan, for their gender bias and still there is a fruitful collaboration between feminist theory and psychoanalysis as there is between feminism and Marxism, in spite of the feminists' critique of Marx and Marxist theory.

Kate Millett's and Mary Ellmann's books provide the inspiration for what is now known as the "Images of Women" approach to literature. This variety of feminist criticism flourished in the United States in the early 70s, the best example of which is a collected volume of essays published under the title *Images of Women in Fiction: Feminist Perspectives*. This approach relies on woman as reader and her experience as reader. Her experience of literature is supposed to tally with her experience of real life. It is thus frankly empirical and mimetic and expects literature to mirror "real" life. It therefore lacks the post-structuralist insight that "real" is something that we construct and that these constructed images and models of women (or men) often control and restrict their real lives. Recent feminist scholarship is alert to the manner in which women's subjectivities are formed by the cultural mores and values. As Rajeswari Sunder Rajan observes,

> The construction of women in terms of recognizable roles, images,

> models, and labels occurs in discourse in response to specific social imperatives even where it may be offered in terms of the universal and abstract rhetoric of "Woman" or "Women" (or the "Indian woman" as the case may be)... If we acknowledge (a) that femaleness is constructed, (b) that the terms of such construction are to be sought in the dominant modes of ideology (patriarchy, colonialism, capitalism), and (c) that therefore what is at stake is the investments of desire and the politics of control that representation both signifies and serves, then the task of the feminist critic becomes what Jacqueline Rose describes as "the critique of male discourse" born of "a radical distrust of representation which allies itself with a semiotic critique of the sign". What is required here is an alertness to the political process by which such representation becomes naturalized and ultimately coercive in structuring women's self-representation.
>
> (*Real and Imagined Women* 129)

If writers like Kate Millett or Mary Ellmann have been busy with "the critique of male discourse" or representations of women by men, the other feminist critics like Elaine Showalter or Sandra Gilbert and Susan Gubar have been pre-occupied with "women's self-representation". If the former deals with woman as reader, the latter focuses its attention on the subject of woman as writer. In the late 1970s three major studies on women writers were published which tried to reconstruct a female literary tradition in British and American literature and history: Ellen Moers's *Literary Women* (1976), Elaine Showalter's *A Literature of Their Own* (1977), and Sandra Gilbert and Susan Gubar's *The Madwoman in the Attic* (1979). These books were enthusiastically welcomed, as they were the long-awaited major studies on women writers. They now have become the modern classics of feminist approach to literature.

Elaine Showalter in *A Literature of Their Own* traces a female literary tradition in the English novel from the Brontes to the present day and demonstrates that the development of this tradition is similar to the development of any literary subculture. She discovers three major phases of historical development which she claims to be common to all literary movements,

> First, there is a prolonged phase of imitation of the prevailing modes of the dominant tradition, and internalization of its standards of art and its views on social roles. Second, there is a phase of protest against these standards and values, including a demand for autonomy. Finally, there is a phase of self-discovery, a turning inward freed from some of the dependency of opposition, a search for identity. An appropriate terminology for women writers is to call these stages, feminine, feminist and female.
>
> (*A Literature of Their Own* 13)

The British female tradition is accordingly divided rather neatly into three phases: The Feminine phase from 1840 to 1880, (2) the Feminist phase from 1880 to 1920 and, (3) the Female phase from 1920 to the present day.

Showalter's study is remarkable for its scholarship and the high regard and love that it shows for its subject. Its real value lies in its rediscovery of lesser known women authors and their work. Because of the efforts of critics like Showalter many unknown and forgotten novelists are now beginning to come into the limelight. However, Indian feminist critics Susie Tharu and K. Lalita have criticized Showalter for not mentioning her debt to Frantz Fanon. They observe:

> Showalter's own political biases probably make it difficult for her to acknowledge the theorist and revolutionary Frantz Fanon as the best-known source for this thesis about emerging subcultures. What is also obscured as a result is her transformation of Fanon's theory, domesticating an idea of revolutionary action to a liberal-conservative one of self-discovery and individual fulfillment as the goal of literary endeavor.
>
> (*Women Writing in India 18*)

Showalter has also been criticized for her unstated subscription to empiricism and bourgeois humanism by some of the radical feminists in the West. They find this allegiance of hers at odds with her feminist ideology.

Another text which enjoys a privileged status in feminist circles along with *A Literature of Their Own* is *The Madwoman in the Attic* written by Sandra M. Gilbert and Susan Gubar. *The Madwoman in the Attic*, on the one hand, aims to describe the "distinctively female literary tradition" (Gilbert and Gubar xi) of the nineteenth century and, on the other, to propound a complex theory of women's creativity. The authors' argument runs somewhat like this: Since creativity is defined as male in the patriarchal culture, the woman writer of the nineteenth century suffers from an intense anxiety of authorship. She possesses a distinctive female power or voice, but she can give expression to it only in a roundabout or indirect manner. This is the reason why she creates the female stereotypes of angel and monster as male writers have done, but in creating these she subverts and revises them. The novelist's anger and anxiety against patriarchal prohibitions take the form of the female monster of, as in *Jane Eyre*, the madwoman in the attic, who actually is the dark double or the repressed self of the woman writer, and who, like her author, has a story to tell which patriarchy tries to suppress.

As Susie Tharu and K. Lalita have noted, the theoretical perspective is really the weakest and most whimsical part of this energetic book (21). The problem in Gilbert and Gubar's approach is that, like Kate Millett before them, they identify the author with the character. They insist that the monster or the madwoman is the novelist's double, "an image of her own anxiety and rage" (Gilbert and Gubar 78). They thus transform all the texts written by the nineteenth century novelists into feminist texts whereas not every book written by a woman writer is necessarily a feminist text; in fact, very few are. Gilbert and Gubar's otherwise magnificent work, *The Norton Anthology of Literature by Women* (1986), stands open to the same charge. In their anxiety to redress the imbalances of the male literary historiography Gilbert and Gubar appropriate women writers of all ages for their twentieth century feminist *praxis*.

The earlier Anglo-American feminist critics were mostly indifferent and sometimes even hostile to literary theory. They looked upon it as something impossibly male and abstract, and also a part of sexual politics. This attitude, however, has changed to a great extent over the years. As Catharine R. Stimpson points out,

> By the mid-1970s, feminist criticism was an international movement with a wide, conflicting range of theoretical concerns. Indeed, the potential partners for feminist critic are a narrative of contemporary critical methods and the quarrels among them. To each partner, the feminist critic brings her questions about women and gender.
>
> (Stimpson 264)

Thus one may find all varieties of feminist critics, from the liberal humanists to the deconstructionists. This creates disagreements and differences among the feminists. For example, there are deconstructionists like Toril Moi who charge Elaine Showalter and others for their empiricism and bourgeois humanism, while a radical critic like Josephine Donovan feels that deconstructionist theory blocks the assertion of political identity (Donovan xi). There are then feminists who would like to do away with gender differences as they lead to the discrimination against and repression of women, while there are others who celebrate these differences between men and women and even valorize womanhood as a part of their political strategy against male domination. In this connection we should take note of the French feminist philosopher Julia Kristeva's programme for the feminist struggle. Julia Kristeva refuses to believe in biologism and essentialism. The feminist struggle, she argues, must be seen historically and politically as a three-tiered one, which can be schematically summarized as follows:

1. Women demand equal access to the symbolic order. Liberal feminism. Equality.
2. Women reject the male symbolic order in the name of difference. Radical feminism. Femininity extolled.
3. (This is Kristeva's own position). Women reject the dichotomy between masculine and feminine as metaphysical. (Moi 12)

According to Julia Kristeva the final goal of the feminist struggle should be the deconstruction of gender identities. But this may appear a utopian desire to the radical feminists who may wonder, as Michele Barrett does, whether "The project to deconstruct the category of women could ever provide the basis for a feminist polities. If there are no 'women' to be oppressed then on what criteria do we struggle, and against what?" (Barrett 96).

Another powerful source of differences and disagreements among the feminist critics, apart from their allegiance to divergent critical theories or political agendas, is their membership of a particular social or cultural group. One charge that is often levelled against American white feminist criticism is that it has not paid sufficient attention to the problems of marginality created by class and race in addition to gender. This may be the reason why the black feminists have felt the need for establishing a separate critical canon for themselves. The situation in Great Britain is somewhat different. Most of the feminists in that country are Marxists or leftists and they work outside the academic institutions. Therefore, in the words of Showalter, "The English contributions to international feminist criticism have been an analysis of the connection between gender and class, an emphasis on popular culture, and a feminist critique to Marxist Literary Theory" (*The New Feminist Criticism* 8). But they too, like their American and French counterparts, have overlooked the dimensions of race, nation, empire, etc., and have therefore been taken to task by their Third World sisters. For example, from her site in the Western academy Chandra Mohanty reminds the First World feminists that "Beyond sisterhood there is racism, colonialism and imperialism" (Mohanty 77).

The Western feminists tend to universalized patriarchy and thereby homogenize women, especially the Third World women. As Chandra Mohanty observes,

> An analysis of "sexual difference" in the form of a cross-culturally singular, monolithic notion of patriarchy or male dominance leads to the construction of a similarly reductive and homogeneous

> notion of what I shall call the "third-world' difference"—that stable, ahistorical something that apparently oppresses most if not all the women in these countries.
>
> (Mohanty 63)

But the problems and the subjectivities of women in the various Third World countries may differ according to their national, historical or local contexts. The ideological construction of woman in India, say, is not the same as that of a woman in Argentina though both of them are supposed to belong to the so-called Third World. Even within India there are differences and divergences. That would, for example, a peasant woman from Konkan have in common with her metropolitan, middle-class sister from Delhi?

The First World feminists also tend to reserve agency and thereby selfhood for the white women and to consign the rest of the womankind to the status of the "other"—an undifferentiated lumpen mass. These gestures on their part are strangely reminiscent of the Western white male's treatment of them which led to the birth of feminism in the first place. Another Indian from her location in the Western academy, Gayatri Chakravorty Spivak, who is generally designated as a deconstructive, neo-Marxist, Third World, postcolonial feminist critic, also, like Mohanty, detects and decries a "colonialist move" in the Western feminist criticism as it "celebrates the heroines of the First World in a singular and individualist, and the collective presence of women elsewhere in a pluralized and inchoate fashion" (Spivak 237). Though critics like Spivak do not deny that Indian women have suffered a great deal of oppression and injustice at the hands of native patriarchies, at the same time they also resist the representation of the Third world women—particularly Indian women—as victims by the mainstream feminists. In the first place, this kind of projection deprives the Indian women of agency and subject position. The Indian feminists would like to empower Indian woman with voice and action and the right to self-representation. In the second place, the representation of Indian women as victims of the native patriarchal structures was a ruse that was often used by the British colonialists for their own material and political benefits. Rajeswari Sunder Rajan, writing on the subject of sati, points out:

> The abolition of sati in 1829 was the first major legislation of the East India Company's administration in India. That it—like the series of laws that were subsequently enacted on behalf of women—served as the moral pretext for intervention and the major justification for colonial rule itself, does not have to be argued further.
>
> (Sunder Rajan 42)

The Indian feminist critics therefore are suspicious of any intervention, howsoever benevolent it might appear to be, by the First world feminists.

Though feminism has now become a global phenomenon and though the feminists of all shades and nationalities share the basic paradigms of feminism with the Western feminists, they at the same time are eager to proclaim their difference from the latter and to carve out a separate identity for themselves. Besides their experience of colonialism also sets some of them apart from their white sisters. That is why most of the postcolonial feminist critics in India—and the Third World—adopt a stance that is feminist as well as anti-imperialist. As said earlier, they also detect this imperialistic streak in the work of Anglo-American feminist critics. Susie Tharu and K. Lalita, for example, from their location in the Indian academy make the following comments on Elaine Showalter's *A Literature of Their Own*,

> We find it quite astonishing, however, that although the period covered by Showalter's book coincides with the age of high imperialism, neither Britain's colonial "possessions" nor the complicity of English women, writers not excluded, in the ideologies of class and of empire are seriously dealt with. In part, as we shall see, Showalter's own schemes replicate an imperialist design.
>
> (*Women Writing in India* 18)

Similar lapses are discovered by them in the otherwise admirable attempts made by Gilbert and Gubar to construct a female tradition in writing and a female historiography. Susie Tharu and K. Lalita therefore proceed to create a separate tradition of Indian women's writing and to rewrite literary history from their position of postcolonial feminists. Their anthology has brought out a rich haul of texts written by women in various Indian languages, right from the days of the Buddhist nuns in the sixth century B.C. to the present day. These two critics have also tried to place women writers and their works in their proper historical context, keeping in mind not only the issues of gender but also those of class, caste, nation, empire, etc.

Another notable feature of Susie Tharu and K. Lalita's contribution is their critique of the manner in which the British imperialists proceeded to reconstruct Indian woman and her subjectivity. Their restructuring of the native woman in the image of the nineteenth century middle-class English woman had not always had an emancipatory effect either on Indian women or on Indian literatures as they both had to be cut and tailored to suit the Victorian ideal of morality and ethics. The editors point out the adverse effect this imperialist intervention had on the native literatures with special reference to the work of the eighteenth-century Telugu poet Muddupalani and her *Radhika Santwanam*. Muddupalani belonged to the class of prostitutes. Also, she had foregrounded a woman's sexual desire and pleasure in her poem. The British government brought a ban upon *Radhika Santwanam* as it "was convinced that the book would endanger the moral health of their Indian subjects" (Tharu and Lalita 4). The continued neglect of this work, though the ban on it was lifted in 1947, leads them to the conclusion that "the interests of empire and of nation are not always in contradiction" (Tharu and Lalita 11).

The feminist critics in postcolonial India have to contend not only against the constructions put upon the "Indian woman" by the colonial discourse or the Western feminist criticism but also have to wage an even more arduous struggle against the entrenched patriarchal structures in the country which still continue to control and restrict the lives of women in one form or the other. Cultural representations of women in the image of a Sita or a Savitri or an Ahilya—women known for their exceptional devotion to their husbands — still proliferate in popular media as well as in serious literature. In most of the popular films and fiction traditional role of women as dutiful daughters, devoted wives, self-sacrificing mothers are valorized. Women who are foolhardy enough to go against these norms, are ridiculed for aping the Western models, are humiliated and chastised and, finally, are made to see the wisdom of accepting their allotted role and place in the family. Side by side of this conventional stereotype there is now what Rajeswari Sunder Rajan calls "the emergence of a 'new Indian woman' in media and official discourse in India today, a construction which serves not only to reconcile in her subjectivity the conflicts between tradition and modernity in Indian society, but works also to deny the actual conflict that women existentially register as an aspect of their lives" (Sunder Rajan 129). Modernity, according to this version, instead of deflecting the Indian woman from her traditional roles and chores, facilitates their easy and efficient performance and thereby vindicates her Indian identity. As Rajeswari Sunder Rajan observes. "The combined hegemony of global consumer capitalism and national state broadcasting is undoubtedly a powerful one in the interpellation and construction of women in contemporary India"(137). These new representations of women instead of doing away with gender differences and gender discriminations perpetuate them under a new guise. The feminist critic in India on the one hand has to resist this process which works in favour of the patriarchal ideology and on the other has to introduce and encourage the kind of self-representations of women which would be useful for a feminist praxis. This is what Rajeswari Sunder Rajan attempts to do in her remarkable study of contemporary Indian culture, *Real and Imagined Women*, which along with *Women Writing in India* is a classic of Indian feminist theory and criticism.

Returning from the Indian scene to the general feminist movement, we could sum up its achievements in the words of

Catharine R. Stimpson:

> This movement has now created and recreated critical maps in five ways: (1) by charting the course of women as writers, who they are, how and why they write, their reception and reputations—a job that Elaine Showalter has named "gynocritics"; (2) by charting the cultural representations of gender, patterns of masculinity and femininity, a complementary task that Alice A. Jardine calls "gynesis"; (3) by showing the complex relations among these representations and patterns of masculine dominance and then asking for the erasure of such patterns (feminist critics are like cartographers of the vanishing rain forest who say both *see* and *stop* the damage); (4) by establishing the unreliability of other maps because they overlook or misconstrue women and the issue of gender; (5) by so doing, stimulating vigilance about the processes of map making themselves.
>
> (Stimpson 25)

The first and foremost contribution of the feminist approach to literature is its deconstruction of the opposition between politics and aesthetics. It has exploded the myth of a value-free criticism—criticism as something neutral, objective or universal. This insight has been borne out by most of the post-structuralist thinkers. The feminists had already put into practice—though perhaps without sufficient critical awareness—what later on came to be known as post-structuralist approaches, approaches like the reader-response theory or deconstruction or the new historicism. The greatest drawback of the feminist approach is thought to be its lack of coherent theory or its inability to offer a definition of it. But I am not sure whether this should be taken as its minus point. In this post-structuralist era why should one want to apply a closure to feminist theory? Feminist criticism, as I said earlier, is a political approach to literature and as such it will keep changing and evolving according to the changing exigencies of the time. The political impact of the work done by the feminists is already beginning to be felt. Today, there may still be people who will be sceptical about the feminist approach to literature, but few can ignore it. And, finally, one look at the college and university syllabi will tell us what the feminist theory and criticism have achieved for women and women writers.

References

Barrett, Michele, *Women's Oppression Today: Problems in Marxist Feminist Analysis*. London: Verso, 1980.

Donovan, Josephine. (ed.), *Feminist Literary Criticism: Explorations in Theory*. Kentucky: The University Press of Kentucky, 1989.

Ellmann, Mary. *Thinking About Women*. New York: Harcourt, 1968.

Gilbert, Sandra M. and Gubar, Susan. *The Madwoman in the Attic: The Woman Writer and the Nineteenth-Century Literary Imagination*. New Haven: Yale University Press. 1979.

Mohanty, Chandra. "Under Western Eyes: Feminist Scholarship and Colonial Discourses," *Feminist Review* 30 (Autumn 1988): 61-88.

Moi, Toril. *Sexual/Textual Politics: Feminist Literary Theory*. London/ New York: Methuen, 1985.

Rogers, Katharine M. *The Troublesome Helpmate: A History of Misogyny in Literature*. Seattle: University of Washington Press, 1966.

Showalter, Elaine. *A Literature of Their Own: British Women Novelists from Bronte to Lessing*. Princeton, N.J.: Princeton University Press. 1977.

Showalter, Elaine (ed), *The New Feminist Criticism: Essays on Women, Literature and Theory*. New York: Pantheon Books, 1985.

Spivak, Gayatri Chakravorty. "Imperialism and Sexual Difference", *Oxford Literary Review*, Vol: 8, Nos. 1-2 (1986): 225-240.

Stimpson, Cathrine R. "Feminist Criticism", in *Redrawing the Boundaries: The Transformation of English and American Literary Studies*, eds. Stephen Greenblatt and Giles Gunn, New York: The Modern Language Association of America, 1992.

Sunder Rajan, Rajeswari. *Real and Imagined Women: Gender, Culture and Postcolonialism*. London/New York: Routledge, 1993.

Tharu, Susie and Lalita K. (eds), *Women Writing in India: 600 B.C. to the Present*, Vol. I, Delhi: Oxford University Press, 1993.

3

The Mad Scientist in the Laboratory: Mary Shelley's *Frankenstein*

Preeti Kapoor

In the early nineteenth century, when the novel of manners and the historical novel were popular, Mary Shelley (1797-1851) wrote *Frankenstein* (1818), a Gothic tale of horror and science fantasy. Mary Shelley had an extra-ordinary parentage, being the daughter of Mary Wollstonecraft, the famous women's rights advocate and William Godwin, the philosopher and political thinker. As both her parents were radical theorists in the political and social field, it had a great impact on Mary's mind and thought. The non-conformism reflected in her fiction and her life can easily be related to the radical views of her parents.

Mary's mother died eleven days after giving birth to her. Though her father married again, and Mary was surrounded by many half-brothers and sisters, yet she found herself emotionally alone. At the age of sixteen, she fell in love with her father's friend, Percy Bysshe Shelley, who was already married. Mary and Shelley eloped in 1814, and when they returned to London after two months, a life full of legal and pecuniary problems awaited them.

Mary was already pregnant when she eloped with Shelley. In February 1815 she gave birth to a premature and sickly daughter, who died twelve days later. This came as a great shock to Mary. Her journal reveals that in spite of trying to repress her sorrow, Mary was unable to come to terms with her loss. On March 19, 1815, she wrote in her journal, "Dream that my little baby came to life again; that it had only been cold and that we rubbed it before the fire and it lived. Awake and find no baby" (quoted in Moers 96). Mary suffered a nearly fatal miscarriage later. She gave birth to three more children, but only one of them survived.

Mary started writing *Frankenstein* in 1815 when she was eighteen years old. By this time she had experienced the feeling of emptiness and the pain of unfulfilled hopes with the loss of her first baby. Mary was aware of the fact that by living with Shelley without the legal sanction of marriage, she had overstepped the limits imposed by society. So she may have considered the death of her newborn child as a form of heavenly punishment for her life of sin. Such a painful experience of her life may have influenced her first novel to some extent.

Frankenstein begins with the letters of an explorer, Robert Walton to his sister, Margaret in England. Walton is the captain of a sea-expedition to the North Pole. These letters, which are four in number, subtly create an atmosphere of mystery and an expectation of the unusual events that follow. In the fourth letter, Walton describes his meeting with Frankenstein, an intelligent scientist, in the icy Arctic region. This is followed by the story of Frankenstein in the first person, as it is narrated to Walton, who records it verbatim in his diary. The setting of the plot in a remote locale and the presentation of the story by means of an indirect narrator conforms to the Gothic literary tradition. The credibility of the bizarre incidents cannot be questioned by the readers for it is also probable that Frankenstein's story is only a figment of Walton's imagination.

Frankenstein is the story of a young and ambitious scientist, Victor Frankenstein. He discovers the secret of infusing life into dead organic matter. He decides that he would create a new human being: "A new species would bless me as its creator and source; many happy and excellent natures would owe their being to me" (50). He collects bits and pieces of flesh and bones from dead bodies and fabricates a giant male human being and animates it. But the body which looked proportionate and beautiful when it was being assembled, assumes a grotesque shape when it comes to life: "when those muscles and joints were rendered capable of motion, it became a thing such as even Dante could not have conceived" (55-56). Frankenstein, overwhelmed with disgust and horror deserts the newborn, yet unnamed monster. The alienated creature comes to know about the strange circumstances of his birth and pursues his creator to be owned by him. Infuriated by Frankenstein's indifference towards him, the monster strangles the scientist's younger brother to death. He then confronts his creator and demands love and sympathy from him. But Frankenstein abhors his ugly creation and rejects his plea. This conflict between the maker and his creation continues and portends disaster for both of them.

Bruno Bettelheim in his book, *The Uses of Enchantment*, discusses the importance of fairy tales and age-old myths in the modern world. He states that fantasies offer meaningful and lasting solutions to deep psychological and existential problems (8-10). This is the basic cause of their popularity even in a scientific age as ours. Mary Shelley's fantastic tale of the scientist's creation of a new kind of human being brings into focus the problematic relationships of the creator with the created object. This creation may be purely biological or intellectual or artistic, and the novel's narrative form has invited several kinds of interpretations suggesting its extremely complex structure of symbols and emotional conflicts.

One of the most significant interpretations of *Frankenstein* relates to the central conflict between the creative person and the object of creation. Ellen Moers discusses the creator's guilt and anxiety experienced by Frankenstein when he perceives the newly-created being taking full shape. Frankenstein is very keen to create a human being, "a resistless, and almost frantic, impulse urged me forward; I seemed to have lost all soul or sensation but for this one pursuit" (51). But when the scientist beholds the monster he has created, he is overcome with a feeling of revulsion and loathing for the ugly creature, "A mummy again endued with animation could not be so hideous as that wretch" (55).

According to Ellen Moers, this is "the trauma of the after-birth" (93)—the post-natal depression often experienced by mothers. The feeling generally associated with the concept of motherhood is that of ecstasy and immense joy. This, one feels, is more of a patriarchal construct. A woman who endures pain and suffers due to a loss of bodily resources and sudden physical separation from her child, may not feel so elated. To the agony of labour-pains a shade of guilt and depression will be added, specially when the mother becomes aware of her peculiar situation as an unwed mother.

Mary Shelley was deprived of the financial and social security which made child-bearing an enjoyable and relaxing experience for a woman. Her own experience of giving birth without the legal sanction of marriage must have added to her guilt and depression. The anxiety and disgust felt by Frankenstein when his task of creation is complete can also be interpreted as the depression which a woman experiences after the delivery of the child.

In *Frankenstein*, Mary also focuses on the other, untouched aspect of the procreative act - the necessity of owning up and providing emotional security to the child by its parent. Frankenstein creates life from non-living matter like God, but deserts the animated creature. The monster pleads in vain for his compassion, "Remember, that I am thy creature; I ought to be thy Adam: but I am rather thy fallen angel, whom thou drivest from joy for no misdeed" (104). The benevolent monster turns into a murderer to avenge himself for the indifference of his maker and goes on a killing spree to destroy many of Frankenstein's loved ones.

The novel is also related to the myth of creation as it reverses the myth and shows a tragic relationship between the creator and the object of creation. In the Book of Genesis in the Bible, the Almighty creates the first man and woman out of a feeling of love for them. He also offers them the Garden of Eden where they may live in comfort. He feels a flood of love for his creations and is proud of them. The Greek myth of Pygmalion also shows a relationship of love between the artist and his object of creation. Pygmalion, a talented sculptor, makes an ivory statue of a beautiful maiden, which he names Galatea. He falls in love with the statue and prays that life may come to it. His prayer is granted and Pygmalion marries the animated statue.

The relationship between the creator and the created being is inverted in *Frankenstein*. The scientist creates a new being out of "bones from charnel-houses" (51) to satisfy his creative urge. The creature is eight feet tall and resembles a giant. As he is artificially assembled, his body is a sort of patchwork and he is hideous in appearance. Frankenstein despises the creature, instead of feeling proud of him. Rather than offering him love, sympathy and understanding, Frankenstein deserts the newborn monster who cries in agony, "Accursed creator! Why did you form a monster so hideous that even *you* turned from me in disgust?" (140). Later Frankenstein pursues the monster to the North Pole to destroy him.

The complex relationship between Frankenstein and the monster can be interpreted with reference to the Greek myths of the birth of gods, in which the relationship between the parent and the child is that of mutual conflict and hostility. In the myths of the birth of Uranus, Cronus and Zeus, each god is afraid of the power of his son and tries to destroy him, but finally is overpowered by the child and is deprived of his authority. Uranus, the god of the sky has a son Cronus who emasculates his father to make him powerless and becomes the god of the sky. Later Cronus comes to know of a prophecy that one day a son of his would assume his position. To prevent this from happening, he swallows each of his five children as soon as they are born. But his wife Rhea hides their sixth son Zeus and saves his life. When Zeus grows up, he wages war against his father, defeats him and becomes the god of the sky (Rosenburg 6-12). A similar kind of antagonistic relationship between Frankenstein and the monster is discernible in the novel.

The monster pursues Frankenstein from Chapter V, as soon as he is animated. But the scientist evades him until he murders Frankenstein's little brother, William. The monster confronts his creator in Chapter X and narrates his sad experiences in an interlude of six chapters. He demands a female companion from the scientist, threatening to kill his friends if Frankenstein does not comply with his request. Frankenstein later travels to the remote Orkney Islands where almost after completing the creation of a female being, he decides to destroy it. The monster then murders Elizabeth, Frankenstein's wife, on their wedding night and the enraged scientist pledges to destroy the monster in Chapter XXIV. He pursues the monster to the Arctic region, until he himself succumbs to death due to fatigue, starvation and the freezing cold. Overcome by remorse by the death of his surrogate father, the monster weeps bitterly, "This is also my victim! In his murder my crimes are consummated; the miserable series of my being is wound to its close!" (244).

Rosemary Jackson explains that a literary fantasy "is a literature of desire, which seeks that which is experienced as absence and loss" (3). Mary Shelley, it seems, took resort to fantasy, when she could not accept the harsh reality of the death of her child. Before creating the monster, Frankenstein thinks, "if I could bestow animation upon lifeless matter, I might in the process of time renew the life where death had apparently devoted the body to corruption" (50-51). *Frankenstein* could be interpreted as a manifestation of Mary Shelley's sub-conscious desire to bring her dead child back to life. But instead of creating a charming child in the novel, the writer creates an ugly monster, who is spurned even by his creator. It is probable that Mary Shelley, when writing the novel, experienced a conflict between her subconscious desire and her conscious mind which was aware of the irrationality of her desire. As a result of this emotional and mental conflict, Mary created a being in the novel who was spiritually as innocent and loving as a child, but whose repulsive physical appearance made him an object of contempt not only of the human society, but also of his own creator.

In order to alleviate his loneliness, the monster asks Frankenstein to create a bride for him, in return of which he would remove himself from society. Frankenstein agrees, but when the creation of the female counterpart is almost complete, realizes the evil consequences of his thoughtless act. Not willing to expose human beings to the assaults of a new race of monsters, Frankenstein tears the female body to pieces: "The remains of the half-finished creature, whom I had destroyed, lay scattered on the floor, and I almost felt as if I had mangled the living flesh of a human being" (188). Frankenstein remembers the day when he had animated the monster and the misery and grief he had experienced due to his careless act of creation, and resolves that he will not repeat the same error. Judy Simons observes that "the image of miscarriage mingles with a sense of slaughter as the creator assumes responsibility for the aborted being, so physically realized" (71). Mary Shelley's careless love for Shelley had caused her a lot of suffering. She had also realized the painful consequences of heedless physical passion due to the deaths of her babies. Similarly Frankenstein's ill-considered act of scientific creation makes life miserable for him.

The monster is given adult dimensions by the scientist and he does not undergo the basic process of physical development common to all human beings. Gillian Beer notes that the monster is "denied the experience of growth" (110) and as a result, is rejected whenever he makes pathetic attempts to enter human society. The creation of the monster is an intellectual activity in which sex plays no roles. Mary Shelley illustrates by means of *Frankenstein* that sex is necessary for life to go on normally. She depicts the havoc that may be caused on earth if man starts a mechanical production of life with the help of intellect and imagination alone.

Walton, the polar explorer, and Frankenstein, the scientist, are similar in their quest for new discoveries, their disregard of danger and their thirst for power and fame. But at the end of the novel Frankenstein dies a miserable death, while Walton survives. Paul O'Flinn points out that Mary Shelley portrays "two models of scientific progress" (26) by means of Walton and Frankenstein. Walton carries the support of his crew in his expedition to the North Pole while Frankenstein performs all his scientific experiments in complete privacy. At a critical juncture during the journey Walton's crew realizes that by continuing their voyage further, they may get trapped and meet a terrible death there. Walton is keen to explore further, but they threaten him with mutiny and force him to turn back; and they return to England, defeated, yet safe and sound. Thus Walton is saved because his ambitious actions are checked by other rational creatures. But Frankenstein is doomed to a life of misery and sorrow because his scientific experiments are done for a purely selfish motive without considering one's social responsibility.

Through *Frankenstein*, Mary Shelley expresses her dislike for man's undesirable interference in natural processes. In the novel, women are denied any involvement in the role of procreation which nature has reserved for them. Instead the creature is fabricated like a machine out of bits and pieces of organic matter. This novel is a feminist critique of the attempt of males to take up feminine roles. Mary Shelley thus gives an early warning of the destruction that may be perpetrated on earth if man usurps the role of creator from God.

The novel is clearly feminist in its portrayal of events. After the death of the scientist, the miserable monster jumps onto an ice-raft in the sea and is carried away into the darkness by the sea waves. His death is not clearly depicted at the end. Rosemary Jackson views the monster as "Frankenstein's lost selves, pieces of himself from which he has been severed and with which he seeks re-unification" (100). The novel is a quest for this unity, which does not take place in life. As the novel concludes, the human part of the personality dies, but the scientific part is still alive. This kind of an open ending, where no permanent solution to a serious problem is offered, is characteristic of feminist writings.

Mary Shelley's *Frankenstein* incorporates a variety of themes and ideas. Basically this novel explores the complex relationship between the creator and the created being. Mary Shelley employs the mode of fantasy to question the male attitude towards the concept of motherhood. She also cautions against man's unnatural obsession with science and his tendency to meddle with natural processes. Due to the multiplicity of ideas woven into this novel, it invites various interpretations for the complete understanding of its different aspects, which makes its study an interesting and rewarding experience.

References

Beer, Gillian. *Darwin's Plots, Evolutionary Narratives in Darwin, George Eliot and Nineteenth Century Fiction*. London: Routledge Kegan Paul, 1983.

Bettelheim, Bruno. *The Uses of Enchantment: The Meaning and Importance of Fairy Tales*. London: Penguin, 1975.

Jackson, Rosemary. *Fantasy: The Literature of Subversion*. London: Methuen, 1981.

Moers, Ellen. *Literary Women*. London: W.H. Allen, 1977.

O'Flinn, Paul. *"Production and Reproduction: The Case of Frankenstein" The Study of Popular Fiction: A Source Book*. Ed. Bob Ashley. London: Pinter Publishers, 1989.

Rosenburg, Donna. *World Mythology*. London: Harrap, 1986.

Shelley, Mary. *Frankenstein* (1818). New York: Book Essentials Promotions, Inc., 1994.

Simons, Judy. *Diaries and Journals of Literary Women from Fanny Burney to Virginia Woolf*. The Macmillan Press, 1990.

4

The Rights of Women in the Nineteenth Century

Neelam Raisinghani

The central theme of this paper is that from time immemorial women have, in general, been forced to occupy a secondary place in the world in relation to men, though they constitute numerically at least half of the human race. This secondary standing is imposed on them by strong environmental forces of educational and social tradition under the control of men. This resulted in the general failure of the Victorian women to take a dignified place as free and independent existents. They were denied the opportunities to stand with men on a plane of intellectual and professional equality. This limited their achievements and gave rise to pervasive social evils.

Commenting on the position of women in 1470, G.M. Trevelyan in his *History of England* writes:

> Wife beating was a recognized right of man and was practised without shame by high as well as low. . . . Similarly the daughter who refused to marry the gentleman of her parents' choice was liable to be locked up, beaten and flung about the room, without

any shock being inflicted on public opinion. Marriage was not an affair of personal affection, but of family avarice, particularly in the "Chivalrous" upper classes.....Betrothal often took place while one or both the parties was in the cradle and marriage when they were scarcely out of the nurses' charge.[1]

The status of women, some hundred years later was still a matter of grave concern. The reality was quite grim and dark from the one portrayed in fiction. Virginia Woolf in *A Room of One's own* writes:

Women have served all these centuries as looking glasses possessing the magic and delicious power of reflecting the figure of man at twice its natural size.

(33)

Even in the eighteenth-century women were still regarded, according to Jane Spencer in her *Rise of the Woman Novelist: From Aphra Behn to Jane Austen*, "as a chattel under the authority first of her father and then of her husband" (12). Girls were educated at home with their mothers or governesses. A knowledge of classical languages or formal schooling was denied to them. They had less education than their brothers. Though there were 'boarding schools' for girls, but they were few and indifferent. "Husbands were often found for girls on the principle of frank barter" (Trevelyan 328). To remain single was considered a great misfortune. Divorce was almost unknown. It was obtainable only through church courts and then to be sanctioned by a special Act of Parliament. Trevelyan reveals that "not more than six divorces were thus legalized during the twelve years of Queen Anne" (*English Social History 329*).

Towards the end of the eighteenth-century the philosophers of Europe and of England began attacking the existing English laws. G.M. Trevelyan in the *English Social History* writes:

This greater sensitiveness to evils which all previous ages had accepted as matters of course was part of the general humanitarian movement.....the supremacy of law was popularized by Blackstone's *Commentaries on the Laws of England* (1765), a book widely read by educated people. The fault was that the law thus idealized was regarded too much as static, as a thing given once for all, whereas, if law is indeed to be the permanent rule of life to a nation, it must be apt to change with the changing needs and circumstances of society.

Nevertheless the prolonged efforts of Jeremy Bentham, the father of English legal reform converted the rising generation. And though the English laws rapidly changed accordingly to the principles of common-sense and utilitarianism laid down by Bentham, the legal rights of women remained a dream.

In the nineteenth century the growth of the factory system and of capitalist agriculture provided women with the opportunities to be employed. Women, who had been deprived of their old means of livelihood by the decay of the cottage industries, owing to the invention of new machines, were employed by the big capitalist farmers, but the growth of high farming and big business turned some of them into ladies of no occupation. Nevertheless these two great revolutions in the nineteenth-century proved to be reactionary forces in English life and also brought a gradual change in the lives of women. Though they lost some of the best things in life, they gained an economic independence, which gave them confidence to fight for their legal rights. The working class women aroused envy in the hearts of other women of the higher class:

> Members of the leisured class like the Bronte sisters and Florence Nightingale were beginning to feel that the independent factory hand, earning her own bread, was setting an example that might be of value to the 'Lady'.
>
> (Trevelyan 369)

The increasing wealth of their men-folk was cutting off the upper-class women from life and its interest. Their idle lives were becoming more artificial. They were 'ladies' too fine to work. The upper and middle-class women still could not think of a professional career.

The growing wealth of the well-to-do classes also gave rise to the evil of prostitution. The economic condition of single women forced many of them to adopt this trade against their wishes. Moreover, the hardness of the social ethical code also drove the once seduced girls to take recourse to prostitution, because the English laws did not provide them any remedy. Elizabeth Helsinger has revealed the pathetic plight of seduced women in *The Woman Question*:

> No single woman, having been seduced, has any remedy at common law neither has her mother, nor next friend. If her father can prove 'service' rendered, he may sue for loss of service. . . In the eyes of this law, female chastity is only valuable for the work it can do.
>
> (II:4)

About the middle of the 19th century the legal position of women was being questioned and discussed. John Stuart Mill in his essays on *Liberty* (1859) and on the *Subjection of Women* (1869) attacked the conventional bondage of women and laid stress on the doctrine of individualism, freedom of life and thought for both men and women.

The reformers believed that a change in the legal position of women would certainly bring a wide-spread social change. It was during the last thirty years of Queen Victoria's reign that the real emancipation of women in England could take place. Elizabeth Helsinger in *The Woman Question: Defining Voices* refers to Queen Victoria herself, who writes years later to her daughter Vicky about her husband Albert whom she adored and called:

> My father, my protector, my guide, and adviser in all and everything, my mother (I might almost say) as well as my husband. I suppose no one ever was so completely altered and changed in every way as I was by dearest Papa's (Albert's) blessed influence.
>
> (I. 64)

The queen, who feels socially and intellectually inadequate represents her age adequately in revealing the conflicting elements of her personality that characterize the age itself. To her newly-wed daughter she writes about conjugal relations:

> There is great happiness and great blessedness in devoting oneself to another who is worthy of one's affection; still men are very selfish and the woman's devotion is always one of submission which makes our poor sex so very unenviable... that despising our poor degraded sex (for what else is it as we poor creatures are born for man's pleasure and amusement and destined to go through endless sufferings and trials?) is a little in all clever men's natures; dear Papa even is not quite exempt though he would not admit it.
>
> (I:73)

The influence of social politics, and natural science started a new era infecting the literature, social life, education and culture. The age old values were dying slowly. The legal reality which was inconsistent with the factual position of women in the Victorian society, started being questioned by feminists like Caroline Dall, Caroline Norton, Barbara Bodichon and Elizabeth Cady Stanton. They all questioned the Marriage Law which advocated the forfeiture of women's power over themselves, and their property after marriage. Elizabeth Helsinger reveals that these feminists challenged the father's right to the custody of children. English law did not acknowledge a woman's control over her children, the father had complete control and authority. In case the father failed to safeguard the interests of the children, courts could intervene. But generally law did not interfere unless the children were very rich or owned property. The mother's claim to the custody of children was overlooked and rejected. She did not have any access to her children against the wishes of the father, children's custody could be entrusted to the person designated by the father in his will. Even the mistress of the father could be the guardian designate. The law turned a deaf ear to the claims of the helpless mother for the custody of her own children. It was in 1836 that the celebrated poet Caroline Norton, who first of all raised her voice to seek the custody of her three sons, who had been sent to an unknown place by her husband to deny her any access to her own children. She turned to law, but in vain. She wrote a pamphlet in 1836 to move the sympathies of the public and the Parliament. To alter the custody laws, she got a Bill introduced in the Parliament by her barrister friend Thomas Talfourd, an M.P. The Bill received strong opposition both inside and outside the Parliament. John Kemble denounced the proposed legislation on an unprecedented attempt "to overthrow the foundation of society". Caroline was called "She devil", "She-beast", "Talfourd's mistress" and "the destroyer of marriage". Anti-feminists like Kemble believed:

> that a woman's whole life and being, her soul, body, time, property, thought, and care ought to be given to her husband; that nothing short of such absorption in him and his interests makes her a true wife.
>
> (Helsinger II:20)

After creating a national sensation, the Infants and Child Custody Bill of 1939 was ultimately passed by the Parliament.

Even in the middle years of the century the secondary education of girls was very ill provided for. They were sacrificed to pay for the expensive education of their brothers. Women were denied entry into the institution of higher education like Oxford and Cambridge. Virginia Woolf resents this injustice in her *A Room of One's Own*.

> But here I was actually at the door which leads into the library itself. I must have opened it, for instantly there issued, like a guardian angel barring the way with a flutter of black gown instead of white wings, a deprecating, silvery, kindly gentleman, who regretted in a low voice as he waved me back that ladies are only admitted to the library if accompanied by a Fellow of the College or furnished with a letter of Introduction.
>
> (7)

The great educational reformer of the thirties was Dr. Thomas Arnold, the Headmaster of Rugby. He encouraged the growth of the public-school system, but the great emancipation and improvement in the condition of women's education was postponed till the last thirty years of Queen Victoria's reign, which is called "the real period of 'the emancipation of women' in England" (Trevelyan 534). In his *English Social History* Trevelyan further reveals that:

> The professional and social emancipation of women went forward on the lines advocated in Mill's *Subjection of Women* (1869), Women's Colleges were founded at Oxford and Cambridge and women's secondary schools were much improved.
>
> (565)

Caroline Dall questioned the Marriage law which advocated the forfeiture of women's power over themselves and their property after marriage. The most famous definition of a married woman's legal status given by the English Jurist William Blackstone in his *Commentaries on the Laws of England (1765)* was:

> By marriage the very being or legal existence of a woman is suspended or at least incorporated or consolidated into that of the husband, under whose wing, protection or cover she performs everything and she is therefore called in our law a 'feme covert'.
>
> (Helsinger II 4)

Under coverture wife was neither liable for her debts, nor could be prosecuted for crimes that were committed by her in her husband's presence. Though coverture granted her protection, it at the same time limited her rights. A married woman did not have any legal right to sign a lease, initiate a law suit, or make a will. The husband had complete control of family finances. She could not lay claim even to her own personal property, earnings or her children. There was no remedy or divorce if the husband ill-treated her. Even after separation, the husband retained control of her property. Though the law recognized that they were one but this *one* was the husband.

In 1855, historian J.W. Kaye wrote for the *North British Review*:

> The larger and more important section of the women of England must be legal nonentities. That the effect of this is to limit the aspirations, to paralyze the energies, and to dramatize the characters of women, is not to be denied. They are born and educated as it were, for total absorption. . . . We make women what they are we reduce

> them to dependence, and then taunt them with being incapable of independent action. Partly by our system of education—partly by our wise laws—we reduce them to the lowest possible level, keep them there, and revile them for not mounting higher.
> (Helsinger II 5)

Victorians felt that only a reformed legal system could bring a social change. Instances of abuse were more common than the recorded ones. Early reformers emphasized the need to protect women from the cruelty of their husbands. Though these reforms hurt the male ego, yet women succeeded in getting the existing laws altered to safeguard their interests. The mother's custody rights were acknowledged. The earnings of some married women were safeguarded by the new laws. They could seek separation on more favourable terms. The end of coverture brought a new legal existence for women. Married women were granted property rights. But still they could not have equal access to absolute divorce and they did not have a right to vote. Trevelyan points out in *English Social History*:

> The Married Women's Property Act released the wife, if she had money of her own, from economic bondage to her husband. The equality of the sexes' began to be advocated in theory, and found its way increasingly into the practice of all classes. The demand for political enfranchisement of women was the outcome of a very considerable degree of social enfranchisement already accomplished.
> (565)

Though the Married Women's Property Act of 1870 enabled women to keep possession of their earnings and to inherit personal property and small sums of money; it still was fraught with compromise and contradiction. It still empowered husbands to retain their control over everything else, either acquired before or after marriage. It was in 1882 only that another act empowered women to keep all real and personal property that was hers at the time of marriage or acquired later. Though still the wife's status was not exactly that of a man, she could dispose of her separate property in a will. She got the right to contract and sue alongwith the responsibility for her debts. With the passage of the Married Women's Property Act, a restraint against anticipation was provided. Earlier, husbands could prevent their wives from freely alienating their property by anticipating future rents and profits. This act was the greatest legal achievement for English women to own and control property. This new legislation put an end to women's absorption in their husbands existence. A woman's separate entity was now recognized by the law.

Many Victorians feared that women would reject marriage, once they were granted the custody of their children and financial independence. The procedures relating to marriage and divorce were so complex that it was not easy for women to seek divorce. English lawyers were trying to simplify these complex procedures. Social reformer couples like Harriet Taylor and John Stuart Mill, Robert Dala Owen and Mary Jane Robinson, Lucy Stone and Henry Blackwell pledged that they do not base their marriages on law which empowers one party over the other (Helsinger II: 23). These reformers stressed the need of mutual affection in conjugal relations, and if the affection ceased to exist, marriage should be dissolved without expense, without dishonour and without publicity. But the Perfectionists advocated a complex system, that made divorce unnecessary. Because of the controversy attached to this issue the majority of feminists avoided it. Only the most radical women espoused the cause of divorce.

Divorce which was almost unknown, was obtainable only through Church-courts and then to be sanctioned by a private Act of Parliament. The whole process was lengthy, expensive and complicated and could be exercised only by men. To obtain a divorce, a wife could not file a suit. Only the husband had the right to seek divorce on the grounds of adultery. Again the injustice of the English divorce laws was discovered by Caroline Norton, who was accused of adultery. But her husband could not prove her relations with Lord Melborne, the Whig Prime Minister and the Jury declared Caroline innocent. But she was forced to live with a man whom she despised. During the unhappy years after the trial Caroline carefully observed the Government's attempts to reform Divorce laws. Disheartened by the unnecessary delay in the reformation of these laws, she wrote a pamphlet, *A letter to the Queen on Lord Chancellor Cranworth's Marriage and Divorce Bill* to raise a woman's voice on this controversial issue. She argued for economic protection and the inadequacy of the Bill presented by Lord Cranworth in the Parliament. She attacked the double standards of the male dominated society. Her contention was that men and women should be subject to the same standards, whereas the House of Lords had social, religious and economic arguments for defending the double standard. Lord Harwicke's Marriage Act of 1753 was changed in 1836 by the Marriage Act of 1836, which provided some relief to women. Trevelyan writes in *The English Social History*, "The Act established Civil Officers called Registrars of Births, Deaths and Marriages—in itself a notable reform consonant with the new era of statistics and exact information" (528). It was a significant piece of legislation in 1857 when the Matrimonial Causes Act was passed by the Parliament, which extended the possibilities of divorce. Jenni Calder in *Women and Marriage in Victorian Fiction*, commenting on the 1857 Act pointed and that, "it was not until 1923 that they could obtain a divorce on grounds of the husband's adultery" (120).

As for political rights, they were not easily achieved. In 1867 John Stuart Mill made before the English Parliament the first speech ever officially presented in favour of women's right to vote. In his writings he imperiously demanded equality for woman and man within the family and a society at large. On his lines English women organized themselves politically under Mrs. Fawcett's leadership. In 1878 an International Congress was held to claim the Rights of women. The question of the right to vote was, however, not raised in this Congress. Women limited their demands only to claiming civil rights. For thirty years the progress of the movement was very slow. But the women of England, America and France had to struggle further to gain full rights. Even the English scientists of the times proclaimed that woman was "a sub-species destined only for reproduction".

Feminism was very timid until about 1903, when the Pankhurst family founded in London the women's social and political union and feminist agitation took on a militant character. It was in the twentieth century only that women's active initiation and action gave a special interest to the 'suffragette' adventure. Women demanded enfranchisement. At first their movement was peaceful, non-violent, marching with banners, invading meetings, provoking arrests, going on hunger strikes, marching to the Parliament with ordinary women and great ladies in line together, but their efforts proved fruitless. In 1912 they took recourse to more violent tactics burning houses, slashing pictures, trampling flowerbeds, throwing stones at the police, ultimately compelling the evasive British Government to yield by granting them right to vote with restrictions in 1918 and the unrestricted vote in 1928. According to English Law, obedience is no longer included among the duties of a wife, and each woman citizen has the right to vote; but these civil liberties remain theoretical as long as they are unaccompanied by economic freedom. A woman supported by a man remains bound in her conditions of vassalage. Only through gainful employment women have traversed most of the distance that separated them from the male, and nothing else can guarantee her liberty in practice.

References

Calder, Jenni. *Women and Marriage in Victorian Fiction*. New York: Oxford University Press, 1976.

De Beauvoir, Simone. *The Second Sex*. Middlesex: Penguin Books, 1972.

Ford, Boris. (Ed.) *The Pelican Guide to English Literature*. Vol. 6. Middlesex: Penguin Books, 1958.

Helsinger, Elizabeth K., 'Queen Victoria and "The Shadow Side". *The*

Woman Question: Defining Voices (3 vols) Vol I. Manchester: Manchester University Press, 1983.

—, 'Law', *The Woman Question: Social Issues, 1837-1883*, (3 vols) II. Manchester, Manchester University Press. 1983.

Mill, John Stuart. *The Subjection of Women (1869)*. London: J.M. Dent and Sons, 1982.

Spencer, Jane. *Rise of the Woman Novelist: From Aphra Behn to Jane Austen*. Oxford: Basil Blackwell. 1986.

Trevelyan, G.M. *English Social History*. Middlesex: Penguin Books; 1944.

Woolf, Virginia. *A Room of One's Own* (1929). London: Grafton Books. 1989.

5

Inching Toward Freedom: Women in Victorian England

Krishna Rathore

In the Victorian period the state of female education was not better than what it had been in the eighteenth century. In the lower classes it was hardly different from that of men but the daughters of well-to-do families had less education than their brothers. There were boarding schools for both, no doubt, but the curriculum was not the same. In the initial stages the same education was given to both without any gender discrimination but once they attained the age of six or seven they were given different education by different sets of tutors. Boys were sent to Grammar Schools and the girls either learnt at home from their mothers or were sent to boarding schools and other places to learn needlework, dancing, singing, music, painting and other accomplishments that would help in running the household efficiently. Boys were taught the classical languages like Latin and Greek but for girls it was a forbidden sphere. A knowledge of the English language, History and a bit of Arithmetic was considered sufficient for them. The girls were not privileged with good secondary education even till the middle years of the nineteenth century. As the 'Public Schools' came in vogue the education of girls was sacrificed to pay for the expensive public school education of their brothers. Feminist theorist Elaine Showalter points out in her book *A Literature of Their Own* that, "for the middle class Victorian girl, the departure of a brother for school was a painful awakening to her inferior status" (41).

Though women were enclosed in private spaces called homes and were denied education, they had not only been always permitted to write letters but were also encouraged to excel in the art of letter writing. Letter writing is a good medium for exploring and expressing emotions in order to maintain relationships. The women transformed their private occupation into public and professional activity and in the process they created a new literary form the novel which voiced their feelings and gave them intellectual and monetary satisfaction. Commenting upon the themes and imagery of the nineteenth century women writers, Sandra Gilbert and Susan Gubar observe in *The Mad Woman in the Attic* :

> The one plot that seems to be concealed in most of the nineteenth century literature by women. . . is in some sense a story of the woman writer's quest for her own story, it is the story, in other words, of the woman's quest for self definition.
>
> (76)

The two books which attacked the bondage of convention and focused the attention on the rights of individual men and women to free life and thought were James Stuart Mill's *On Liberty* (1859) and *The Subjection of Women* (1869). The publication of these two books was the turning point between the early and the later Victorian age. The last thirty years of Queen Victoria's reign can be taken as the years, which brought about marked improvement in women's education. The 'Secondary schools' were much improved and women's Colleges were opened at Oxford and Cambridge. These years were also the years of professional and social emancipation of women on the lines forwarded by Mill's book *The Subjection of Women*. Women's education was a debatable issue; one side wanted to deny it in order to keep wives in due subjection, while the other side, led by the chief literary men of the times, ascribed the frivolity and the gambling habits of ladies of fashion to an up-bringing which debarred them from more serious interests.

Men had set a code of behaviour for women if they expect protection. From the work of eighteenth and nineteenth century women writers we get an understanding of the tactics which have been employed by men in order to have the life long consent of women to follow the set-code of behaviour which fulfills the demands of patriarchy. Women's defeats, compromises and conciliatory moves all are recorded in their work. These writers also tell us how and why women put up with some shameful or humiliating acts and questioned others. They also show that girls are brought up in a restrictive atmosphere which is different from the atmosphere in which their brothers grow up. They emphasize the point very strongly that women are the progenitors as well as the victims of patriarchal institutions and question as to why women being women differentiate among their children on the basis of gender. The tragedies of women often follow from their own characters because they themselves are responsible for giving momentum to patriarchal cultures by giving their agreement and consent. The paths on which women move are confused paths and pull them in different directions.

Alice Browne in her work *The Eighteenth Century Feminist Mind* observes that at the end of the eighteenth century a number of women writers called for an improvement in women's position. They emphasized that change was needed in three areas. The first point called for women's education to be equal to that of men and denied and rejected the intellectual superiority of men. The second point concerned the legal and economic weaknesses of women's position especially if they were married. The third point attacked the double standard in sexual morality: "for men to demand chastity of women, but not of themselves, was immoral, absurd and damaging to men as well as to women" (1).

The social status of women was greatly affected by the Industrial Revolution which brought about the sudden decay of the home industries which involved the labours of the whole family. The new machines separated the home from the work place and as a result the closing years of the eighteenth century had a great deal of unemployment and misery for women and shattered the economy of numerous small rural households. The independence and the utility of women was eroded by the move towards industrial living. As trade expanded and commercial production gradually took over spinning, weaving, brewing, baking, soap and candle-making, the importance of the single woman waned. The unmarried women who was an asset to the household of pre-industrial era became a burden in the post industrial era. The growth of prostitution in the period can be attributed to the erosion of women's other economic opportunities and the harshness of the ethical code of the times, which drove a girl once seduced to prostitution.

Trevelyan points out in the *English Social History* that as the move to the factories could not materialize at once, they started going into the fields alongwith menfolk for hoeing and weeding. But here too the invention and the implementation of the farm machinery enabled farmers to dispense with many kinds of hand work and female employment in agriculture became restricted. In the old system, farmer's wives had active participation in the activities associated with farm work and life, but the Agricultural Revolution and big business dissociated them from active involvement turning some of them into ladies of no occupation and other into field labourers or factory hands. The women who went to work in the factories gained economic independence and in due course set an example for women who aspired to become independent. Trevelyan also observes that the "early Victorian lady and her mother of the Regency period has nothing in the world to do except to be paid for and approved by man" (501). No doubt there were leisured women like Jane Austen, Maria Edgeworth and Hannah More who utilized their time and became authors but most of the ladies suffering from too much leisure fed on the popular romances and tried to imitate their fashionable heroines. It was expected of a lady to do as little work as possible and, except for dancing, they were not supposed to exercise their bodies at all.

In the post-Industrial England the middle class ideology about the proper sphere of womanhood developed. A woman was required to be a pure and perfect lady accepting her secondary status and showing contentment in the confines of the home. In Victorian England women were more controlled by space. The patriarchal structures enclosed women in the private space of home where they led inert and useless lives. Lee R. Edwards comments in *Psyche as Hero* that "Bourgeois and patriarchal structures fused in their mutual insistence on female subordination, lock women into a coercive imaginative structure. The presumption of female piety and moral goodness is a staple of bourgeois ideology" (21). Men assured women that they were not inferior to them, just different and these differences were explained to them in detail by men. Conduct books or courtesy books for women were in circulation, Dr. James Fordyce's two volumes on female conduct Sermons to Young Women (1765) and *Character and Conduct of the Female Sex* (1776) are noteworthy. These books contain all those characteristics which are considered good and amiable in a woman and every thing is explained in detail. According to Fordyce, women are created for domesticity and they are to be defined in relation to men.

Independence in a woman was almost viewed as a sad necessity and was seen as either the result of the failure of the man to provide for her or a failure of woman to get a husband for herself. The state of an unmarried woman was pitiable. On one hand her helplessness was encouraged and on the other she was deprived of her economic strength. Jenni Calder observes in *Women and Marriage in Victorian Fiction* "As the Victorian age took shape necessities became conventions and as the walls closed in on the Victorian heroine and the Victorian marriage two features grew into dominance, statis and boredom" (56).

The 1801 census revealed a drastic increase in the number of females making Victorian marriage an ideal to be longed for but granted to few. There was shortage of husbands in the aristocracy due to the laws of primogeniture which deprived the younger sons of their share in the ancestral property. The elder son was the sole inheritor of the large fortune while the younger ones had to be satisfied with the minimal. As a result the younger sons married out of their class into the professions. Lower down the social ladder men in trade were encouraged not to marry until they found themselves capable of supporting a wife. Marriage became the core of social aspiration.

Leonore Davidoff remarks in *The Best Circles Society Etiquette and the Season* that right from childhood girls were taught self effacement and modesty. They were encouraged to feel shame about their bodies and even hide natural conditions like menstruation and pregnancy. The Victorian married women was required to bear the pain of illness in silence. A woman was not supposed to voice her experiences and her anguish in public. She was indeed free to record them in her private diaries or confide in one or two intimate women friends. There were strong taboos against sharing them with men. It was her sole duty to make her marriage successful even if the husband strayed.

The state of the old maid was the most pathetic one. She could participate in just one clear growth area of Philanthropy and Charity leading the life of self-abnegation. She had to derive dignity from service to the poor which men got from the ideals of work.

Women have both sustained and questioned the patriarchal pressures and the works of women writers show the resistances that the subordinated ones put up. The female authors had to adopt different strategies to avoid being judged by the male dominated publishing industry as the prototype of their sex. Charlotte Bronte had to conceal her identity behind Currer Bell and Mary Anne Evans had to surface as George Eliot, because of the pressures of male dominated publishing industry. The critical response was that if written by a man it was excellent but if by a woman it was scandalous.

Thus choices were limited and status both within marriage and outside it, both with it and without it was low and subordinate. Society was slow to concede them position and the law was even slower. But public opinion throughout the second half of the century progressed towards change.

References

Browne, Alice. *The Eighteenth Century Feminist Mind*. Brighton: Harvester, 1987.

Calder, Jenni. *Women and Marriage in Victorian Fiction*. London: Thames and Hudson, 1976.

Davidoff, Lenore. *The Best Circles Society Etiquette and the Season*. London, 1973.

Edwards, Lee R. *Psyche As Hero: Female Heroism and Fictional Form*. Middletown Connecticut: Wesleyan University Press. 1984.

Gilbert, Sandra and Gubar, Susan. The *Mad Woman in the Attic*. New Haven: Yale University Press, 1979.

Showalter, Elaine. *A Literature of Their Own*. Princeton: Princeton University Press, 1977.

Trevelyan, G.M. *Illustrated English Social History*. Pelican, 1967, rpt in Penguin Books, 1986.

6

Better Deal for the Better Half: Mill and Harriet Taylor on the Subjection of Women

Sarojini

In the English speaking world the feminist movement might be said to have begun with the publication of Mary Wollstonecraft's *Vindication of the Rights of Women* in 1792. It made very little impact on its contemporaries, partly because it was so obviously a child of the French Revolution, and partly because of its impassioned style. It aroused more derison than sympathy. Moreover a woman crusading for women is less persuasive than a male champion for the women's cause. The male voices, however, were rare and solitary. In 1825 William Thomson in his "Appeal of one half of the human race" contended that there would be no progress until women were given equal opportunities for education and equal political rights. In the mid 19th century John Stuart Mill lent the weight of his philosophical authority to the cause of feminism. His famous treatise *On the Subjection of Women* (1869) is a clear, cool-headed, well argued plea that compelled the reader to wonder that so self-evident a cause should need a champion. Written in his characteristic manner, he presented his views with cogency and comprehensives.

His essay provides the women's movement with a philosophic rationale and is a landmark in the long history of women's struggle for political, legal and economic rights.

Mill's interest in the woman question goes back to the "very earliest period when I had formed any opinions at all on social and political matters" (*Subjection* 125). He was reprimanded at the age of seventeen for scattering tracts through the streets of London which advocated birth control. But Mill's commitment to women's issues acquired a new dimension after he met Harriet Taylor in 1830, as he tells us in his autobiography:

> What is true is, that until I knew her, the opinion was in my mind, little more than an abstract principle. . . . But that perception of the vast practical bearings of women's disabilities, which found expression in the book on the "Subjection of Women" was acquired mainly through her teaching.
>
> (*Autobiography* 207)

In 1832 just at the outset of their friendship, Mill and Harriet wrote essays on "Marriage and Divorce", a subject of mutual interest. It arose out of Harriet's intellectual incompatibility with her husband. These essays throw some light on Mill's preoccupation with the feminist cause which later led to his writing of *The Subjection of Women*. Taking into account the prevalent civil disabilities of married women, wherein a woman was entirely dependent for her social position on her marital status, Mill felt that the indissolubility of marriage was a boon to women. He strongly felt that divorce would be of no use to women so long as society was based on inequality. In fact the indissolubility of marriage served as a safeguard for a woman in such a society. Hence, he held that before dealing with divorce one must first consider the question of marriage. "Determine whether marriage is to be a relation between two equal beings or between a superior and an inferior, between a protector and a dependent, and all other doubts will easily be resolved" (*Essays* 73).

He aptly pointed out that everything finally centered on the debate on the status of women in society and pleaded in all earnestness for the equality of the sexes and improved education for women to release them from their dependence on men. But he was reluctant to advise women to become career oriented:

> It is not desirable to burthen the labour market with a double number of competitors. In a healthy state of things, the husband would be able by his single exertions to earn all that is necessary for both. . . it will be for the happiness of both that her occupation should rather be to adorn and beautify it (life).
>
> (*Essays* 74-75)

Compared to Mill, Harriet is more radical in her views which she expressed in her essay 'Enfranchisement of Women' written in 1850. She argues at length against the domestication of women. She categorically states that education and social indoctrination are responsible for such a notion. Women are wives and mothers only because there is no other career open to them. On grounds of maternity they are excluded from active life: "There is no inherent reason or necessity that all women should voluntarily choose to devote their lives to one animal function and its consequences (*Essays*, 104). She demolishes the argument that equal employment opportunities for women would create unemployment. She pointed out that in order to alleviate the unemployment problem, child labour needed legislative regulation. That would also protect children from exploitation. Withholding women's right to employment was not a solution to the problem. Harriet strongly believed that a woman's contribution to the family income would raise her status from the position of a servant to that of a partner:

> A woman who contributes materially to the support of the family, cannot be treated in the same contemptuously tyrannical manner as one, who, however she may toil as a domestic drudge, is a dependent on the man for subsistence.
>
> (*Essays* 105)

If Harriet is more radical in her views, Mill is more rational in his approach. Having resolved the issue of the status of women, he considers marriage as an institution. Marriage, he states, is a necessary social institution for no man is complete without a woman. However, he advocates free choice in marriage. It should not be a necessity for a woman. Nor should she be expected to cling to a marriage which is better dissolved. Given the equality of the sexes, he feels, divorce will be in the interest of both the parties. These were ideas, indeed, much ahead of his time. He was aware that his advocacy of divorce would create complex social problems. The innocent children of such broken marriages would be the greatest suffers. To counteract such a danger, Mill suggested delay in having children till both partners had tested their compatibility. His advocacy of birth control was bound to meet with stiff resistance in an age when contraceptives were taboo. Hence provision for children remained a problem. He suggested communal living as a solution.

Harriet, however, differed with Mill on the question of children. She strongly felt that a woman ought to take entire responsibility of her own children. Instead of regarding children as a means of binding her to the man who feeds her, she should think carefully how many children she should have. Harriet's demand for a mother's legal rights over the children points to the increased responsibilities of women that the equality of the sexes entails. Rights cannot be demanded without accepting corresponding duties. Harriet understood that freedom of choice and a wider range of life goals would undercut women's desire for a bountiful maternity. She was adamant in her demand of complete equality in every sphere of life and equal admission to all social privileges.

What characterized Mill's involvement with women's disabilities was that he ceased to look upon the rights merely as an abstract theory. He made them a living principle of action. Particularly after Harriet's death Mill imbued with a passionate fervour to keep her memory alive, drafted *The Subjection of Women* (1861) at the suggestion of his daughter. In keeping with his mood he dedicated the treatise to his wife with whom he had shared these views. Right at the start Mill pointed out that the primary object of the treatise was to explain the grounds of his belief in women's rights.

Before writing *The Subjection of Women* Mill was well aware of the enormous cultural resistance he was working against in advocating an anti-patriarchal doctrine. He set about it courageously and persuasively, presenting each issue in its historical perspective, demolishing every counter argument with logical reasonings. Mill's approach consisted of two enquiries, viz., investigation of historical facts and analysis of human nature. The historical perspective led him to examine whether the long survival and widespread existence of male dominance provides an argument in its favour. In the course of his analysis he examined the social organization of early man, the origin of law and the evolution and development of present institutions. To him the inquiry indisputably proved that the belief in the subordination of women was purely hypothetical. Just because from the dawn of history every woman was found in a state of bondage to some man, it does not follow that she should continue to be so. All laws based on despotism and muscular strength have been abolished or are in the process of being replaced. The continued fight against slavery and colour prejudice is proof enough of erroneous laws having persisted owing to the force of custom. The peculiar character of the modern world is:

> That human beings are no longer born to their place in life, and chained down by an inexorable bond to the place they are born to, but are free to employ their faculties, and such favourable chances as offered, to achieve the lot which may appear to them as most desirable.
>
> (*Subjection* 143)

Hence women's subordination is a breach of the fundamental law, "a single relic of an old world of thought and practice exploded in everything else, but retained in the one thing of most universal interest (*Subjection* 146). Justice and expediency demand that due to the fatality of birth, higher social functions ought not to be closed to half the human race.

Analysis of human nature was the other course Mill followed

to examine the belief in the superiority of men over women. He firmly believed in the power of society to mould human nature. A person's character, Mill believed, resulted not only from innate qualities but from environment and education, Mill's central argument in *The Subjection of Women* was based on the assumption that it was an irrepressible tendency of human beings to usurp power over their fellowmen in the absence of proper laws and restraints imposed by society or institutions. Mill pointed out that the unlimited power given to husbands over their wives evokes the latent tendency of selfishness in husbands and offers them a licence for cruelty and despotism. Under the prevalent law, Mill declares, wives could be forced to endure the worst forms of slavery and bondage known to history. Unlike most other slaves, a wife could be put on duty all hours of the day or night, she had no legal means of findings redress from a tyrannical husband. Worst of all she could not refuse her master but had to submit to being made the instrument of an animal function against her wish.

Mill refutes the assumption of women's inferiority with a number of arguments. He holds that with the right type of education, training and opportunity, women would do as well as men in any profession. By means of social indoctrination, men had successfully held women in subjection for centuries. There was no scientific proof of their intellectual inferiority. He asserted that the domestic and social circumstances in which women lived sufficiently explained almost all the differences between man and woman, including the sentimental myth of woman's moral superiority.

Mill's attack on the prevalent laws of marriage was directed to bring out the inhumanity of the situation. Society has appointed marriage to be the destination of all women. Foul means are employed in its execution. Girls are bartered or disposed of, without their consent, in marriage, treated as personal property by their husbands, compelled to obey them and in general treated as slaves. A wife is not allowed to own property or have legal right over her children. If she leaves her husband she can take nothing with her. If the husband chooses, he can compel her to return by law or by physical force. Mill points out the dangers of such despotism and draws attention to the serious results of the abuse of this institution. He gives constructive suggestions for the division of rights and duties in a marriage based on individual abilities and mutual consent. No laws can be constructed on an unequal foundation. The reciprocity of relationship which binds men and women can only result in personal and social pleasures. He goes on to describe the ideal relationship in a marriage:

> What marriage may be in the case of two persons of cultivated faculties, identical in opinion and purposes, between whom exists that best kind of equality, similarity of powers and capacities with reciprocal superiority over them—so that each can enjoy the luxury of looking up to the other, and can have alternately the pleasure of leading and of being led in the path of development. . . I maintain with the profoundest conviction that this, and this only, is the ideal of marriage.
>
> (*Subjection* 235)

In *The Subjection of Women* Mill revolutionized the traditional concept of a wife. He has rescued her from the prevailing glorification of female submissiveness and demolished the myth of "delicacy" and "femininity" which meant a total dependence upon a husband. He envisaged a completely new relationship based on equality which would lead to a greater fulfilment of man's quest for wholeness. Both in precept and example, Mill was a fully liberated man.

Mill's battle has been won because he demanded identifiable goals—the vote, education, right to property, divorce and employment. But the more difficult battle is still on—the mysterious inflexibility of the male mind towards women. There is still a considerable residue of the mental cliches which regards men as persons but women as merely women.

References

Mill, J.S. *Autobiography*. Oxford University Press, 1944.

Mill, J.S. *The Subjection of Women*, *Essays on Sex Equality: John Stuart Mill and Harriet Taylor*, ed. Alice Ross, University of Chicago Press, 1970.

Mill J.S. "Early Essay on Marriage and Divorce", *Essays on Sex Equality*, ed Alice Ross.

Taylor, Harriet. "Enfranchisement of Women", *Essays on Sex Equality*, ed Alice Ross.

7

Aurora Leigh: A Woman in Search of a Vocation

Santosh Gupta

Elizabeth Barrett Browning (1806-1861) considered her long narrative poem, better classified as a "novel-poem", *Aurora Leigh* (1857) to be "the most mature" of her work, one into which her "highest convictions upon Life and Art" have entered (*AL* 374). This poem deals with some of the subjects very close to the writer's own heart, and central to the Victorian age. Her views on child labour, prostitution, gender and class conflict were unconventional and she expressed the views in this poem. Her heroine's quest for an independent status as a professional poet, and her questioning of many of the society's institutions bring forth Elizabeth's own struggles and intense experiences. Elaine Showalter calls this work to be an "autobiographical discussion" of the feminist issues (23). The conflicts that women in the Victorian age faced between their aesthetic vocation and feminine roles are dramatically portrayed in Aurora's struggle to succeed as a poet.

Aurora Leigh, made a tremendous appeal to its age. It ran into five editions within the first two years of its publication, and thirteen editions by 1873. It was highly acclaimed by poets, critics and general readers (Miller 70; Woolf 216). John Ruskin, who a year earlier had found much to criticize in Robert Browning's poems in *Men and Women* considered *Aurora Leigh* to be "the greatest poem in English language, unsurpassed by anything but Shakespeare" (Miller 68). Emily Dickinson was also a devoted admirer who knew the whole of the poem, some 10,000 lines long, by heart, and called the writer the "Queen of poetry of her age" (Moers 40).

The subsequent fall from public favour and critical regard of this minor classic as well as its author is intriguing. Some critics, mostly feminist critics, regard the poem's formal, stylistic and intellectual achievement to be still engaging and impressive. Virginia Woolf considers the poem to be "with all its imperfections a book that still lives and breathes and has its being" (218). The feminist and aesthetic issues that emerge in the poem remain significant and unsettled in the 20th century as well, making the bold and forthright treatment by Elizabeth Barrett modern and relevant to the reader today.

Elizabeth Barrett seriously believed in the poet's strong involvement with the social and cultural issues and problems of his or her own time. Just as the prose novelist had faced the contemporary social evils, using the novel to awaken society's conscience, she felt that the poet's concern is not "to rhyme the stars and walk apart", but, (s)he should be concerned with the people and the problems of the contemporary age. She wrote to Robert Browning on the subject of poetry: "I am inclined to think that we want new forms as well as thoughts. The old gods are dethroned. Why should we go back to the antique moulds, classical moulds as they are so improperly called? . . . let us aspire rather to life" (*Letters* I, 45-46, quoted by Bush 270-271).

Elizabeth Barrett brings centrestage the issues of gender roles, women's struggle for an equal and just treatment, and class conflict in her poems. Her non-conformism had "shocked mammas in England" (Bush 269). She questions popular Victorian concepts of a woman's vocation, her status in marriage, family and society, as well as the notions of virtue and charity. She acknowledges the significance of socially constructed norms of gender and sex, and addresses herself to these issues through the characters of Aurora Leigh, Marian Erle, and Romney Leigh in *Aurora Leigh*. Instead of projecting helplessness as the typical feminine behaviour she portrays strong-willed women who pursue their goals with determination and intelligence. The heroine, Aurora, wants to become a poet, and earn a living through her publications. She wishes to realize fully her intellectual and creative talents. She seeks to acquire a status as an independent and responsible person; she wishes to attain selfhood on the basis of her feminine separateness. The poem gradually shows the mutual needs of men and women, in their search for a relationship of mutual affection and respect. This relationship is possible only after a period of self awareness, self analysis, and after both men and women discard their pride and prejudices.

The poem beings with the heroine, Aurora Leigh, looking back at her initial struggle, and her success as a poet. Now a well recognized poet, she thinks over her concept of the nature of poetry. She considers poets to be "the only truth-tellers now left to God/The only speakers of essential truth/opposed to relative, comparative and temporal truths;" (Bk 1, 387). She then talks about her childhood, the loss of both her parents and then the journey to England to be brought under the care of her aunt. Aurora's aunt occasionally expressed her disapproval of the marriage of her brother (Aurora's father) with an Italian woman, when she found the young girl resist her efforts to mould her into a meek and "feminine" English maid. The young girl resisted, but felt disturbed by the restriction and disapproval. Aurora recalls how she had been drawn to the world of books at an early age, when she sat "nibbling" like a mouse, poring through the books piled up in her father's library (before his death). She remembers her early decision to become a poet. At the touch of poetry, she says, her soul, "Let go conventions and sprang up surprised/Convicted of the great eternities/Between two worlds" (Bk 1, 386). But she had to keep her ambition secret from her aunt for fear of censure. Book I effectively presents the undercurrents of anxiety, tension and suppression that Aurora experiences, as a young woman who is aspiring to be a poet.

Book II of *Aurora Leigh* is a dramatic confrontation between the two leading characters, Aurora and Romney Leigh. Book II opens on a beautiful early morning on a day in June. It happens to be an important day for Aurora, being her 20th birthday. It is also the day when her cousin Romney proposes marriage to her. Cousin Romney plans to devote his life to social reform, and to helping poor men and women. He asks Aurora to become his wife, and to help him in his mission in life. Aurora, after expressing her own plans for the future turns down the proposal.

Aurora's quest for selfhood and freedom to pursue her own plans comes into conflict with her society's intention to restrict her freedom, by binding her into the domestic role. The open green world of nature where Aurora loves to spend her time offers her a sense of freedom, while the life within her home, with her aunt and others, reinforces the socially accepted role. Romney's reaction to Aurora's plans reflects his disdain towards a woman's self-awareness, and her ambition to become an independent being. He doubts her ability to become a good poet, as she is a woman, and then says, that even if she could do so, it would hardly matter. The world is so full of pain and evil that what it needs is not poets, but devoted selfless workers to help humanity. Her ambition to become a poet is a selfish, self-centered wish, neglecting the more worthwhile, serious work in the world.

What Romney tells Aurora reflects the deep-rooted Victorian views regarding women as poets, women's status in society and a patriarchal arrogance. The "feminine" woman was a devoted wife, mother and helpmate to man. Men expected women to provide love and care, to look after their families and also other weak and suffering persons. Romney tells Aurora that women make "doting mothers and perfect wives", they can become "sublime Madonnas and enduring saints", but he further says. "We get no Christ from you and verily, we shall not get a poet, in my mind" (Bk II, 394).

A woman's true vocation was to give herself up to the care of others, and to work self-effacingly to further the interest and honour of man. Women attain self-fulfilment in their self sacrifice in these roles, in relation to men and children. Submission to male authority in a cheerful and humble manner were high on the list of feminine virtue, and their passivity, an applauded quality.

Romney's views expressed to Aurora in their discussion were not his alone. These views were being discussed propagated and consolidated throughout the latter half of the 18th and the entire 19th century England, America and Europe. Books on conduct, treatises on moral education expressed in strong language the views regarding women's role in family and society. It was repeatedly emphasized that the education of women was not meant to give them ideas of freedom in thought and action; rather, the young Christian woman (should) be determined "not to live for herself as much as others, . . .above all, to not to live for this world, so much as for eternity".[1] Many Victorian texts written by male as well as female writers were attempts at defining 'womanliness' as also 'feminine sphere' of duties. John Ruskin's essay "Of Queen's Garden" published in *Lilies and Sesame* (1865) was an influential text, which expressed the opinion that women should be educated "not for self development but for self-renunciation"; it brings out the conflict between a woman's self awareness and her duty to renounce her self for the sake of others (Dyhouse 174). This conflict between the needs of the individual and those of society was heavily turned against women's self awareness, by relating her social duty with strong shades of moral duty.

Romney's offer of marriage to Aurora is not an offer of mere personal needs, gratification and companionship. He relates it to his larger, more selfless mission of helping society's down trodden people. It gives him and with him, if Aurora agrees to be his wife, to Aurora also a noble and worthwhile occupation. The poets merely dream of "beautiful" and "happy pastorals" while he would be devoting his (and her) life to help the 'hungry orphans' beaten and bullied wives, with 'unweaned babies.'

Romney's rhetoric of selfless service to social cause undermines the woman's dream to pursue poetry as a self-satisfying career. Her aspiration to achieve a status and profession is suggested to be unsocial, as it seems to be self-centered. The critical, disapproving language and tone are heavily against feminine freedom from domestic role and search for a vocation other than being just a woman, in relation to men. Elaine Showalter says that during the Victorian age, "women were not accustomed to choosing a vocation: womanhood was a vocation in itself". Moreover the vocation to write was all the more against that 'feminine' conduct, for it required "a genuine transcendence of female identity" (26). The choice of a woman to write thus created strong reaction in others, and led to deeply felt currents of anxiety and guilt.

Carol Dyhouse points to the curious contradiction in the moral views of the Victorians, as they applied the concept of self-renunciation to men and women. She says, "In a man's education self-denial was more generally associated with the activist ethics of self-help, hard work and self-reliance," but in case of women, self-denial was regarded as related to the "passive virtues of patience, resignation and silent suffering" (175). In a society that "enshrined independence as one of the highest human virtues", "the desirability" of keeping women "totally in dependent roles" was constantly being emphasized (175).

The Victorian resistance to women writers who were keen to pursue a literary career caused many young aspirants to suppress their desire; Charlotte Bronte went through a prolonged phase of anxiety and tried to channelise her creative urge into other activities, such as teaching children. When she wrote to the Poet Laureate Robert Southey for advice, he wrote clearly against the idea of a literary career: "Literature" he wrote to her, "cannot be the business of a woman's life and it ought not to be" (Gaskell 127).

Aurora's defence of her choice of career begins by hinting at Romney's male arrogance towards women. Like other men, he too cannot regard women as independent beings, he thinks them "mere complement of his sex". On religious and humanitarian ground she asks that women be treated as individuals capable of responsible actions: "You forget too much that every creature, female as the male,/Stands single in responsible act and thought" (Bk II. 396). She tells him that she cannot agree to marry him for she has chosen another vocation: "I too have my vocation, work to do,/The heavens and earth have set me" (Bk II. 398). She further questions Romney's opinion of women's abilities. If he thinks that a woman lacks intellectual and moral maturity, then they cannot also be expected to share with men their (men's) difficult and tedious plans. How are then women asked to undertake the most difficult task of regarding and looking after children? She says,

> May God
> Be witness, 'twixt us two!
> To stand alone, yet strong enough to bear
> Such leaners, on my shoulders? poor to think
> Yet rich enough to sympathize with thought?
> Incompetent to sing, as blackbirds can
> Yet competent to love, like Him?" (Bk II. 396).

Aurora refuses to give into the rhetoric of Romney. He tells her that if he considers her "Sex" to be "weak for art", he thinks it "strong for life and duty", and in a romantic, heroic manner, asks her to "come hand in hand" with him to help the poor and suffering men and women. She thinks that the image evoked of companionship does not in real life work in that manner, for she finds the man-woman relationship after marriage becomes an unequal one. In the name of 'Love' she finds women cheated in marriage. Women are often 'surprised' by men when they talk to women of love and marriage; women give in "And catch up with it any kind of work/Indifferent, so that dear love go with it" (Bk II. 397). Women become willing slaves and bear the burden of men's missionary work, without complaining, and without getting any recognition for their contribution. She is not prepared to sacrifice her own wishes for a career, where she feels she could also prove to be equally useful to society.

Aurora does not agree with Romney in his description of poetry as an indulgence in dreams of beautiful meads and pastorals only. It is the artists, the poets, who give mankind visions of a new, better and more just world, preparing them for creating a new world. The poet is a prophet, a visionary: "God bid him speak to prove what lies beyond/Both speech and imagination. . . . " Even social reforms can be successful only when the minds of men have been prepared for changed conditions. She tells him "It takes a soul/To move a body: it takes a high-souled man/To move the masses, even to a cleaner sty" (Bk II. 398). She rejects Romney's materialistic vision of human beings, and says "We'll not barter, sir,/The beautiful for barley."

Finally her reason for not accepting Romney's proposal of marriage is an emotional one. She feels that Romney's proposal does not convey any sense of love for her. All he needs is a 'helpmate', 'a Sister of Charity', not really a wife. She tells him, ironically, that he is already wedded to his social cause: "Sir, you were married long ago,/You have a wife already, whom you love,/Your social theory" (Bk II. 399). She would want a more warm and loving relationship, and a more equal status within marriage.

Aurora's strong-worded and spirited defence of her choice brings her into conflict of choices and norms of woman's behaviour. After Romney leaves her, her aunt expresses shock and disbelief at the impudence of an almost penniless and lonely girl like her for having turned down a proposal of marriage from a rich and fine person like Romney. An important consideration in favour of Romney is also the fact that after the aunt's death Aurora will not have even a house of her own. All the Leigh property would belong to Romney. But this information given by the aunt to move Aurora to reconsider her views, only makes her more adamant. A few months later the aunt dies and Aurora moves to London to start working and living alone, as a professional writer. In her words and acts Aurora defies the socially accepted ideas of woman's role within family and society. Her search for working for herself, and attaining self-reliance, and economic independence are pursued with a determination that reveal a toughness within her. She aspires to become a literary woman and her rebellion, her struggles against convention and family pressures, especially her rejection of marriage on usual terms, all these are, as Ellen Moers calls it, the "heroic matter" of the poem and Aurora emerges in the poem as a strongwilled determined woman (Moers 40). She rejects the arrogant and highly chauvinist attitude of Romney and prepares to face all odds in order to pursue her career. She says "I choose to walk at all risks" (Bk II. 393). She finally agrees to marry Romney (in Bk IX), after he is suitably changed, and ready to value her love and devotion with much greater respect.

In pursuing a literary career Aurora's sense of conflict with the social norms of femininity became more intense than it would have if she had chosen some other career. Writing poetry was particularly an unsuitable and unlikely choice for a woman, for the poet's act of articulation requires an intense and sharp sense of self-consciousness. Such self-awareness could not fit in with the woman bound within socially constructed gender roles. A woman's desire to be part of her society and to be accepted as "feminine" clashes with her aesthetic career causing inner anxiety and self deprecation.[2] That Aurora later experiences such negative feelings about her success as a poet and she seeks emotional fulfillment in love for Romney expresses these conflicts that were part of woman's search for herself, her vocation and a new role within society. Elizabeth Barrett expresses powerfully, both, the aspiration and struggle of the young woman, and her later, subsequent clash between the desire to be an individual being, and to be loved. *Aurora Leigh* remains an important novel-poem for it challenges many of the dominant patriarchal ideas about women's roles and functions; it challenges restrictions put on women's self expression; it "denounces the gospel of self-sacrifice", and attacks "patriarchal religion". Like some other Victorian feminist texts it expresses their "search for new heroines: new role-models, and new lives" (Showalter 99).

The second Book of *Aurora Leigh* has the pace and tight

structure of a well-constructed play. It presents in fast-moving scenes the proposal of marriage, discussion of their ideological differences by Romney and Aurora followed by the later events: a new proposal, more gently termed, sent in a letter by Romney, and Aurora's more gentle refusal, her aunt's death and Romney's efforts to give Aurora some financial help, which she again refuses and her decision to move to London. The pace of movement takes the reader headlong, interested as much in the succession of events as in the characters. Aurora thrice refuses to accept Romney's offers, two of marriage and the third one of help, giving her full opportunity to express her strong sense of independence and the determination to work for herself. The poetic language is so regulated that the quick repartees, passionate exchanges and mild ironical and humorous hints make the reading extremely interesting. The language helps in building up a quick flow of conversation, bringing it very close to the pace of real spoken language.

What most impresses in Book II is the presentation of the characters. Romney's pride and prejudices are as vividly sketched as the sharp wit, quick temper and strong will of Aurora. The aunt's more conventional views and the young girl's sense of conviction build up the conflict of ideals and norms held by the rebellious girl and her society. Virginia Woolf praises the characterization; she feels that the intensity and brilliance of characters makes this novel in verse come superior to many prose novels. Elizabeth Barrett, she says, is able to give "a sense of life in general, of people who are unmistakably of their own time, all brightened, intensified and compacted by the fire in poetry." In this respect, Woolf says, *Aurora Leigh* "succeeds" (217).

The poem presents several contrasts that make the relationships more dramatic and effective. There are in Book II itself some contrasts between choices, ideology and emotions. The first of these contrasts is seen within the young heroine's search for freedom and selfhood, moving within the congenial open green world, where Romney comes as an intruder, inviting her to give up her search, and accept another, more approved role of wife and to be bound within domestic enclosure. She is asked to give up her freedom and accept a secondary, subservient role. The contrast between the patriarchal norms and views and Aurora's feminist quest, the choices of the mission of philanthropy and prophetic artistic role is presented in this unusual love story.

In *Aurora Leigh* Elizabeth Barrett Browning finds an artistic form for expressing the deep currents of anxiety, doubt and self-contrary emotions that were/are experienced by female artists. These frustrations and inner division of emotions are the lot of the "highly gifted girl" whose fate Virginia Woolf recreates in the story of the imaginary sister of Shakespeare she talks about in *A Room of One's Own* (1929). Both Browning and Woolf have been important influences on later feminist writers for both have given deep attention to the peculiar problems that women face when choosing a vocation, especially, the literary, creative vocation.

Notes

1. Mrs. Sarah Ellis, *Daughters of England* (1845) quoted by Carol Dyhouse, "The Role of Women: from Self-Sacrifice to Self-awareness", *The Victorians: The Context of English Literature*, ed. Laurence Lerner, London: Methuen and Co. Ltd., 1978, 174.
2. Sandra M. Gilbert and Susan Gubar give instances of continuing male critics' reluctance to accept acknowledged women poets on literary aesthetic basis. Women poets, they point out, are seen as writing either in spite of their femininity or as a form of compensation for not gaining emotional fulfillment in personal lives—issues relating to gender that are never raised in discussing a male poet. "Women Poets", *Literature in The Modern World: Critical Essays and Documents*, ed. Dennis Walder, Oxford: Oxford University Press in association with The Open University Press, 1990, 27-28.

References

Browning, Elizabeth Barrett. *Aurora Leigh*, Dedication, In *The Collected Works of Elizabeth Barrett Browning with Two Prose Essays*, 1904, Oxford University Press, rpt. 1951.

Bush, Douglas. *Mythology and the Romantic Tradition in English Poetry*, 1937, New York: The Norton Library, 1963.

Dyhouse, Carol. "The Role of Women: from Self-Sacrifice to Self-Awareness", *The Victorians: The Context of English Literature*, ed. Laurence Lerner, London: Methuen and Co. Ltd., 1978.

Gaskell, Elizabeth. *Life of Charlotte Bronte,* (1857), London, Everyman, 1919.

Gilbert, Sandra M. and Gubar, Susan. "Women Poets", *Literature in the Modern World: Critical Essays and Documents*, ed., Dennis Walder, Oxford: Oxford University Press, and The Open University Press, 1990.

Miller, Betty. *Robert Browning: A Portrait.* London: J. Murray, 1952.

Moers, Ellen. *Literary Women.* New York, Doubleday, 1978.

Woolf, Virginia. "Aurora Leigh". *Collected Essays*, Vol. I, (1925), London: Chatto and Windus, 1966.

8

Women Without Men: Family Patterns in *Cranford*

Veena Singh

Elizabeth Gaskell's *Cranford* is perhaps one of the first novels to present an all female society. There would be nothing surprising about an all male novel for the world of men opens out on to adventure, travel and explorations, but an all women novel makes several significant statements about marriage, family and society. It defines female space, projects and questions feminine roles and opens out patriarchal structures. In itself a totally female society is not creative: it is sterile and barren and does not procreate. It tends to become limited and closed and adopts hypocritical pretensions. Cranford is a small village inhabited, as the opening sentence indicates "Cranford is in possession of the Amazons: all the holders of houses, above a certain rent are women" (i). Their ability to pay rent establishes their independence and self sufficiency, but the ironical tone is also apparent in the use of the word Amazon with its masculine connotations. Patricia Beer has also observed in this connection that these women:

> do seem able to manage without men in the same way that they are able to manage without money: in fact, poverty and lack of men are equated as facts of life which can be combated by gentility and proper organization.
>
> (155)

At first sight the men are dispensable commodities and women manage with single-sex families. This view is not sustained for long. Gradually the narrative moves into various directions—the physical peripheries in the cottage occupied by Captain Brown and his two daughters, the social periphery occupied by the doctor, the trades people and the magician who entertains, and the nostalgic recapitulation of the past by the Jenkyn sisters, the extended families through the servants and the connections of Mary Smith with the present paternal figure of this society. Mary's father is Matty's financial adviser.

Most of the women are elderly spinsters, frigid and conservative in their attitude and disapproving of courtship and love. They shy away from expressions of desire and hide their emotions behind closed doors, darkness or muffled handkerchiefs. It is a world of incomplete lives and relationships, wary of its own passion and desire. In this society of the Amazons there are pictures of incomplete families. Into this world, inhabited by the single women, comes the sixty year old widower Captain Brown with his two daughters—Miss Brown, forty years old and Miss Jessie Brown, ten years younger than her sister. This incomplete family is further reduced by the fatal accident of the Captain. The sickly Miss Brown too dies, leaving Miss Jessie the lone survivor of the family. Like Jessie, the Jenkyns sisters are also the remnant of a family, their parents being dead and their brother lost. Miss Mary Smith, the narrator, who is a family friend of the Jenkyns, is a motherless child and her family consists only of her father and herself. The Barker sisters, who set up a milliner shop are also only by themselves.

Through indirect means the writer brings the missing members of the family into existence. For instance Matty relives the past through the letters exchanged between her dead parents. The letters throw light on the courtship, early married life of the parents and about their brother Peter's going away from home. The reading of these letters reconstructs the age that was—the life the Rector's family at the vicarage. In Arthur Pollard's words:

> Though Mrs. Gaskell suggests that the degree of satisfaction which husband and wife respectively derived from their letters may have varied in extent, she shows also how the letters symbolize the enduring affection between them.
>
> (71)

The strong bond of wedded love gives the couple strength and support in their ultimate sorrow when Peter runs off from home. Matty remembers how her father, "a strong man", when he saw "dumb despair" in her mother's face could not keep a hold over himself. But when the mother saw this, a gentle sorrow came over her countenance and she said, "Dearest John! don't cry; come with me, and we'll find him" (54). This sort of understanding and caring love for each other reinforces the importance of a family. Like the letters, the meeting of the old lovers, Mr. Holbrook and Matty in a store, and then the visit to his bachelor home—"a place which might have been her home" (31) is also a way of reclaiming of the family.

Besides these families, there are what could be called extended families. Mary Smith, the narrator is not directly related to Matty but at crucial moments—moments of distress and need—she is always by her side. Not only is her presence a consolation and a comfort for Matty but she also fulfils Matty's psychological need as she unwinds her heart to Mary. At the time of financial crisis it is Mary Smith who carves out plans for Matty's future. Martha, the maid, offers her savings to Matty when she loses her money in the shares and at the end Matty agrees to live with Martha and her husband Jem Hearn. This warm relationship between the master and the servant is no less than the bonds of kinship or family ties.

In the course of the novel along with truncated families some bright pictures of complete families also come up. Mrs. Gaskell brings into Cranford Lady Glenmire, who marries the doctor Mr. Hoggins. Initially this news creates shock waves in this society for it is a union between nobility and a commoner—an idea much against the false notion of decorum and decency prescribed in this society. This marriage points to the crumbling of the rigid social order. Another marriage that takes place is the marriage of Jessie Brown to her suitor Major Gordon. The spinsters return "with wonderful account of her house, her husband, her dress and her looks. For, with happiness, something of her early bloom returned" (22). The marriage further finds its completeness in the form of their daughter Flora. Another family is that of the magician Signor Brunoni and his wife. This couple has undergone tremendous hardships and bereavement and they symbolize love and mutual fidelity. Their daughter Phoebe brings happiness into not only her parents' lives but also to Matty and others. The Signor we are told has a twin brother, who in the words of his wife is a "very helpful and good brother" (110).

In the world of the Amazons men may have been pushed to the periphery, and "if gentlemen were scarce, and almost unheard of in the genteel society, they or their counterparts—handsome young men—abounded in the lower classes" (24). Martha has a lover whom she ultimately marries. Fanny too had a lover. In fact, we are told that "the pretty neat servant-maids had their choice of desirable followers" (24). The servant-maids openly express their desire to marry and settle down. This is in contrast to the single women who delude themselves into believing that they can live or manage without men, little do they realize that their singleness is either by compulsion (as they are widows) or for reasons of thwarted love, or circumstance (like Matty's) and not by choice.

The concept of family is very closely related to the positive concepts of love, fidelity, sacrifice, fame, security, companionship, reverence, honour and motherhood. If the Jenkyns couple are an embodiment of love, the Browns stand for sharing and fidelity. For family honour Rector Jenkyns publicly reprimands his son Peter and as a consequence loses him. Jessie delays matrimony so as to be able to nurse her sick sister. After her father's funeral she comes back, puts off her mourning dress, and even smiles, "as if to reassure us of her power to endure" (18). Her sisterly love compels her to hide the news of her father's death from her dying sister as she wants to spare her this shock. Morality, the sense of right and wrong, takes up a different meaning in the changed circumstances. On one hand Matty succumbs to parental pressure and gives up Mr. Holbrook on the ground that her father believed that he was not "enough of a gentleman" being much below her rank (29). On the other hand Lady Glenmire crosses social barriers of class and wealth and marries Dr. Hoggins. Family and motherhood are inseparable. The concept of motherhood is stressed upon and almost glorified in chapter XI of *Cranford*. Mrs Brown for the sake of her infant leaves her husband in India and alone undertakes a hazardous voyage back home. It would be relevant to mention here that Mrs. Gaskell herself was very attached to her family. Her husband and her children were her first priority (L-480 and L-584). She kept a diary in which she faithfully recorded her day to day experiences in rearing her children, particularly her first-born. Motherhood was an exalting experience for her. She believed that a woman's natural fulfilment lay in marriage and motherhood. In a letter to Lady Kay-Shuttleworth in 1850 she wrote:

> I am always glad and thankful... that I am a wife and mother, and that I am so happy in the performance of those clear and defined duties, for I think there must be a few years of great difficulty in the life of every women who foresees and calmly accepts single life.
>
> (L-72)

and again in 1860 she wrote to Charles Eliot Norton:

> I think an unmarried life may be to the full as happy, in process of time, but there is still a time of trial to be gone through with women who naturally yearn after children.
>
> (L-453)

Mrs. Gaskell's own role as a wife and a mother, as reflected in her letters and personal diary that she maintained, in no way clashes with her role as a professional writer. She experienced and believed in the contentment, strength and support that came from family. The ladies of Cranford have all had their "years of great difficulty" and their "time of trial".

If the family instills certain values in a human being, sex deprivation results in falsehood and hypocrisy. The Victorians were timid of talking about passion. Their attitude was one of indirectness. But no matter how indirectly expressed, love and passion remained the centre of human action. The restraint and the control which social conditions made necessary, only helped to highlight the hidden passions which in themselves were explosive. These single women who flit through Cranford, at their personal level succeed in sublimating sex, and reconcile to male absence but the longing for male company and nostalgia for the family remains. For instance the strict and stern Miss Jenkyns "a model of feminine decorum" for the ladies of Cranford, when told of a gentleman sitting in the drawing room with his arm round Miss Jessie, responds "the most proper place in the world for his arm to be in" (22). Miss Matty explicitly talks of a strange yearning at her heart whenever she sees a mother with her baby. The recurring dream of a little child "clasping her dear little arms" around her neck (107) is an overt expression of her suppressed desire. Such honesty keeps breaking through. Some more examples of this are to be found: Miss Pole, the most eloquent manhater, hangs a man's hat in the lobby to scare burglars (89), Miss Matty looks upon a husband as a great protector, in whom one can find intellectual, emotional and physical security. She says:

> I don't mean to deny that men are troublesome in a house. I don't judge from my own experience, for, my father was neatness itself... but still a man has a sort of knowledge of what should be done in difficulties, that it is very pleasant to have one ready to lean upon.

Juxtaposed to these images of frustration are pictures of fruition in love. Stories of Martha and Jessie, but the happiest of these is the story of Lady Glenmire and Dr. Hoggins. Mrs.

Gaskell subtly brings out the vitality of Lady Glenmire and the virility in the "broad and radiant" Dr. Hoggins. The lady is said to have "a kind of attraction". Falling in love has brought back "something of the flush of youth" in her. Her lips look "redder and more trembling full than in their old compressed state" (117). On hearing of this relationship first, the ladies of Cranford see in it an element of danger and degradation but soon accept it. Arthur Pollard is of the opinion that:

> Hoggins is the surgeon, the bringer of healing. He restores Signor Brunoni. His is the true magic, but Brunoni also is shown as a force making for life. His story and that of his wife is a history of courage, struggle, tenderness and affection. They, together with other characters from outside such as Lady Glenmire and Peter Jenkyns, are used to demonstrate some of the insufficiencies of Cranford society. (84)

Patricia Beer also holds this view. The return of the long lost brother, Peter Jenkyns, she views as a "saving arrival". She writes:

> He is not a husband, it is true, but he is a protector, a companion, a financial support and a restorer of harmony to the whole of Cranford, even inducing Mrs. Jamieson to speak to the fallen, radiant impenitent Mrs. Hoggins. (159)

By the time the reader approaches the end of the novel it is evident that the opening sentence about the Amazons is meant as an ironic exaggeration. The world of Cranford widens out to accept outsiders and normalcy. The closed world of the spinsters disintegrates giving place to a healthy growth, more families, marriages and children. The social structure that these women had evolved for themselves by pretending not to know that they know falters, as in essence, it was an artificial one. The concepts of honour and class, social respectability have undergone a change. Now "friendly sociability" is established in Cranford (60).

In the early pages of the novel there are several deaths Captain Brown, Miss Brown, Miss Jenkyns all die but by the end of the novel children are being born, further more there is talk of "the probable children" (156). The spinsters will no more be disturbed by the idea that society would crumble down.

> As most of the ladies of good family in Cranford were elderly spinsters, or widows without children, if we did not relax a little and become less exclusive by-and-by we should have no society at all. (64)

For Mrs. Gaskell, as a Victorian, as a woman and as a writer, the concept of family, which has no substitute or alternative, seems to be the heterogeneous family.

References

Beer, Patricia. *Reader, I Married Him*, London: The Macmillian Press, 1974.

Chapple, J.A.V. *Letters of Mrs. Gaskell*, Ed. J.A.V. Chapple and Arthur Pollard, Manchester: Manchester University Press, 1966.

Gaskell, Elizabeth. *Cranford* (1853). Ed. Elizabeth Porges Watson, Oxford University Press, 1980.

Pollard, Arthur. *Mrs. Gaskell, Novelist and Biographer*. Manchester: Manchester University Press, 1965.

9

The World of *Cranford*: A Structural Approach

Veena Singh

Cranford has often been read and put aside as a woman's novel and dismissed as light reading. Few critics have concerned themselves with its narrative structure. Angus Easson is perhaps one of the few to have acknowledged its distinctiveness. Comparing it to *Our Village* by Mary Russell Mitford (1787-1855) Easson comments:

> Martin Dodsworth in a perceptive essay insisted that 'The fundamentally serious concerns of her book have been neglected for a belle-lettristic study of incidental detail, and while I query his suggestion that we should treat the novel as symbolic of a conflict within the mind of the author, I do want to argue for a serious concern with the pattern of behaviour and feeling for the pathos which (along with evident comedy) lies in the book.

Other critics like Vineta Colby and David Cecil comment in passing on it. Colby in her book *Yesterday's Woman* hardly devotes a full paragraph to it. (248-49). Cecil in his book *The Early Victorian Novelists* (240) finds nothing "remarkable" in *Cranford* and faults it for its happy ending. As recent a book as *Elizabeth Gaskell* by Tessa Brodetsky has not much to say on *Cranford*. One reason for the neglect of *Cranford* lies in its episodic structure, and the nature of its comedy. But it is perhaps the dominance of women characters and its difference from the industrial novel which has led to its isolation from the main body of Mrs. Gaskell's work.

There is, however, a need to view *Cranford* as part of Mrs. Gaskell's work and relate the writer's creative talent as manifest in other works also to this. *Cranford* continues a tradition of comedy; it also works out the psychological inferences of this comedy. The canvas is narrow but through her narrative strategies the writer manages to encompass a wider world. This paper is an attempt to examine the various strategies Mrs. Gaskell uses to achieve this.

When Mrs. Gaskell began writing *Cranford* she never knew that what was meant to be one episode in *Household Words* would become a series of short stories, each complete in itself but tied together by the involvement of the narrator, Mary Smith, in the affairs of Miss Matty, and through her with the other residents of Cranford. The stories are also held together by Mrs Gaskell's constant craving 'for the country' (Letter 421).[1] For Mrs. Gaskell, Cranford was symbolic of the town where she was brought up and which enshrined many of her cherished memories. As she herself says in a letter to William and Mary Howitt in May 1838, "I was brought up in a country town and my lot is now to live in or rather on. . . before me." (Letter 8).

In *Cranford* the narrator, Mary Smith, who may be viewed as the alter ego of Mrs. Gaskell, is given the freedom that Mrs. Gaskell did not have. She moves from industrial Drumble to Cranford with ease, and only in one instance, when her father falls ill, does she have to leave Cranford against her own will. These flights into the countryside were what Mrs. Gaskell yearned for and for this reason perhaps she described the book as "the only one of my own books that I can read again. . . but whenever I am ailing or ill, I take Cranford and . . . I was going to say enjoy it! (but that would not be pretty!) laugh over it afresh!" (Letter 562).

Then again, in a letter to Eliza Fox in 1854 Mrs. Gaskell writes "Nature intended me for a gypsy-bachelor: that I am sure of. Not an old maid for they are particularly fidgety and tidy, and punctual—but a gypsy bachelor" (Letter 206).

Having based *Cranford* on her childhood memories of Knutsford, Cheshire, Mrs. Gaskell then proceeds to fill it with characters and incidents based more on real life than on fiction. The world of Cranford is made to appear a social and a historical reality. Mrs. Gaskell gives dates and details of persons and things. The parents of the Jenkyns sisters had got married in 1774. There are other references to historical and political events like the Napoleonic wars, also to the literary events. Johnson is clearly a much respected writer—the respect inherited from an earlier generation. The references to Dickens put him within a contemporary framework, a writer who is slowly becoming popular but not widely respected. There are other details which refer to a lifestyle which is threatened by the rise of industrialization. The china, the furniture, the plates, the eating habits and the thinly sliced bread and butter sandwiches, are all described in detail in order to provide a realistic framework. But the characterization and the literary craftsmanship instilled in Mary Smith's presentation of life in Cranford creates an independent world of creative fiction.

When Mrs. Gaskell wrote the first episode of *Cranford* (which forms the first two chapters of the book) for *Household Words* she also meant it to be the last, a one-time flashback to childhood and an escape from the suffocating atmosphere of Manchester where she "never felt well" as she wrote to Eliza Bridell-Fox. (Letter 421) She even "killed" Captain Brown very much against her will as she told Ruskin in a letter (Letter 562). But the popularity of the episode and the immense satisfaction that she herself derived led her to write many episodes which form the content of *Cranford*.

Published in *Household Words* between December 1851 and May 1853 the world of *Cranford* comprises a small town, with a limited number of houses, and a pre-dominantly female population. In Mary Smith's words "Cranford is in possession of the Amazons" (*Cranford*). It is a fairly well regulated world with rigid conventions of behaviour and rules of everything, for seating, for invitations, for visiting and calls, for serving tea and playing cards. It is a world which gives the impression of thriving on appearances. If on the one hand there was "unacknowledged poverty" (3), on the other there was the "acknowledged gentility"(7). Inhabited mostly by widows and spinsters "with a distaste for mankind" (7), it appears to be a static, closed world. And in case one is to view the work as a collection of episodes, it would not do to examine the direction of the narration.

The action and the narration of all the successive chapters can be traced to the first, which is titled "Our Society". Beginning with a description of this Amazonian town, we are told how the "ladies of Cranford are quite sufficient" (1). Into this world enters a man who is bold enough to invade their territory and brazen enough to talk about his poverty. In almost everything, he is in direct opposition to this female world—in his frankess, in his commonsensical approach, his sense of humour and in his choice of books. He prefers to read the books of Dickens to those of Johnson. Miss Jenkyns' death liberates Miss Matty from the overpowering presence of her sister; thus, the two unacknowledged leaders are both dead—Captain Brown and Miss Jenkyns—by chapter II of the book. A new centre has to be found, but is sadly missing. If Miss Pole is capable of some initiative, Mrs. Jamieson has claims to social superiority.

With the deaths of Miss Jenkyns and Captain Brown the closed society of Cranford opens up. The self-imposed close confines of the women of Cranford get diffused at multiple levels and various social activities burst forth, bringing the air and freshness of spring after a cold, dismal winter. Romances like the relationship between Holbrook and Miss Matty, Martha and Jem Hern and marriages like that of Jessie Brown with Major Gordon and Dr. Hoggins with Lady Glenmire get talked about and eventually reach fruition. In the process class barriers also collapse as in the case of Lady Glenmire marrying Doctor Hoggins—a case of human values winning over social conventions.

Also the bastions of privacy that the people of Cranford had raised crumble with the advent of the outside world into their lives. Signor Brunoni brings the hocus-pocus of the east followed by the long lost Peter with his "stories that sounded so very much like Baron Munchausen" (152) and the hyperbolic fantasies that he weaved. A little later the outside world again encroaches into Cranford in the form of the failure of the bank, which raises questions of ethics and morality for Miss Matty.

One crosses through several time barriers while reading *Cranford* Mrs. Gaskell uses her skill to portray events in a see-saw fashion going from present to past and back again with faultless ease. Miss Matty goes back in time with "Letters interchanged between my ever honoured father and my dearly beloved mother, prior to their marriage in July 1774" (43). Visions of her parents are aroused with feelings of happiness and joy. But when it comes to reading her late sister's letters there is agony and suffering for her. She is not very happy burning the letters but does so as it has to be done. "We must burn them, I think. . . . No one will care for them when I am gone" (44). Mrs. Gaskell's ability to conjure up a minute detailed description is at its best:

> And one by one she dropped them into the middle of the fire; watching each blaze up, die out, and rise away, in faint, white, ghostly semblance, up the chimney, before she gave up another to the same fate. The room was light enough now, but I, like her, was fascinated into watching the destruction of those letters, into which the honest warmth of a manly heart had been poured forth.
>
> (44)

Another leap into the past occurs when Thomas Holbrook is brought into the story when Miss Matty overhears him at the shop. Memories of the affair of her youth are brought back and relived when Miss Matty and Mary Smith pay a visit to his house. It is a lengthy visit—"a long June day" (30), and for Miss Matty it is a reliving of the past-even though briefly.

The episode relating to Peter is partly in the nature of a flashback with a swift change to the future when he ultimately returns:

> The effect is of the passing of the present time over the past, which by most delicate stimulus and association still touches and can affect it.
>
> (*Cranford* ix)

The class structure that the women of Cranford had erected to protect their insularity and the sharp cleavages that kept the classes apart crumble with the advent of the outsiders like Brown, Holbrook, the magician and Peter into their midst. Behaviour patterns begin to change as a result of the radically different behaviour of these people. Miss Matty agrees to open a tea-shop to earn a livelihood even though her friends decide to help her out financially (137). This shows the juxtaposition of values and the contrast that was growing between the past and the future. Lady Glenmire's decision to marry Dr. Hoggins even though "she has married for an establishment" (115) is indicative of social non-conformity in the world of Cranford.[2]

Gradually the society of Cranford becomes unfettered and veers towards normalcy in the generally accepted meaning. People open out, become less hypocritical and the focus shifts from sandwiches and cards to babies and fashions. Little Flora Gordon brings happiness in the lives of the Jenkyns.

Mrs. Gaskell's innate sense of literary timing and craftsmanship is seen in the various techniques and strategies she adopts to maintain the pace of narration and keep the reader's interest alive in subsequent episodes. After describing three deaths in quick succession, she balances the gloom and misery with exotica as presented by Signor Brunoni and exaltation symbolised by the long-awaited return of Peter, just in time to bolster Miss Matty's flagging spirits and health. The tedium of Captain Brown's death is broken with the reviving of memories of Miss Matty's love affair of days gone by. The geographical confines of Cranford, the town, is diffused with Holbrook's fancy for travelling, his last visit to Paris that ultimately leads to his death and the adventures of Peter leading to his amassing a wealth of adventure and stories which made him "such a favourite at Cranford. . . for their quiet lives were astonishingly stirred up by the arrival from India—especially as the person arrived told more wonderful stories than Sindbad the Sailor" (153-154).

Another outside "interference" that Mrs. Gaskell used as part of her narrative strategy was the reference to the misfortunes of the Town and County Bank (119) and Miss Matty's moral involvement by way of her ownership of shares in it. With poverty considered taboo, at least in conversation, Mrs. Gaskell used the heart-rending incident of the farmer's five-pound note being rejected at the store (122) to highlight the pathos that lack of money could create. However, on the other hand, "When Mrs. Forrester, for instance, gave a party in her baby-house of a dwelling, and the little maiden disturbed the ladies on the sofa by a request that she might get the tea-tray out from underneath, every one took this novel proceeding as the most natural thing in the world" (3). Even when "our hostess" pretended not to know that cakes were sent up for tea "though she knew, and we knew, and she knew that we knew, she had been busy all the morning making tea bread and sponge cakes"(3).

With the element of fantasy accounted for by Signor Brunoni and Peter, Mrs. Gaskell counter-climaxes this with the element of fear and panic brought about by the robberies. Through Mary Smith's doubts as to whether Miss Pole "really would enjoy the little adventure of having her house broken into," Mrs. Gaskell hints at the deep-seated sexual repression that plagues the women of Cranford, who are very early in the book described as widows and spinsters. Sex, no doubt, is an important subject in *Cranford* and there is a lot that suggests that there is sexual unfulfilment in the lives of these spinsters and widows. These women show a profound fear and at the same time a queer curiosity about men. The most humorous remark in this regard comes from Miss Pole, "My father was a man, and I know the sex pretty well" (96). Miss Matty's frustration at not experiencing motherhood and her suppressed desire for the pleasures of a family life are expressed as she tells Mary Smith:

> I am afraid I lost the knack, though I am just as fond of children as ever, and have a strange yearning at my heart whenever I see a mother with her baby in her arms. . . do you know, I dream sometimes that I have a little child—always the same—a little girl of about two years old. . . .
>
> (107)

Similarly, when Holbrook dies she wants to mourn his death as his wife but is inhibited from doing so because of social considerations. These are examples eloquent of sexual repression. Chapter X 'The Panic', as the subtitle suggests, brings into focus more sharply the sexual frustration of these women. The journey in the sedan chairs, the panic generated by the attack on Mrs. Jamieson (93) and by the various gossips and rumours that get "afloat in the town" all have sexual connotations. But the shock of Cranford being the place where carts

> Went about in the dead of the night, drawn by horses shod with felt, and guarded by men in dark clothes, going round the town, no doubt, in search of some unwatched house or some unfastened door.
>
> (89)

And the panic helps in bringing about emotional normalcy among the residents.

Thus, we see that by the time the novel ends "our society" is no more the closed, unnatural, dark, repressed world of the Amazons. Instead it is a world which has purged itself of certain insufficiencies, coarseness, hypocrisy and suppression in all fields. Now a balance has been struck and the distance between Drumble and Cranford and between Johnson and Dickens has been narrowed. The very fact that the book has been reprinted time and again is proof of its appeal, which at one level is because of its delicate, sensitive humour,[3] blended with irony and wit at times to expose hypocrisy, and at another level its genuine concern with important human issues like class, money, taste and sex.

Notes

1. Reference to the numbering of letters is according to the numbering in *Mrs. Gaskell's Letters* ed. Arthur Pollard and J.A.V. Chapple, Manchester: University Press, 1966.
2. In this connection Arthur Pollard comments: "The question of rank and class is centred critically upon Mrs Jamieson. All the behaviour of this self-conscious aristocrat is boorish. Not only does she ignore Mrs. Fitz Adam, but in lesser details also Mrs. Gaskell takes care to expose her bad manners. . . and her greater concerns for her pet dog, Carlo, than for her social acquaintance (79). Mrs. Jamieson exploits her rank, and it is therefore appropriate that her relative and social equal, Lady Glenmire, should explode her pretensions (*Mrs Gaskell, Novelist and Biographer*, 1965:82).
3. Mrs. Gaskell is perhaps the only woman writer of her generation to have this quality. She continues Jane Austen's tradition of wit and irony, but as she shifts it occasionally to a pastoral background, it is softened in its impact. Mrs. Gaskell's humour is often overshadowed by her social and human concerns which have dominated her image as a writer.

References

Brodetsky, Tessa. *Elizabeth Gaskell*, Oxford: Oxford University Press, 1986.

Cecil, David. *The Early Victorian Novelists: Essays in Revaluation*. (1934). Constable of Company Ltd., 1957.

Colby, Vineta. *Yesterday's Woman*. Princeton: Princeton University Press, 1974.

Easson, Angus. *Elizabeth Gaskell*. London: Routledge and Kegan Paul

Ltd., 1979.

Gaskell, Elizabeth. *Cranford*, ed. Elizabeth Porges Watson. Oxford University Press, 1980.

Pollard, Arthur and Chapple J.A.V. ed. *Mrs. Gaskell's Letters.* Manchester: Manchester University Press, 1966.

Pollard, Arthur. *Mrs Gaskell, Novelist and Biographer.* Manchester: Manchester University Press, 1965.

10

The Coming of Age of Shakespeare's Sister: Woolf's *Room*

Savita Goel

Virginia Woolf has contributed greatly to the exploration of feminine values. She has brought to the feminine cause "something much more interesting and profound than an advocacy of equal rights" (Bennett 76). She endeavours to comprehend the patriarchal structures of power and resents the forms of economic, social, educational and professional inequalities and the disappointments, deprivation and anguish that they inflict disproportionately on women. She stresses the fact that women should have more space within the prevailing social structures and yearns to deconstruct the existing status quo.

A Room of One's Own, based on the lectures on 'Women and Fiction' delivered by Woolf at Newnham and Girton in 1928 is a profound study of women's writings and their professional problems within a male-dominated tradition and illustrates the insuperable difficulties that Shakespeare's equally brilliant fictional sister encountered. Woolf contends that some of the reasons for the limited achievements of women in the field of arts are lack of opportunities, money, education and privacy, and domestic servitude, demands of motherhood, male hostility and above all, the absence of any nurturing female tradition, for "we think back through our mothers if we are women" (Woolf 83). At the outset, she makes it clear that women must be economically independent and possess a room of their own if they are to write fiction.

Woolf is concerned about the "safety and security of one sex and the poverty and insecurity of the other" (29). She examines the economic inequality between the two sexes with her fantasy of her two days spent at Oxbridge, a traditional male college and Fernham, a college for women. She adopts a tone of "mock humility and reverence towards the institutions and traditions of the male colleges in order to make fun of their patriarchal assumptions of authority and knowledge" (Morris 74). She describes her encounter with this world of "privileged elitism" (74) as she is driven back from the smooth turf reserved only for Fellows and Scholars. Even the guardian of the library prohibits her entry to the library regretting "that ladies are only admitted to the library if accompanied by a fellow of the College or furnished with a letter of introduction" (Woolf 2). Woolf contrasts the two realms—of the privileged and the under-privileged and it is not only in the restrictions that she encounters "a world which has never questioned its assumptions or its right to privilege" (Rosenthal 222). It pervades the lushness of setting, the magnificent buildings where an unending stream of gold and silver flows, the splendid equipment, the lavish meals and the "yellow flame of rational intercourse" (Woolf 15). In Oxbridge life seems very pleasant, "how sweet its rewards, how trivial this grudge or that grievance, how admirable friendship and the society of one's kind, as lighting a good cigarette, one sunk among the cushions in the window-seat" (15).

However, the geniality and the dignity which are the products of luxury, privacy and space, the sumptuous confectionery, wines and partridges of Oxbridge do not exist at Fernham, instead there is plain gravy soup, prunes, custard and beef "with its attendant greens and potatoes—a home trinity, suggesting the rumps of cattle in a muddy market" (22) and a building of ordinary red bricks with wild unkempt grasses. If women had possessed all the prerogatives which their male counterparts have then, "we could have been sitting at our ease to-night and the subject of our talk might have been archaeology, botany,. . . . If only Mrs. Seton and her mother before her had learnt the great art of making money . . . we might have been exploring or writing" (26). The inadequacy of resources at Fernham reveals that financial dependency narrows down individual energies and potentialities and curbs the intellectual growth. It is futile to ponder on what might have happened if Mrs. Seton and her mother had amassed great wealth, because "in the first place, to earn money was impossible for them, and in the second, had it been possible, the law denied them the right to possess what money they earned" (27).

Woolf probes deeper into the question of women's poverty and their imperceptible contribution to literature. She points out that women are relegated to the purely biological realm, their 'natural' creativity is seen as centered around child-bearing and child-rearing and they are denied a social identity. She visits her friend Mary Seton at Fernham and finds a photograph of Mary's mother on the mantelpiece who appears to be a symbol of domestic slavery like Mrs. Murgatroyd in *The Voyage Out*. "She was a homely lady; an old lady in a plaid shawl which was fastened by a large cameo. . ." (26). She has thirteen children by her husband, a minister of the church. It is practically not feasible to make a fortune and rear thirteen children, "no human being could stand it" (27).

The writer protests against the injustices done to women. Her protests were concerned with her personal grievances, the predicament of middle-class women like herself, but ultimately they assumed a more universal significance. Having consulted Trevelyan's *History of England*, she concludes that women "live like Bats or Owls, labour like Beasts, and die like Worms" (67) and have always been the passive victims of unalterable male oppression. All kinds of tortures were inflicted on women who did not marry the person of their parents' choice. They were married when they were still infants, the husband was the "lord and master, so far at least as law and custom could make him" (48) and wife-beating was his right. Comparing women's real life with her portrayal in fiction, Woolf points out that "imaginatively" she is of utmost significance but "practically" she is a non-entity. She observes, "Some of the most profound thoughts in literature fall from her lips; in real life she could hardly read, could scarcely spell and was the property of her husband" (50).

Woolf examines the social and psychic mechanisms that construct and perpetuate gender inequality. She wonders why women who were the constant subject of Elizabethan poetry were unable to pursue the art that obsessed them. She imagines that Shakespeare had an extremely brilliant sister Judith, who did not get an opportunity to receive education and was expected to "mend the stockings or mind the stew and not moon about with books and papers" (53) although she was equally adventurous and imaginative, "as agog to see the world as he was" (53). She protested against her betrothal to the son of a neighbouring wood-stapler and escaped to London where she had a sad realization that being a woman she cannot act and get any training in her craft, nor can she have dinner in a tavern or stroll the streets at midnight. At last Nick Greene, the actor-manager took pity on her; she found herself pregnant by that man, committed suicide and "lies buried at some cross-roads where the omnibuses now stop" (54). Chastity in those days was employed as a fetish to prevent women from expressing themselves freely. Women poets or playwrights underwent a great mental stress which might have led them insane or even killed them. If they survived, whatever they wrote was twisted and deformed, issuing from a strained and morbid imagination.

The plight of women ameliorated to some extent in the nineteenth century and the careers of Bronte sisters, George Eliot and other women writers amply portray that great talents were no longer destined to be buried at the crossroads although they had to face innumerable problems. They were confined within their normal domain of the home and the family by men who thought that "women writers were women first, artists second" (Showalter 73). They believed that women should "confine themselves to making puddings. . . playing on the piano and embroidering bags" (Woolf 76) and it was preposterous for women to know and achieve more than tradition has pronounced necessary for their sex. Charlotte Bronte in the moments of intense concentration left her story to attend to some personal grievance. She was starved of her proper experience, "she had been made to stagnate in a parsonage mending stockings when she wanted to wander free over the world" (80). Their restricted freedom of movement, liberty to seek experience and cultivate the mind circumscribed their artistic achievements and their subject matter. Woolf envisages that Bronte's genius would have profited greatly if it had not spent itself in solitary visions over distant fields and if she possessed greater knowledge of the busy world. Similarly, if Jane Austen was affected in any way from her circumstances, it was in the cramped life that was imposed on her. Women writers have suffered enormously due to lack of personal autonomy, propitious ambience and privacy. In the early nineteenth century the middle class family possessed a single sitting-room and if women wanted to write, they wrote in this room amidst its constant distractions. Emily Bronte and George Eliot had an innate genius for poetic plays and biography but when they took to writing they naturally wrote novels which required lesser concentration.

The lives of women are a record of unacknowledged work and accomplishments. Men get due credit for their achievements but there are "no yard measures. . . that one can lay against the qualities of a good mother or the devotion of a daughter or the fidelity of a sister, or the capacity of a housekeeper" (92). Renowned writers like Johnson, Goethe and Cowper were oblivious of the fact that it was a woman at home who paved their path to greatness while she herself lived in obscurity. They derived not just comfort, flattery, emotional and physical gratification from the opposite sex but a lot more that their own sex was unable to supply. Women yielded to men a "renewal of creative power" (94) by the contact of contrasting ways of life.

Woolf asserts that values prevailing in the current fiction are values which have been "made by the other sex" and it is the "masculine values that prevail" (80-81). Male critics always treat books written by females as if "texts themselves were women, and they impose on them the same kind of stereotypes that generally characterize thinking about women" (Ellman 33). They tend to exclude or to marginalize women's writing by expurgating its permitted subject matter or by considering its subject matter to be insignificant, unrepresentative and irrational. The critics assume, "This is an important book, . . . because it deals with war. This is an insignificant book because it deals with the feelings of women in a drawing room" (Woolf 81).

Elaine Showalter in *A Literature of Their Own* traces the process of women's literary history and their effort for recognition as writers and insinuates that women's fictional writing can be visualized in three major phases in response to the changing social and cultural milieu in which they worked. These three phases are also reflected in *A Room of One's Own*. The first phase was characterized by men's insistence on women's inferior creative powers. Women generally imitated the dominant male modes and internalized their aesthetic and social values and writers like George Eliot, George Bell and others endeavoured to conceal their identity by adopting male names. George Eliot failed to create for herself her own mode of expression, simulating instead the prose style of great male novelists "committing atrocities with it that beggar description" (84). Similar was the case with Charlotte Bronte.

The second phase of women's writings was characterized by their protest against prevailing attitudes and conditions, against female entrapment in a male-centered ideology and demanding greater autonomy in their lives and writings. Jane Austen and Emily Bronte, representatives of this phase, succeeded in writing as women write, not as men write. They felt confident of their own values and judgements and exploited their own "peculiar gifts instead of trying to emulate the gifts proper to masculine mind" (Sackville-West 620) and they alone "ignored the perpetual admonitions of the eternal pedagogue—write this, think that" (Woolf 82).

In the final phase, literary daughters can think back through literary mothers, as a female tradition has been established. The female writers, "looking at and revering such precursors, are also haunted and daunted by the autonomy of these figures" (Gilbert and Gubar I:195). They have succeeded in liberating themselves from reacting to patriarchal values and male hegemony and have turned inward seeking their autonomous female identity. Mary Carmichael, an imaginary modern novelist, is a symbol of emancipated women, and men are no longer to her "the opposing faction" and "travel, experience and knowledge of the world" (Woolf 100) are accessible to her. She possesses a sensibility that is "wide, eager and free" (100). She describes a whole range of experiences and employs an innovative style and theme in her novel. She writes, "Chloe liked Olivia" and "Chloe liked Olivia for the first time in literature. Cleopatra did not like Octavia and how completely *Antony and Cleopatra* would have been altered had she done so" (89). Myriad male-authored texts have portrayed relationships between women primarily in terms of sexual rivalry and betrayal. Woolf recognizes "the representation of affection between women as a near revolutionary quality in women's writing" (Morris 61) and suggests that the representation of mutual love and faith "will light a torch in that vast chamber where nobody has yet been" (Woolf 91). She seeks to create a feeling of sisterhood, a new sense of cordiality and kinship among women, in order to overcome the hostility that women in the past had for other women as a result of isolation and vulnerability within a male canon.

Uncannily perceptive in her vision, Woolf visualizes that her book would act like a stormy petrel for the opposite sex and would arouse a great opposition, so to pacify them she subtly contends that neither purely masculine nor purely feminine mind can create a great work of art and it is fatal for creative writers to think of their sex. Fiction written by men seems incomprehensible to women because they write with "only the male side of their brains" (109). Mr. Galsworthy and Mr. Kipling describe the world of men and enforce only male values. Neither has a spark of the woman in him (110). Thus, all their qualities seem crude and immature and seem to lack suggestive power. Similarly, it is improper for a women to stress any grievance or plead for a cause or to speak consciously as a woman "for anything written with that conscious bias is doomed to death" (112). Some kind of union has to take place in the mind between the woman and the man, some "marriage of opposites has to be consummated" (112) before the art of creation can be achieved. It is when this fusion takes place that the mind is fully fertilized and uses all its faculties. Coleridge, too, believes that a great mind is androgynous. Woolf portrays the ideal state of men and women, a state in which they exist in absolute harmony in the scene of the young couple meeting and taking a cab. Perhaps, Woolf wrote all this to evade any controversy.

A book, Woolf writes, is not made "of sentences laid end to end, but of sentences built, if an image helps, into arcades or domes" (84). The spatial pattern in *A Room of One's Own* is built up of contrasts and symbolizes the relationship and the status of the two sexes. Initially, a fictional woman character longs for the smooth turf but had to satisfy herself with the gravel path. The space now contracts and she yearns to enter the library but is prohibited and finally desires to possess a room of her own which is a symbol of detachment, calm, freedom, autonomy, means, opportunity and of one's own self.

Virginia Woolf visualizes the resurgence of 'new women'. She compares the oppressed women with strange creatures that had been "under the shadow of rock these million years" (92). Economic and social emancipation will enable them to perceive light and "a piece of strange food - knowledge, adventure, art" (92) coming their way. Women should involve themselves in activities which are not traditionally feminine to speed up the dissolution of rigid sex roles. She imagines that in a century women will cease to be the protected sex and suggests, "Remove that protection, expose them to the same exertions and activities, make them soldiers and sailors and engine drivers" (46). Once women assume new roles a corresponding transformation in their entire vision will take place. Being extremely optimistic about the future of women, she asserts that although Shakespeare's sister did not succeed in proving her talents and was buried at the cross-roads, she has resurrected in "you and in me" (122) and in all other women because great talents never perish, "they are continuing presences; they need only the opportunity to walk among us in the flesh" (122). All women possess a spark of creativity in them which can never be suppressed by men, if they develop indomitable courage, determination and a habit of freedom in themselves.

References

Bennett, Joan. *Virginia Woolf: Her Art as a Novelist*. Cambridge: Cambridge University Press, 1964.

Ellmann, Mary. *Thinking about Women*. Macmillan, 1964.

Gilbert, Sandra M., and Susan Gubar. *No Man's Land: The Place of the Woman Writer in the Twentieth Century*, 2 vols. New Haven: Yale UP, 1988.

Morris, Pam. *Literature and Feminism*. (1993). Oxford: Blackwell Publishers, 1995.

Rosenthal, Michael. *Virginia Woolf*. London: Routledge and Kegan Paul, 1979.

Sackville-West, V. Review of *A Room of One's Own, Listener*. 6 November 1929: 620. in *Virginia Woolf: The Critical Heritage*, eds., Robin Majumdar and Allen Mclaurin. London: Routledge and Kegan Paul, 1975.

Showalter, Elaine. *A Literature of their Own: British Women Novelists from Bronte to Lessing*. Virago, 1982.

Woolf, Virginia. *A Room of One's Own.* (1929). Flamingo: Harper Collins Publishers, 1994.

11

Killing the Angel in the House

K.V. Surendran

A major interest of feminist critics has been to reconstitute all the ways we deal with literature so as to do justice to female points of view, concerns and values. The civilization has been described as male-centred and in all the cultural domains women have been subordinate and often inferior to men. The prevailing concepts of gender are largely cultural constructs that were generated by the patriarchal biases of our civilization. They are male-centred and organized and conducted in such a way as to subordinate women to men in all cultural domains; familial, religious, political, economic, social and artistic.

Some years ago, while speaking at a seminar on "Women in the Media" in Trivandrum, a senior correspondent of a leading Malayalam publication justified his paper's notorious anti-women-journalists stand. They were physically weaker and more vulnerable and hence could not be sent on "tough" assignments, he said. Besides, the reporter's room in a newspaper office was no place for a woman because the all-male staff was used to making jokes about "a woman's anatomy."

At a similar conference in Bombay, a senior woman social worker, who ought to have known better, argued vehemently for having red light areas in all major cities. These were needed, she said, because men from the rural areas who came without their families needed a sexual outlet. If these were not provided, "young women like my friend here", she said, hugging an astonished journalist who was sitting next to her, "would be in danger".

These incidents speak volumes about how society treats women. As we all know, the most highly regarded literary works focus on male protagonists—Oedipus, Ulysses, Hamlet, Tom Jones, Captain Ahab, Huck Finn and not Lady Macbeth, Cleopatra, Cordelia or Desdemona.

Virginia Woolf has often been described as an important precursor in feminist criticism. Her *A Room of One's Own, Three Guineas* and numerous other essays on women authors have their focus on the "patriarchal" society which prevented women from realizing their creative possibilities. In this article an attempt is made to take a close look at *Killing the Angel in the House*, Virginia Woolf's collection of essays taken from two selected volumes *A Woman's Essays* and *The Crowded Dance of Modern Life*. Of the seven essays under consideration "Profession for Women" and the "The Intellectual Status of Women" will get special focus. Woolf's pioneering works in feminism *A Room of One's Own* and *Three Guineas* have also been considered for the purpose.

The basic claim that is put forward in the discussion that follows is that *Killing the Angel* is a revolt against male chauvinism, male domination and neglect of women. It is a fight to restore self respect and an effort to establish equality. In a sense it is a manifesto declaring that women can no longer be held in subjection by men. Woolf daringly announces that women will no longer remain as living, marrying and bearing children in dull obscurity. Conventions can no longer stiffle them nor will they go without getting proper education. She argues that all activity of the mind should be so encouraged that there will always be in existence a nucleus of women who think, invent, imagine and create as freely as men do, and with as little fear of ridicule and condescension. Woolf has noted in *Three Guineas* that all the weapons with which an educated man can enforce his opinion are either beyond the grasp of women or so nearly beyond it that even if they used them they could scarcely inflict one scratch (24). This situation is certainly going to change.

The Angel in the House is the heroine of a famous poem by Coventry Patmore. The woman who is idealized in this poem is "the woman that men wished women to be". It is not the woman who is described in *A Room of One's Own*, that is, the woman who works year after year and finds it hard to get 2,000 pounds together (21). It is also not the woman who has a room of her own and has the habit of freedom and the courage to write exactly what she thinks (108). It is the woman who makes "a fortune and bears 'thirteen' children", as Woolf puts it (23).

In the essay "Professions for Women" read to the National Society for Women's Service and published posthumously, Woolf fights against the concept of idealized woman who she describes as intensely sympathetic, immensely charming, utterly unselfish and as one who sacrifices herself daily. She is so constituted that she never has a mind or a wish of her own, but prefers to sympathize always with the minds and wishes of others. She is pure and her purity is supposed to be her chief beauty and her blushes her great grace.

Woolf says that in those days every household had its Angel. For her it was a phantom and killing a phantom was harder than killing a reality. But she claims to have successfully killed this phantom and what remains is a "young woman in a bedroom with an inkpot". As she observes in *A Room of One's Own* in a century's time women will have changed completely. She has more or less rightly predicted that in a hundred years women will have ceased to be the protected sex. She has also foreseen a situation where they will take part in all the activities and exertions that were once denied to them.

> The nursemaid will heave coal. The shop woman will drive an engine. . . . Remove that protection, expose them to the same exertions and activities, make them soldiers and sailors and engine-

drivers and dock labourers, and will not women die off so much younger, so much quicker, than men that one will say, 'I saw a woman today', as one used to say, 'I saw an aeroplane'. Anything may happen when womanhood has ceased to be a protected occupation.

(40)

Woolf wonders why the women writers are impeded by the extreme conventionally of the other sex. Perhaps she herself has the answer to this question: "Even in the 19th century a woman was not encouraged to be an artist. On the contrary, she was snubbed, slapped, lectured and exhorted. Her mind must have been strained and her vitality lowered by the need of opposing this, of disproving that" (*A Room of One's Own* 53). At the same time she asserts that the values of women differ very often from the values which have been made by the other sex; "yet it is the masculine values that prevail. Speaking crudely, football and sport are 'important'; the worship of fashion, the buying of clothes 'trivial'. And these values are inevitably transferred from life to fiction" (70). Men sensibly allow themselves great freedom, but never realize the extreme severity with which they condemn such freedom in women, which is highly objectionable. Woolf goes on to say that there is nothing to prevent a woman from being a doctor, a lawyer or a civil servant and by discussing the obstacles which are immensely powerful and by defining them the labour can be shared and the difficulties solved.

"The Feminine Note in Fiction" is a very brief essay which is a review of W.L. Courtney's *The Feminine Note in Fiction*. Mr. Courtney believes that there is something called the feminine note in fiction. Woolf observes that Courtney is trying to define its nature in the book though at the start he admits that the feminine and masculine points of view are so different that it is difficult for one to understand the other. Woolf has maintained in *A Room of One's Own* that women's books should be shorter, more concentrated than those of men, and framed so that

> they do not need long hours of steady and uninterrupted work. The nerves that feed the brain would seem to differ in men and women,

> and if you are going to make them work their best and hardest, you must find out what treatment suits them what alternations of work and rest they need, interpreting rest not as doing nothing but as doing something but something that is different; and what should that difference be?
>
> (75)

These things, according to Woolf, are to be discussed and discovered, all this is part of the question of women and fiction.

In her essay "Women Novelists", a review of R. Brimley Johnson's *The Women Novelists* first published in *The Times Literary Supplement* she tries to argue that though men are the best judges of men and women of women, there is a side of each sex which is known only to the other. Woolf goes to the extent of saying (*A Room of One's Own*) that one has a profound, if irrational, instinct in favour of the theory that the union of man and woman makes for the greatest satisfaction, the most complete happiness. She says:

> In each of us two powers preside, one male, one female; and in the man's brain the man predominates over the woman, and in the woman's brain the woman predominates over the man. The normal and comfortable state of being is that when the two live in harmony together, spiritually co-operating. If one is a man, still the woman part of his brain must have effect, and a woman also must have intercourse with the man in her. . . It is when this fusion takes place that the mind is fully fertilized and uses all its faculties. Perhaps a mind that is purely masculine cannot create, anymore than a mind that is purely feminine, I thought.

At the same time she admits that though many instincts are held more or less in common by both sexes, there are certain areas which are "reserved" exclusively for men. For example, to fight has always been the man's habit, not the woman's "scarcely a human being in the course of history has fallen to a woman's life; the vast majority of birds and beasts have been killed by you, not by us" (*Three Guineas* 14). According to her fighting is a source of happiness and excitement, and it is also an outlet for manly qualities, without which men would deteriorate (15-16).

Woolf remarks that George Eliot and Miss Bronte may have adopted male pseudonyms not only with a view to obtaining impartial criticism but in order to free their own consciousness, as they wrote, from the tyranny of what was expected from their sex. It shouldn't be forgotten that all the great women of fiction were, until Jane Austen's day, not only seen by the other sex, but seen only in relation to the other sex (*A Room of One's Own* 79).

Arnold Bennett published a collection of his essays *Our Women: Chapters on the Sex-discord*, in the autumn of 1920. His basic assertion is that women are intellectually the inferior of men. In the essay "The Intellectual Status of Women", Woolf sharply reacts to this in a rejoinder to the review of Bennett's book in the *New Statesman* by her friend Desmond Mac Carthy under the pseudonym, Affable Hawk. The essay begins with the famous and provocative statement made by Samuel Butler. When asked what he thought about women, he said: "I think what every sensible man thinks", and when pressed further he would add "sensible men never tell". In *A Room of One's Own* Woolf is at a loss to know why Butler is of the view wise men never say what they think of women. She is of the view that wise men never say anything apparently! They never think the same thing about women. She quotes Pope who said: "Most women have no character at all" (30).

Bennett describes women as inferior to men in all respects. he says that the literature of the world can show at least fifty male poets greater than any woman poet. With the possible exception of Emily Bronte, no woman novelist has yet produced a novel to equal the great novels of men. No woman at all has achieved either painting or sculpture that is better than second rate, or music that is even second rate. Nor has any woman come anywhere near the top in criticism. Bennett asks whether anybody can name a celebrated woman philosopher, or a woman who has made a first rate scientific discovery or a woman who has arrived at a first rate generalization of any sort.

Affable Hawk agrees with this viewpoint and says that though it is true that a small percentage of women are as clever as clever men, on the whole intellect is a masculine speciality. Though some women have genius, it is in a lesser degree than Shakespeare, Newton, Michael Angelo, Beethoven and Tolstoy. The average intellectual power of women is also a good deal lower. To these views Woolf's response is that the 17th century produced more remarkable women than the 16th, the 18th century than the 17th, and the 19th century than all these put together. She compares some of the earlier writers and novelists to those of more recent origin and claims that the advance in intellectual power seems to be not only sensible but immense.

Perhaps Woolf is at her best in defending women in *Three Guineas* where she says:

> both the Army and Navy are closed to our sex. We are not allowed to fight. Nor again are we allowed to be members of the Stock Exchange. Thus we can use neither the pressure of force nor the pressure of money. . . . We cannot preach sermons or negotiate treaties. Then again although it is true that we can write articles or send letters to the Press, the control of the Press—the decision what to print, what not to print—is entirely in the hands of your sex. (23)

Her main argument is that women are forcibly prohibited and that is why they cannot express the gifts in writing, music or painting. As she makes it clear in *A Room of One's Own*, "A woman must have money and a room of her own if she is to write fiction. . . . One cannot think well, love well, sleep well, if one has not dined well" (19). For her it is not a perennial puzzle "Why no woman wrote a word of that extraordinary literature when every other man, it seemed, was capable of song or sonnet". The condition of women was such that it was almost impossible for a woman to give expression to her feelings. It was a time when wife beating was a recognized right of man, and was practised without shame by high as well as low. The daughter who refused to marry the gentleman of her parent's choice was liable to be locked up, beaten and flung about the room, without any shock being inflicted on public opinion (41-42).

Woolf laments that though imaginatively woman is of the

highest importance, practically she is completely insignificant.

> She pervades poetry from cover to cover; she is all but absent from history. She dominates the lives of kings and conquerors in fiction, in fact she was the slave of anybody whose parents forced a ring upon her finger. Some of the most inspired words, some of the most profound thoughts in literature fall from her lips; in real life she could hardly read, could scarcely spell, and was the property of her husband.
>
> (43)

The conditions which made it possible for Shakespeare to exist were that he would have had predecessors in his art, would make one of a group where art was freely discussed and practiced, and would himself have the utmost freedom of action and experience. These conditions have never been the lot of women. The women from the earliest times to the present day have brought forth the entire population of the universe and this occupation has taken much time and strength. That is why she says in *A Room of One's Own* that

> If only Mrs. Seton and her mother and her mother before her had learnt the great art of making money and had left their money like their fathers and their grandfathers before them, to found fellowships and lectureships and prizes and scholarships appropriated to the use of their own sex, we might have dined very tolerably up here alone off a bird and a bottle of wine.
>
> (22)

She concludes by noting that all activity of the mind should be so encouraged that there will always be in existence a nucleus of woman who think, invent, imagine and create as freely as men do, and with as little fear of ridicule and condescension.

"Two Women" is a review of the "Letters of Lady Augusta Stanley" and Lady Barbara Stephen's "Emily Davies and Girton College" first published in the *Nation and Athenaeum*. She begins the essay by saying that upto the beginning of the 19th century the distinguished woman had almost invariably been an aristocrat. It was the great lady who ruled and wrote letters and influenced the course of politics. The two women she describes—Miss Emily Davies and Lady Augusta Stanley—are to a large extent studies in contrast. Lady Augusta was no more highly educated in a bookish sense than the middle-class women whom Miss Davies championed. But the two women, so different in every other way have come together over the education of their sex:

> Women remain as a vast body, living, marrying, bearing children in dull obscurity until at last one begins to wonder whether there was something in their condition itself in the age at which they married, the number of children they bore, the privacy they lacked, the incomes they had not, the conventions which stifled them, and the education they never received which so affected them that though the middle class is the great reservoir from which we draw our distinguished men it has thrown up singularly few women to set beside them.
>
> (34)

"Memories of a Working Women's Guide" is an introduction to a volume entitled *Life As We Have Known It* by Co-operative Working Women. She is against the idea of writing a preface to a book and is of the view that "books should stand on their own feet" (44). Woolf maintains that though the range of expression is narrower in working women, their limited expression has a force and an emphasis, of tragedy, of humour, which the faces of ladies lack. The basic question that she addresses here is "how could women whose hands were full of work, whose kitchens were thick with steam, who had neither education nor encouragement nor leisure remodel the world according to the ideas of working women?" She finds the emergence of 'Kitchen Writings' a good beginning. Whatever has been expressed has been a work of labour and difficulty. "The writing has been done in kitchens, at odds and ends of leisure, in the midst of distractions and obstacles" and for the same reason they are admirable, maintains Woolf.

"Ellen Terry" the last piece in the collection was first published in 1941. Ellen Terry filled the stage and all others were pushed into the background as electric lights are rendered superfluous in the sun. Shakespeare could not subdue her; nor Ibsen, nor Shaw. The stage could not hold her, nor the nursery. But there is, says Woolf, a greater dramatist then Shakespeare, Ibsen or Shaw. There is nature. "Here is so vast a stage, and so innumerable a company of actors, that for the most part she fobs them off with a tag or two" (77). While other actors are remembered because they were Hamlet, Phedre or Cleopatra, Ellen Terry is remembered because she was Ellen Terry, concludes Woolf.

In sum, *Killing the Angel*, is a strong outburst against the men who have ill-treated women and ridiculed them for no obvious fault of theirs. There has always been an overlap between women's activism and women's studies and there have been periods when the relationship between academics and activists have been strained. The tension has never been fully resolved. But over the years a greater understanding has emerged of the different roles each group of women must play. One can only say that the issue of the disparity between men and women is very much there and the whole issue should at least be looked at from an impartial view. As Woolf remarks in "The Intellectual Status of Women", "the degradation of being a slave is only equalled by the degradation of being a master". The confined moulds of role-models is destructive to the whole social fabric.

References

Woolf, Virginia. *Three Guineas*. London: The Hogarth Press (1952).

—. *A Room of One's Own*. London: Granada Publishing, (1979).

—. *Killing the Angel in the House*. Harmondsworth: Penguin Books, (1995).

12

Jean Rhys's *Wide Sargasso Sea*: A Re-writing of History

Veena Jain

> "Re-vision—the act of looking back, of seeing with fresh eyes, of entering an old text from a new critical direction is for us more than a chapter in cultural history, it is an act of survival".
>
> —Adrienne Rich

For Rhys, the act of looking back and revising *Jane Eyre* was an act of "pitting two cultures and two genders" against one another. It was an act of reliving her childhood, of visiting her birth place and showing "the otherside" to her twentieth century readers. In a letter to Selma Vaz Dias, she wrote:

> I've read and re-read *Jane Eyre* of course and I am sure that the character must be "built up". I wrote you about that. The creole in Charlotte Bronte's novel is a lay-figure, repulsive which does not matter, and not once alive which does. She is necessary to the plot, but always she shreiks, howls, laughs horribly, attacks all and sundry off stage. For me (and for you I hope) she must be right on stage. She must be at least plausible with a past, the reason why Mr. Rochester treats her so abominably and feels justified, the reason he thinks she is mad and why ofcourse she goes mad, even the reason

> why she tries to set every thing on fire, and eventually succeeds. Take a look at *Jane Eyre*. That unfortunate death of a Creole. I'm fighting mad to write her story.
>
> (*Letters* 156)

The story which came out in the shape of her widely acclaimed novel *Wide Sargasso Sea* opened several avenues of interest for critics. Many critics like Dennis Porter, Michael Thorpe and Joyce Carol Oates have treated the novel in relation to *Jane Eyre*. Others like Marsha Z. Cummins and Nancy R. Harrison have concentrated on its technical felicity. Still others as Kenneth Ramchand, Mary Lou Emery and Nunez Harrel have focused on its West Indian background. Thomas F. Staley has seen *Wide Sargasso Sea* in its modern context.

I would like to approach *Wide Sargasso Sea* from the historical point of view looking at it from three angles.

(a) As a reworking of the colonial past of West Indies.

(b) As recreating the life of mad Mrs. Berthra Rochester which makes *Wide Sargasso Sea* a prologue to *Jane Eyre*.

(c) As a novel of alienation, emphasizing the historical uprootedness of its characters. Rhys's linking of history to personal consciousness thus enlarges the panorama of human experience.

The rediscovery of Bertha Rochester in *Wide Sargasso Sea* by Jean Rhys paradoxically was also a rediscovery of Jean Rhys herself after a period of thirty years. After the publication of *Wide Sargasso Sea* in 1966 and its wide reception when she was awarded the W.H. Smith Literary Award, her earlier works came into focus. As the war broke out her earlier works as *The Quartet, After Leaving Mr. Mackenzie, Voyage In the Dark* and *Good Morning Midnight* which were published between 1927 and 1939 went out of print. In 1949 she was spotted by Selma Vaz Dias who broadcast a dramatized version of her novel *Good Morning Midnight*. Selma encouraged her to write and it took her ten long years of hard work and pain before she fully entered the psyche of the creole lunatic.

> Eventually I got back to being a creole lunatic in the 1840's. Quite an effort, some times am almost there, sometimes I think I'll stay there.
>
> (*Letters* 156)

Ford Madox Ford had perceived her genius quite early, when in 1927 in an enthusiastic preface to *The Left Bank* he remarked, Jean Rhys had a "terrifying instinct for form and a terrific, an almost lurid passion for stating the case of the underdog "(Quoted by Wyndham 5). This passion made her interested in a character, "Whether beast or human being, one could not, at first sight tell. It grovelled, seemingly on all fours, it snatched and growled like some strange wild animal, but it was covered with clothing and quantity of dark, grizzled hair, wild as mane" (*Jane Eyre* 295).

Rhys placed her novel in the West Indies, the islands of Jamaica, the period after the Emancipation Act of 1834. Her central figure Antoinette, is a product of the conflicting pressures on the white minority by the black negro community who is suddenly released into power from years of subjugation. Antoinette feels, "I often wonder who I am and where is my country and where do I belong and why was I ever born at all" (*Sea* 102).

The restlessness of her identity is the restlessness of Jean Rhys. Born in 1894, in Dominica (West Indies) one of the Windward islands, she was the daughter of a Welsh doctor and a third generation Dominican Creole mother. She came to England when she was sixteen, but could never feel a sense of belongingness in this country. She remained an outcast most of her life, travelling and leading a bohemian life in the countries of Europe. "Her sense of being an outsider", feels Linda Bamber "certainly has roots in her personal history"(3). In her autobiography, *Smile Please*, Rhys recalls her childhood which was insecure and lonely. "Meta had shown to me a world of fear and distrust, and I am still in that world"(32). She knew that the rejected white Creole woman became the "White Cockroach" In *Wide Sargasso Sea* who shared the status of the underprivileged and the underclass. Thus rejected by the white world and spurned by the blacks,

Antoinette struggles to find her identity in the Caribbean Islands.

As a white creole girl, Tia, her negro friend clearly states her situation: "Old time white people nothing but white nigger now and black nigger better than white nigger" (*Sea* 25). When Annette, Antoinette's mother, marries Mason, the rich English man from England to restore her fortune, her house is set on fire and her handicapped son dies. She has to perforce leave Coulibri and with it she leaves a part of herself. Her disintegration begins, she loses a sense of belongingness and as her husband leaves her in the hands of her caretaker negro servants, she goes mad. She becomes a victim of sexual exploitation.

Similarly when Antoinette marries Rochester, again an Englishman from England, not for recovering her fortune, but as an arrangement made by her father and brother (the two powerful male figures who control her life) her sense of belongingness is threatened. Her formative years are shaped by the negro folk songs, dances, 'vodoo' or 'O beah' and the lushful tropical landscape of the Caribbean islands. Wrenching her from her familiar surroundings, Rochester takes her to an alien country among alien people. It is in this context that Rhys places her young, beautiful, sensitive Antoinette lifting her from the third storey of the attic at Thornfield Hall. The "intemperate", "unchaste", middle-aged Bertha is a lonely suffering figure in *Wide Sargasso Sea*.

The West Indian setting is not incidental to the novel. It is its central focus. The West Indian experience of an expatriate, an alien and the white creole woman links it to the motif of the oppressed, the slave and the female. The dominant forces of suspicion, hatred and fear are revealed in the acts of natives, when Annette's horse dies and their house at Coulibri is set on fire.

Elizabeth Nunez Harrel in her essay "The Paradoxes of Belonging: The White West Indian in Fiction" states the conflict of the white creole woman in relation to history:

> In the English speaking Caribbean these women must bear the guilt of the horrors of slavery inflicted by their own white ancestors upon

> the people whose country they call their own. And they must do so in solitude, for England and Europe wishing to obliterate from their memories the part they played in the brutal history of the Caribbean have set them adrift with this guilt.
>
> (281)

Rochester is the guilty England and Antoinette must bear the guilt of the horrors perpetrated on the natives. As England's purely mercenary interest in the Antilles cannot foster any hope of reciprocal understanding, similarly Rochester's marriage to Antoinette solely for a rich dowry cannot develop true love and friendship.

Rochester's inability to understand Antoinette's feelings and passions is England's failure to comprehend the negro world. Rochester takes his "plunder" (Antoinette) back to England in both *Jane Eyre* and *Wide Sargasso Sea*. But the difference between Bronte's Rochester and Rhys's Rochester lies in their attitudinal differences and the place they hold in their relationship to their women.

Bronte's Rochester is loved by Jane in spite of his moral lapses as he has some redeeming qualities. The quality of remorse and an ability to give himself are some of his endearing traits that make him acceptable to Jane and to the Victorian hearts. He is the "Byronic hero" the "superior male" but with a doubtful past which is reflected in Adele, his former mistress's daughter.

For these moral lapses the Victorian heroine could forgive Rochester. But when Rochester tries to play further deception by making a bigamous proposal, Jane immediately refuses him and "flees temptation". Rochester becomes unacceptable to Jane, not only for his deception but because she realizes that in marrying Rochester, her fate could be like Bertha's. With his class superiority, as his mistress, he could have the power to break her. Hence Bronte's Rochester had to be "chastened" and "purged" in a fire at Thornfield before being acceptable to Jane. Jane had to become Rochester's equal in social status as well.

The masterful warm and understanding Rochester of *Jane*

Eyre becomes the hard hearted cruel oppressor in the second part of *Wide Sargasso Sea*. He becomes the narrator himself. Hence, though a little more honest than his Brontean prototype, he also becomes "the omnipotent God like creator of Bertha's narrative text" (Fayad 443). Rhys does not allow for any sympathy for him from her twentieth century readers.

Rochester comes to the West Indies to make a fortune by marrying a rich heiress like his counterpart in *Jane Eyre*. Unable to fathom the mysteries of nature and disconcerted by the overpowering edenic yet wild setting of the islands, "The orchids threatening like an octopus, tentacles bare of leaves hanging from a twisted root" (*Sea* 19). Rochester attributes this wildness to Antoinette. The inexplicable menacing feeling is transferred to Antoinette. He begins associating her with wildness, sensuality and primitive passions. Faced with primitive passions of his innermost self, an entrance into the inner recesses of being, Rochester begins to feel the threat of Antoinette's world overpowering him. Their blissful honeymooning days at Granbois soon end when Daniel Cosway the self-claimed brother of Antoinette and the "Iago-like" figure intensifies Rochester's mistrust and fear in his letter.

Daniel's letter is an important document which lays bare the hidden feelings in Rochester. It gives him the excuse to brand Antoinette as a slave and rename her "Bertha". It gives him the excuse to denounce her sexuality and consider her an unworthy Victorian English woman. "She'll moan and cry and give herself as no sane woman would or could" *Sea* 165) Antoinette's desperation for his love takes her to Christophine her negro nurse. Christophine mixes a drink for Rochester. After making love to her, on awakening, he feels a repulsion for Antoinette and swears that she has poisoned him. It is actually the revulsion of Antoinette's power over him, over his passions. Out of hatred, fear and desperation and a strong desire to hurt Antoinette, he makes love to Amelie the slave girl in the next room. Rhys is unable to forgive Rochester for this unfeeling act. She explains Rochester's behaviour in a letter to Diana Athill:

> The 'love' drink on obeah night merely releases all his misery, jealousy and ferocity that has been piling up, in Mr. R. for so long. He pretends to think he's been poisoned, that's only to pile up again everything against her and so excuse his cruelty. He justifies it that way (it's often done) I do not think it justifies him at all. I do not think it explains him a bit.
>
> (*Letters*, 269)

Antoinette begins breaking up. When finally Christophine her negro nurse asks Rochester to set Antoinette free by giving her half her money so that she could live her own life, Rochester is filled with a deep jealousy and he decides to take Antoinette with him to England to make her a prisoner in the attic at Thornfield. He himself feels justified in indulging in a licentious affairs, but denies human contact and warmth to her. He has lost the capacity for remorse.

We see the result of her imprisonment in the final act where the two novels are linked together. Antoinette turns into Bertha, a bundle of violence and passions and begins to live in a world of memories and dreams. She attacks Mason, sets fire to Rochester's clothes and then to the house. Rhys explains her madness through these incidents and justifies her actions. In her mind, reality and dream are mixed up. Dreams, for the Rhys heroine are an escape from the harsh cruelties of this world. She survives through these dreams and hallucinations. Time becomes relational in the heroine's mind, and Rhys in this way links the past and the present. When Tia, her childhood friend beckons, she signifies feeling, remorse and an affinity with her childhood world: of the blacks, of her mother and Aunt Cora. Antoinette makes the final triumphant jump and finds release from her prison. In her last act, she defies Rochester — her oppressor and victimizer. Bertha of Rhys is a victim and the Bertha of Bronte is a victimizer.

Bronte could find "an escape into wholeness" for her heroine. The same optimism could not be shared by the author of *Wide Sargasso Sea*. Sexuality was a potent force to be shunned and avoided in the Victorian ethical norms. Jane who has a rich cultural background of religion, ethics and heritage possesses a strong morality to control her feelings. Her instinct for self-preservation, saves her from sexual exploitation. She is passionate but with a strong sense of self control. In the famous Gypsy-scene, in *Jane Eyre* she deftly side tracks the overtures of Rochester. Paradoxically, it is the Victorian heroine who finds ways of self fulfilment in a male dominated society. Rhys's Antoinette and Rochester cannot hope for a union in the colonial setting. Antoinette as a white creole girl in Indies has no culture or heritage to fall back on. Religion gives a brief respite. Sexuality is openly experienced and also discussed by Rhys, whereas the references to sexuality are "veiled" in *Jane Eyre*.

Gilbert and Gubar in their brilliant analysis of the 'doubles' in *The Mad Woman in the Attic* even go to the extent of considering Bertha Rochester as the 'veiled' sexual self of Jane, Rhys brings the problem of sexual repression out into the open. Antoinette's madness is the result of her sexual castration and lack of human contact. Jane accepts Rochester's double standards. Antoinette retaliates by involving herself with Sandi.

Nevertheless, Antoinette becomes a victim of sexual exploitation and in the absence of sustaining values, moral or psychological she is set adrift in the unbridgable gulf of *Wide Sargasso Sea*. Antoinette becomes a symbol of displaced personality, of social and cultural exile. In her portrayal of individual consciousness Rhys resembles Joyce, Hemingway and Dorothy Richardson. Rhys's raw material from Bronte's novel transforms it into a modern experience of insecurity, alienation and despair.

References

Bamber, Linda. "Jean Rhys", *Partisan Review*, Vol. 49, (1982), 93-100.

Baer, Elizabeth R. "The Sisterhood of Jane Eyre and Antoinette Cosway" in *The Voyage In: Fictions of Female Development*, Elizabeth Langland, Marianne Hirsch and Elizabeth Abel. Hanover and London: University Press of New England, 1983.

Bronte, Charlotte, *Jane Eyre*. 1847. New Delhi: Peacock Press, 1994.

Cummins, Marsha Z. "Point of View in the Novels of Jean Rhys: The Effect of a Double Focus", *World Literature Written in English* 24 (1984), 359-73.

Emery, Mary Lou. "The Politics of Form: Jean Rhys's Social Vision in *Voyage in the Dark and Wide Sargasso Sea*", *Twentieth Century Literature* 28 (Spring 1982), 418-29.

Fayad, Mona. "Unquiet Ghosts: the Struggle for Representation in *Jean Rhys Wide Sargasso Sea", Modern Fiction Studies* 34 (Autumn 1988) No. 3, 437-52.

Gilbert Sandra M., and Susan Gubar. *The Madwoman in the Attic: The Woman Writer and the Nineteenth-Century Imagination*. New Haven: Yale University Press, 1979.

Harrel, Elizabeth Nunez. "The Paradoxes of Belonging: The White West Indian in Fiction", *Modern Fiction Studies* (Summer, 1985), Vol. 3 No. 2.

Harrison, Nancy, R. *Jean Rhys and the Novel as Women's Text*. Chapel Hill and London; the University of North Carolina, 1988.

Oates, Joyce Carol. "Romance and anti Romance: From Bronte's *Jane Eyre to Rhys' Wide Sargasso Sea*". *Virginia Quarterly Review*, 6 (Winter 1985), 44-58.

Porter, Dennis. "Of Heroines and Victims: Jean Rhys and Jane Eyre", *The Massachusetts Review I* 17 (Autumn 1976), No. 3, 540-77.

Ramchand, Kenneth. *The West Indian Novel and its Background*, London: Faber and Faber, 1970.

Rhys, Jean. *Jean Rhys: Letters 1931-66* ed. Francis Wyndham and Diana Melly. Harmonds worth: Penguin Books Ltd., 1985.

—, *Smile Please: an Unfinished Autobiography* ed., Diana Anthill. London: Andre Deutsch, 1979.

—, *Wide Sargasso Sea*, London: Penguin Books, 1968.

Staley, Thomas, F. *Jean Rhys: A Critical Study*. Austin: University of

Texas Press, 1979.

Thorpe, Michael. "The Other Side: *Wide Sargasso Sea and Jane Eyre*", *Ariel* 8 (177), 99-127.

Wyndham, Francis. *Introduction to Wide Sargasso Sea*. London: Penguin Books, 1968, Reprinted from *Art and Literature*, No. 1.

13

Writing Postcoloniality and Feminism: A Reading of Jean Rhys's *Wide Sargasso Sea*

C. Vijayshree

W.D. Ashcroft in a strikingly perceptive analysis of "postcolonial" and "feminist" positions identifies them as "intersecting marginalities" (23). I would like to begin by reflecting on this particularly powerful trope associated with both postcolonials and women: that of margin. If as this trope suggests culture is like an enclosed space, then the place of postcolonials and of women has been politically/traditionally situated away from the centre, on the fringes, on the periphery. To be both a postcolonial and a woman, therefore, involves double marginalisation and postcolonial women's texts, as a result, are pitted against two different forms of hegemony: patriarchy and colonial authority. While theoretically speaking, such location of postcolonial women's texts is more than convincing, in practice it is not easy to draw the outlines of the area of overlap of these two liminalities with any degree of fixity. There, of course, are the uneasy questions such as: Which comes first, gender or race? Which is more urgent—contesting the colonial hegemony or combating the male authority? These issues generated spirited debates among the postcolonial feminist scholars (Trinh 1989, Mohanty 1991, Suleri 1992). What appears to be problematic in critical formulations, sometimes gets uncannily resolved in a creative work. This is what I would like to demonstrate in my reading of *Wide Sargasso Sea* (1966), which, I consider, is a paradigmatic text for postcolonial feminist discourse.

I

Wide Sargasso Sea is a significant text for all those who are interested in the evolution of feminist thought in postcolonial societies. Rhys offers here a re-visionist re-writing of Charlotte Bronte's *Jane Eyre* (1847), what has generally been celebrated as a cult text of feminism in the Anglo-American feminist studies. The point Rhys makes is to show how a text which counters hegemony of one kind may consciously or unconsciously perpetrate other forms of hierarchisation and domination. To be more precise, the Victorian novelist, Bronte makes a strong case for woman's freedom in plotting the relentless struggle waged by her protagonist Jane against male domination and patriarchal oppression; but at the same time, Bronte's portrayal of the Caribbean Creole, Bertha, in the same novel belies the author's tacit connivance with the imperialist ideology, Bronte's novel has been generally acclaimed as a powerful feminist tract and her protagonist is often praised for her "passionate protest against patriarchal authority" (Rich 106). Rhys finds an alternate point of entry into Bronte's text, and views the world contained in it from the perspective of Bertha, the invisible woman in the attic in Bronte's story. With this shifting of perspective, the textual patterns in the master narrative change dramatically and a reworlding from within occurs, and the imperialist bias in the original text stands exposed. It is fascinating to see how Rhys reworks the ideological, formal and linguistic patterns of he master narrative through a complex network of intertextual quotation and allusion advancing what may truly be called a counter-discourse, the discourse that counters all forms of inequality and domination and clearly shows that those who are urging autonomy on one level cannot remain complacent to or a part of discrimination process at another level. Rhys's text advances an oppositional reading of the canonical text not only on the thematic plane but also within the rhetorical apparatus of formal and linguistic reformulation.

Most of Rhys's work is concerned with reading, writing and rewriting. She shows a consistent and unrelenting engagement with the literary and ideological traditions of England and Europe. "As woman and colonial, she challenges assumptions which commanded universal or natural status, examining these with the eye of the outcast, the object, the other" (Gregg 409). Rhys constantly invokes and interrogates the canonical texts of the main stream such as *Kubla Khan, Wuthering Heights, Jane Eyre, Nana, A Passage to India* and *Ulysses* effecting a deliberate deconstruction of the androcentric and Eurocentric paradigms contained there in. The very first text she countered in her revisionist movement was *The Bible* itself. Her revolutionary writing began with her provocatively titled essay, "The Bible is Modern" (Gregg 408) which establishes the tenets of a Rhysian poetic of counter-discourse which is later shaped by an agenda of revaluation of the cultural (mis)representations of colonized in the British/European texts of the nineteenth century, the great age of imperialism. Whenever these master narratives, allude to Caribbean life, or attempt constructions of Caribbean reality, Rhys sharply reacts to the political implications of these constructs and often attempts a rewriting of such texts from an insider's point of view. For instance in "Tempi Perdi" a short story Rhys wrote in the 1930's, she parodies Marcel Proust's *A la Recherche du temps perdu* exposing the latter's inability to comprehend the culture and beliefs of the indigenous people of the West Indies. Again in "The Insect World" she counters the picture of the West Indies projected in *Nothing So Blue* (1927) written by Elma Napier the daughter of Sir William Gordon Cumming, taking serious objection to the latter's stereotypical depiction of "the surly natives". Rhys herself states her suspicion of the political motives of English literary texts thus:

Now I am almost as wary of books as I am of people. They are

> capable of pushing you into the limbo of the forgotten. They can tell lies—and vulgar, trivial lies—and when they are so many all saying the same thing they can shout you down, and make you doubt not only your memory, but your senses.
>
> (Temps Perdi 145)

Her own literary work, therefore, is inspired by a desire to transform the imperial / androcentric codes of cognition and recognition contained in the dominant discourse. *Wide Sargasso Sea* comes as the culmination of Rhys's concern with rewriting.

II

Charlotte Bronte's *Jane Eyre* is itself a novel of female protest and it addresses the problems of growing up in a patriarchal nuclear family structure. The protagonist Jane, orphaned and presumably defenceless discovers the strength of her own personality by the challenges of several contrasting environments—the Reed household where she is despised and ill-treated; Lowood school where through education she finds directions for her own struggle; Thornfield where she encounters adult conflicts of sex and love; Whitcross where she acquires the semblance of a family; and Ferndean where she is at last wed. It is the Thornfield section and Jane Eyre's love relationships with Rochester, the master of the Thornfield estate that provide the take-off point for Rhys's narrative. It is here that Jane meets Bertha Mason, Rochester's first wife, a Caribbean Creole who is now kept in solitary confinement in an attic on account of her madness. Here is Bronte's description of Bertha as seen for the first time by Jane:

> In the deep shade at the end of the room, a figure ran backwards and forwards. What it was, whether beast or human being, one could not, at first sight tell: it grovelled, seemingly, on all fours; it snatched and growled like some strange wild animal: but it was covered with clothing and a quantity of dark grizzled hair, wild as a mane, hid its face.
>
> (321)

Bertha's madness is almost accepted as a given by Jane since it is explicable in terms of heredity—the mad daughter of a mad mother. Furthermore, Jane feels no sense of kinship or empathy towards the strange woman turned into a beast and therefore readily accepts Rochester's version of Bertha's "intemperate and unchaste behavior", and is quite willing to forgive his uncouth and ungentlemanly ways toward his wife. Her sympathies are aligned more towards Rochester who has lived through horrors in the hell of West Indies and continues to confront the memories of that nightmarish past in his mad wife—Bertha. Jane, however, is unwilling to become Rochester's mistress and make moral compromises. She therefore turns down his proposal and leaves Thornfield. The conflict is resolved through an accidental turn of events wherein mad Bertha sets the mansion on fire reducing all of Rochester's earthly possessions including herself to a heap of ashes. Rochester himself is left blind and incapacitated. Jane, in the last section marries Rochester rehabilitating her much afflicted lover and securing for herself the status of a legitimate wife.

III

Jean Rhys born on the Caribbean island of Dominica to a Welsh doctor and his English Creole wife went to England for higher education. It was during this period when Rhys was sixteen or seventeen, that she first read Bronte's novel. She was moved by the plight of Bertha and at once decided that she would try and write her a life. *Wide Sargasso Sea* written almost three decades later is the life of Bronte's Creole lunatic. Rhys retells the story of the shadowy figure in Bronte's text retrieving the shrieking, howling, violent mad woman from her banishment in the attic and placing her "right on stage". Rhys's concern is with the antecedents of Bertha's insanity, with the material and psychic forces that have driven her to the present state. To quote Rhys:

> For me . . .She [Bertha] must be right on stage. She must be at least plausible with a past, the *reason* why Mr.. Rochester treats her so abominably and feels justified, the *reason* why he thinks she is mad and why of course she goes mad, even the *reason* why she tries to set

everything on fire and eventually succeeds . . . .

(*Letters* 156-157)

In probing the causes of Bertha's madness Rhys not only presents the case study of Bronte's mad woman in the attic, but also renders an insider's account of the racial-harassment suffered by the Creole community and thus re-incribes the colonial history of the West Indies from a Creole point-of-view. As Ellen Friedman rightly observes: "Rhys enters and re-imagines Bronte's text—glossing and subverting, reversing and transforming it—writing it into her own time and her own frame of reference" (117).

Rhys's objections to the master narrative are two-fold: ideological and technical. Ideologically she opposes Bronte's silencing of the Creole Woman in what is meant to be a text of feminist revolt. Technically, she finds Bronte's portrayal of Bertha flawed and unconvincing. Rhys firmly asserts: "So I will struggle and make it as convincing as possible" (*Letters* 296). However, Rhys's task too is not easy: even as she is attacking what Gayatri Spivak calls "the unquestioned ideology of imperialist axiomatics" (181) contained in the master narrative, she is still working within the structural and formal conventions of the English novel. The novelist, therefore deconstructs the discursive norms of the form too working from with in, and this linguistic and formal decentering completes the total textual revolution targeted by Rhys in rewriting Bronte's canonical text. How does Rhys actually realize this?

Firstly, she moves freely away from the chronological time frame of the original text. *Wide Sargasso Sea* is set in the 1830's in the West Indies of post-Emancipation Act period, and in thus locating her story at a specific historical time different from that of the master text, Rhys is straight away setting records straight and fitting the narrative into proper historical matrix. In other words, she clearly spells out the details of the historical forces that shaped the life and experience of Bertha Mason and the likes of her, the members of decayed Creole aristocracy at emancipation. Since the freeing of slaves in the islands, the white landowners have lived in a state of undeclared war forced to employ their formal slaves as servants and utterly helpless without them. The old ruling class, rendered powerless thus, lived under certain fear of being murdered at any time. Paranoia became the condition of life at isolate estate homes such as Coulibri and mental dis-ease was the natural outcome of such a situation. Both Antoinette [Bronte's Bertha is restored to her original identity and renamed Antoinette by Rhys] and her mother are a part of this social formation and read as such, their mental aberration falls in place.

Secondly the narratorial voice is now accorded to the non-speaking subject of Bronte's text and silences in the original text are powerfully articulated. Bronte's Bertha is proverbial: she groans, screams, mutters and laughs but she never speaks; but Rhys's Antoinette on the other hand argues, reasons and speaks back asserting her own individual identity. The master text, privileges "the individualist female subject" Jane who, "not-quite/not-male" articulates herself in such a way that the "native female" [ ] "is excluded from any share in this emerging norm." (Spivak 245) Rhys's rewriting gives voice to the silenced "other" and consequently the hidden story kept under repression in the original narrative in unearthed. This is the tragic tale of Antoinette's mother: Annette. Annette, as a former slave owner's widow is hated by the emancipated black natives of the island; the other Creole women in Jamaica do not communicate with her since she is from another island; the whites consider her racially inferior, and subjected to such multiple stratifications, she practically lives in solitary confinement in her island home: Coulibri. She marries an English gentleman Mason in her desperate attempt to move up the social ladder, in vain. While Annette feels the hostility in the air, Mr. Mason fails to understand her anxiety and considers her fears unnatural and her reactions abnormal. A riot breaks out, their home is set on fire, the family manages to flee but this outburst of violence leaves Annette a psychological wreck. She is later left in the care of black servants who ill-treat and sexually abuse her and finally she dies in their custody, What Antoinette inherits from her mother, thus we understand, is not the psychic condition of insanity, but a family history of suffering, alienation, anxiety and anguish. Antoinette's speech is generally swift and elliptical; her narration is in no way that of a mad woman but is shaped by "the naivete and the hope, the terrors and the longings that haunt her" (Porter 542). The mad woman in the attic is thus retrieved through her own narration.

Rhys provides yet another angle of vision as she allows Rochester to present his own version of his unsuccessful marriage to the Creole heiress, Antoinette. However, by the time Rochester takes over the baton of narration, the reader is adequately equipped with a knowledge of Antoinette's past, as well as her personality and is sufficiently informed of the dynamics of socio-political locale of the text. The British gentleman's version of his Caribbean experience is, therefore, not taken at its face value. Moreover, the conventional and class-conscious nineteenth-century English man influenced by the politics of imperialism stands exposed through his own narration. When the two versions of the story are taken together, Rochester-Antoinette relationship provides a powerful allegory for colonial domination and authority. Antoinette, the Creole heiress is an anomaly created by colonial transactions of interracial sexual relations. Early in life she recognizes she belongs nowhere: as a white she is hated and constantly othered in her own native Jamaican world; she is treated as an outcast by her own race. While natives contemptuously call her "white cockroach", Europeans refer to her reproachfully as "white nigger". As she tells her English husband: "So between you, I often wonder who I am and where is my country and where do I belong and why was I ever born at all" (85). She is caught in an irresolvable crisis, an atmosphere of indispensable despair and ineluctable doom.

Rochester is the archetypal colonizer driven by strong aspirations for material prosperity. Marriage to Antoinette is looked upon as a business arrangement by means of which "caste and class are traded off against a substantial sum of cash" (Porter 544). Yet he cannot respond to her in a human way because he carries with him the presumptions of his country, color, class and race. He cannot comprehend the power of her passion and associates her with the magic of West Indies. He fears her and looks upon her with suspicion.

Two themes of colonialism and male sexuality come together most strikingly during the meeting between Rochester and Antoinette's half brother Daniel Mason. The latter's accusations of Antoinette's infidelity and intemperance readily appeal to Rochester's estranged mind. Now his wife appears doubly contaminated racially as a Creole, morally as an "impure" women. Rochester's indifference makes Antoinette anxious and in a desperate attempt to win him back, she administers a love potion, on the advice of her Obeah maid. Rochester now is convinced that she is "mad" and though he knows that their marriage is over, he would not release her: "She's mad, but mine, mine" (137). Antoinette is take a captive to England, kept in confinement at Thornfield (Thorn-field), where she rapidly becomes the image of Rochester's shame and guilt, a moving monument of human exploitation arising out of racial and gender discrimination.

Finally, Rhys works out a complex network of intertextual connections between the master text and her own version of it. Besides the conscious character parallelism discussed above, one finds several situational analogies between the two texts. At the conclusion of the novel, Rhys directly connects her novel with *Jane-Eyre*—the master text. In part III of the *Wide Sargasso Sea* Antoinette describes a fiery dream in which she sees herself setting fire to the Thornfield mansion and leaping to death. What Bronte's Bertha actually does at the end of *Jane Eyre*, is only a dream in Rhys's novel. However when Antoinette awakes from the dream she realizes: "Now at last I know why I was brought here and what I have to do" (190) Through this unusual intertextual collage and quotation Rhys edges Bronte's canonical imagery, plot and characterization with a subversive revision of them. In doing so, she brings into the master text an important aspect obviously absent in it earlier: the racial difference. Rhys thus achieves a transforming invasion and rupture, releases the repressed, edges the canonical with the subversive, the patriarchal with the feminine, the imperialist with the anti-colonialist and successfully clears a space from where all forms of hegemony and domination may be confronted and contested.

References

Ashcroft, W.D. "Intersecting Marginalities: Post-colonialism and Feminism", *Kunapipi* 1989, 11 (2): 23-44.

Bronte, Charlotte. *Jane Eyre* (1847). Harmondsworth: Penguin. 1966.

Friedman, E.G. "Breaking the Master Narrative: Jean Rhys *Wide Sargasso Sea*" in E.G. Friedman and M. Fuchs (ed.) *Breaking the Sequence*, Princeton: Princeton University Press. 1989.

Mohanty, Chandra T. "Under Western Eyes: Feminist Scholarship and Colonial Discourse", *Boundary 2* 1984, 12 (3), 13 (1): 333-58.

Porter, Dennis. "Of Heroines and Victims: Jean Rhys and *Jane Eyre The Massachusetts Review* 1976, 17: 540-52.

Rich, Adrienne. "*Jane Eyre*: The Temptations of a Motherless Woman", *On Lies, Secrets and Silences.* London. Macmillan.1980.

Rhys, Jean. *Jean Rhys: Letters 1931-1966.* London: Andre Deutsch. 1984.

Rhys, Jean. "Temps Perdi" in Kenneth Ramchand (ed.) *Tales of the Wide Caribbean*. London: Heinemann. 1986.

Rhys, Jean. *Wide Sargasso Sea*. Harmondsworth: Penguin Books. (1966) 1975.

Spivak, Gayatri, C. "Three Women's Texts and a Critique of Imperialism", in Catherine Belsey and Jane Moore (ed.) *The Feminist Reader*, (1985) 1989 London: Macmillan, 175-197.

Suleri, Sara. "Woman Skin Deep: Feminism and the Postcolonial Condition". *Critical Inquiry* (1992), 18 (4) 756-69.

Trinh T. Minh-ha. *Woman, Native, Other: Writing Postcoloniality and Feminism*. Bloomington, Ind: Indiana University Press. 1989.

14

The Epistemology of Inequality: A Look at the Second Sex

Santosh Gupta

The twentieth century has seen an unprecedented upsurge of women's resistance to collective male authority both in theory and praxis. Reacting strongly to the Victorian age's imposition of gendered roles pushing women into frozen, static images of femininity, the women have pushed back state-supported male-dominated hegemony of patriarchal ideology. The concerted efforts of women to change their cultural situation and their enquiry into the meaning of gendered identities have been strengthened immensely in the initial stages by the theoretical formulations of writers like Virginia Woolf and Simone de Beauvoir. These writers were concerned with redefining the nature, role and status of women in society.

Virginia Woolf's *A Room of One's Own* (1929) and *Orlando* (1928) probed cautiously, a little too artfully and diffidently, into the socio-cultural situation of women over the ages, and the actual control of all political, economic and social power by men. Important as her questioning was, its full impact was not felt immediately, for the playful, tentative and self-conscious style tended to reduce the seriousness of the enquiry.

Simone de Beauvoir's *The Second Sex*, coming about twenty years after *A Room of One's Own* establishes the importance of woman's questioning of her social and intellectual milieu. The book proceeds to examine the knowledges created so far as having been created by men and posits its own specific point of view as the woman's point of view. Recognizing the need to look back at the history of ideas, as well as the history of cultures and societies, Beauvoir relates feminist struggle to the larger social, historical reality. She looks at the many existing definitions, analysis and data that have worked together to construct the image of woman as the "second sex" – incidental, non-autonomous and dependent upon the male for defining even her identity.

Simone de Beauvoir (1908-1986), became associated with the philosopher Jean-Paul Sartre and other existentialists during 1925-30 and played an important role in the existentialist movement. She taught at the universities at Rouen, Marseilles and Paris. Her novels, short stories and autobiography examine human character in terms of its potentialities, exercise of choice, and struggle against the social conventions. In all her writings she has emphasized the idea that a character is forever in the process of becoming conscious as an undetermined being, realizing itself through committing a wholly autonomous act. Such an act requires great courage, and a perpetual state of effort, but it is only in such acts that one becomes fully self-aware.

The Second Sex is Beauvoir's exploration of the nature of woman's life and status in society. One of the most significant feminist texts written so far, it lays down basis for women's questioning of knowledge and the validity of feminist study. It attempts, Beauvoir says, to "clarify and understand" woman's life, rather than ask for more rights and privileges. It is primarily an epistemological quest, trying to remove the confusion and mystery surrounding the concepts, "woman", and "womanliness". She considers it very important for women to understand the hidden political male bias of all forms of knowledge that are defining and explaining woman's nature. The hegemony of thought derived from patriarchal prejudices has, she points out, been reflected in the new sciences, distorting their perception of "reality". The Victorian world which includes the "Atlantic community", of England, France and the United States, "an extreme polarization of sex roles accompanied the imposition of the ordering vision; this was probably the change that had most impact on the lives of Victorian Women" (Hellerstein, Hume and Offens 2-3). The 'Ordering Vision' was formed by the ideas of sociologists, anthropologists, biologists and political scientists. In France, the socialist Pierre Joseph Proudhon sought to prove women's subjection to male authority and justify their confinement to household drudgery, on the basis of their inferiority. Auguste Comte praised women for their civilizing role, but he, too, believed that women had weak brains and bodies. Social anthropologists, armed with evolutionary theories of Charles Darwin, were connecting the subordination of women in society to the processes of struggle for survival on another level, and gave patriarchy scientific underpinnings. Herbert Spencer the most important Darwinist of his time, argued that evolution had placed women in the home and that the dictates of social survival necessitated rigid sex roles and male domination. "Patriarchy was now equated" say Hellerstein, Hume and Offens, "not only with nature, but with the forces of progress and civilization as well" (3).

The well-fortified ideology supporting the notion of female inferiority and male domination could not be shaken easily and called for a radical and thorough examination. Simone de Beauvoir's strongly non-conformist, existential stand enables her to stand out of the existing structure of knowledge and show the underlying structure of power. Her standpoint begins with the very basics of philosophical analysis. Rejecting essentialist, deterministic theoretical approaches she bases her analysis on the ground roots of lived experience. Rather than negotiate for space within the male hegemonic structure, she makes her protest by taking a stand in direct opposition.

In her Introduction to *The Second Sex* Beauvoir raises some important issues and defines her methodology. She begins with the problem of nomenclature. Can the problems be resolved by calling men and women by the common term "humanity?" Beauvoir finds that the difference of sexes are undeniable facts, seen at every step. One look at humanity walking across the streets shows, she says, the "humanity is divided into two classes of individuals whose clothes, faces, bodies, smiles, gaits, interests and occupations are manifestly different" (14).

Asking the question "What is Woman?" is in itself an indication of the different status and significance of the two sexes. She remarks that a man never feels the need to explain himself. She says, "A man is in the right in being a man; it is the woman who is in the wrong . . .". Man enjoys the prime position in the "hierarchy of sexes" as Beauvoir calls it; he becomes "the absolute type" whereas woman is "relative to him" (15). This she finds to be a surprising condition distorting the co-existence of man and woman in nature. This inversion in stature makes her raise some questions regarding the origin, imposition and continued existence of woman's subordinate submissive position. At what stage in history and for what reason did this unequal status of women come to prevail?

Most of the definitions of 'woman's nature' come from male thinkers, says Beauvoir, a fact that is reflected in the masculinist bias of their views. Aristotle, St. Thomas, Bousset, all have defined woman as secondary, inferior and relative to man. Beauvoir remarks, "man has defined himself as the absolute, the Norm, and Woman as the 'Other'. Thus, humanity is male and man defines woman not in herself but as relative to him; she is not regarded as an autonomous being" (15).

Beauvoir's questioning of existing knowledge is based on her clearly stated perception of knowledge as originating in a specific point of view—of a person whose sex, social background and political position play an important role in shaping his epistemological activity. No knowledge can be treated as being totally impersonal, objective and universal. The sexist attitudes of the earlier thinkers represent the views of their sex but not necessarily the truth about woman.

Here again Beauvoir finds it surprising that though man has treated woman as the "other", woman has never resisted or reciprocated this gaze. She has never reacted in the most natural way by turning man into the "Other" for her. Woman's acceptance of her objectified image and unwillingness to resist this situation further reduces her status.

In order to understand woman's submissive behaviour, as well as the treatment of the society, Beauvoir looks into history of ideas, of religion, myths and social praxis. The reason for woman's submission is seen as located within the entire culture and its ideas about man-woman relation, not in some fixed essential human nature, or some hidden mysterious element in woman. Woman has always been, she says, "man's dependent, if not his slave; the two sexes have not shared the world in equality" (19).

Beauvoir's political awareness of the tensions between man and woman is strongly reflected in her analysis of the unequal relationship. Different forms of knowledge have been, she argues, instruments of male imposition, similar to other political, imperialistic impositions. Man's domination over woman's body, mind and life is one of the many forms of colonizations that are found in the world. She puts at par different types of slavery—of a sex, a race or a class, and says, "whether it is a race, a caste, a class or a sex that is reduced to a position of inferiority, the methods of justification are the same" (22). The Black or the Jew are reduced to a type, a fixed image, an "other" against whom the Master recognizes and establishes his achievement. The subjectivity, existential freedom of these persons comes into conflict with their subordination. But the "compulsions of the situation" enforce an "inessential" status and women, like other oppressed human beings, have been forced into inauthentic, inessential roles.

In the Introduction Beauvoir emphasizes the importance of feminist knowledge. Women need to write about their experiences for they can tell the meaning of being a woman in a patriarchal society. A woman should not be merged into the universal terms 'human' or 'mankind', for, she says, "We know the feminine world, more intimately than do the men, because we have our roots in it, we grasp more immediately than do men what it means to a human being to be feminine and we are more concerned with such knowledge" (26).

The Second Sex is a massive book. Beauvoir writes in the way "men write" (Spacks 22), using her vast scholarship and philosophical position to look into the various theories about man and woman relationship. She examines scientific, social and political theories, literary works, prevalent and popularly held myths, fantasies and beliefs about woman's body and mind. Her keen insight engages with the existing data, and she points to the inadequacies of the theories, constructed by men and imposed on the women. Her feeling for the oppressed classes whether women, Blacks or the Jews, her feelings for social justice make her, as Spacks says, "angry", (23) but her anger remains controlled by her learning and her greater desire for intellectual thoroughness. *The Second Sex* becomes an extremely moving and forceful book, conveying the deep sense of pain at the injustice and deprivation experienced by "half of the humanity". The book had startled millions of women all over the world as it was translated into several languages in different countries.

The book is divided into two parts. Part I consists of three sections, Section I called "Destiny", deals with the definitions of woman—her body, feelings and mind; the analysis of family given by Historical Materialism; Section II, "History", is an anthropological view of the development of society—its phases, emergence of patriarchy, capitalistic economy and the changing of status of women; Section III, looks at literary works of men, examines their presentation of women, the section is called "Myth". It examines the images of woman constructed by men as part of ideology used to convert the subjectivity, freedom of woman into stereotyped images of the "other".

The second part of the book has a totally different perspective. It is concerned with "Woman's Life Today" and examines the life through its different stages—childhood, adolescence, youth, marriage or otherwise, and later, old age. Woman's social, psychological experiences are of various kinds, and Beauvoir attempts a panoramic analysis, looking at "Lesbian", "Prostitute", "Narcissist" and "The Woman in Love". Final section looks towards the woman of the coming ages, "The Independent Woman".

At the beginning of her analysis she takes up the assumption of scientific studies, the idea that human beings, like other living forms, do not have fixed essences or physical beings, but are formed through a process of development and interaction with the given environment. She examines the biological details of reproduction, the role played by male and female and their association with the progeny. The woman bears the full responsibility and her body is particularly made for the procreative role. In this role, she becomes, Beauvoir says, the "victim of the species" for her physical situation confines her to home for longer period and she is more closely bound to the nurturing and caring of the little child(ren). But this is not, Beauvoir says, a sufficient reason for woman's lesser significance in family and society. She thinks that the woman's role is harder, more difficult and carries greater responsibility than the man's; woman and man "together, create a living being" and should be treated at par. Beauvoir discusses at length the importance of the bodily phenomena, and makes the statement, "the body being the instrument of our grasp upon the world, the world is bound to seem a very different thing when apprehended in one manner or another" (60). But this data does not sufficiently explain the "setting up (of) a hierarchy of the sexes; they fail to explain why woman is the other" (60).

Taking on psychoanalytical theories, Beauvoir finds Freud's explanation of female psyche distorted, and, reflecting male bias. He is unable to explain why a girl-child envies the male child, why she feels a sense of shame for herself and her body. Beauvoir relates this to the cultural environment of privileging the man, his body, desires and personality. The girl-child perceives from her early consciousness the power vested in the male, and learns to look up to him for support, indirectly relating to his power.

Psychoanalytic theory also fails to provide an adequate analysis of female erotic desires. By treating female psychology as an inversion and reflection of the male, Freud fails, Beauvoir says, to deal with the complex combination of desire, fear, attraction, repulsion and passivity that is seen in woman's sexual behaviour. Beauvoir's discussion of this aspect of female behaviour is bold, perceptive and detailed. She insists that the male scientific psychological approaches have proceeded on unscientific grounds and have failed in their task. Her analysis and perception have influenced later feminists who were uncomfortable with Freudian theories and have used women's experience to build their theories. In questioning major theoreticians such as Freud, Karl Marx and Fredric Engels, she draws attention to the incomplete, inadequate explanations in their theories. The emergence of capitalism explains why man began to accumulate wealth, why women were forced inside domestic realms, but, she says, it does not explain woman's subordination, and the unending universal subordination.

Beauvoir's analysis of woman's life within family and society in section II (Part I), called "History" (contemporary feminists would call it 'Her-Story') and in section III, "Myths", take the discussion further, in her critical, questioning manner. She draws the conclusion that the devaluation of woman was a part of the evolutionary process of the society, but she does not consider it to have been "necessary". Man and woman could have worked on a collaborative basis, and both would have led better lives. She feels strongly that the powerful, aggressive person, the master, becomes bound to the slave, the weaker, subdued, "other". This struggle of power destroys the nature of relationship and she looks beyond towards a society where both man and woman would value the freedom and dignity of the other.

In making woman submit to man, Beauvoir finds, family plays an important role. The 'lies' that the woman is fed upon are accepted by her, for she "finds it to be easier, but these lies damage and corrupt her by designating as her true vocation this submission, which is the temptation of every existent in the anxiety of liberty" (77).

Woman herself is held responsible ultimately for accepting an inferior status and perpetuating the secondary position. Woman will have to emerge out of the designated position and struggle for her freedom. Beauvoir criticizes women writers for their inability to go beyond self-expression and analysis of their condition. The writing women can play an important role in generating feminist awareness, but mostly they forfeit this right by submitting to male domination and by seeking male approval (669).

At the end of the analysis Beauvoir reiterates the value to the society of women's upliftment. Man and woman relationship will be profoundly altered, for the better, if their relations are based on an equal footing. She emphasizes the importance of family ties when she says, "To emancipate woman is to refuse to chain her to the relation she bears to man, not to deny them to her" (686).

Simone de Beauvoir's impact on feminist theory has been tremendous. She provides feminist theory a methodology, a justification and a self-confidence in her use of the wide ranging scholarship and a clear, definite philosophical point of view. In questioning the very basic assumptions of universality and objectivity of given knowledges, Beauvoir prepares a strong basis for the validity of feminist theory.

Patricia Meyer Spacks feels that Beauvoir's manner and use of male norms in judging women writers reflects her implicit acceptance of male standards. She suggests that "we may question the value judgements" Beauvoir makes about men and women writers (Spacks 21). It suggests, she says, "an a priori tendency to take them (the women writers) less seriously than their male counterpoint" (22).

Even while recognizing such criticism of Beauvoir, *The Second Sex* remains highly impressive for its intellectual vision and imaginative vibrancy. Its descriptions of various aspects, stages and types of woman's life give the book an appeal that is very powerful. Spacks admires Beauvoir for her ability to use the data from everyday experience, and convert it into general and abstract images of woman, and remarks that "ultimately, this scholarly book is imaginative literature..." (6). Spacks comments that Beauvoir writes in the manner of man in using several kinds of information and in dealing with ideas with confidence and ease, but Beauvoir's 'anger' reflects her feminine background. Beauvoir expresses her anger, and "she is 'angry', as a thinking woman can hardly fail to be, her anger expresses itself in her essentially masculine postures of defense. Trying to write as she believes only men have written-lucidly, logically. . . she indeed demonstrates her power as a thinker, but also her power as a woman" (24).

To be an intellectual woman is one of the tasks of the women writers. Beauvoir asks women to look for new role models, to ask their own questions, and create a knowledge system of their own. Giving prime importance to the ground root of experience—the body, she looks at the femaleness of the female body. Beauvoir's bold and unhesitating enquiry has influenced the latter feminists for she emphasized the need to accept the reality, to look beyond the present and to work for an equal world.

References

de Beauvoir, Simone. *The Second Sex* (*Le deuxieme sexe* 1949), Paris, trans and edited H.M. Parshley. London: Jonathan Cape.

Hellerstein, E.O., Hume, L.P. and Offens, K.M. ed. *Victorian Women: A Documentary of Women's Lives in Nineteenth Century England, France, and the United States*. Brighton: Harvester Press, England, 1981.

Spacks, Patricia Meyer. *The Female Imagination*, (1972). New York: Avon Books, 1975.

15

Simone de Beauvoir's *Memoirs of A Dutiful Daughter*

Madhuri Chatterjee

Simone de Beauvoir remains one of the famous post-war woman writers of France. Her great study of women *The Second Sex* (1949) has become a landmark in the history of feminism where she voiced the proposition which was to shift questions of sexuality and gender on a radically new terrain: You are not born a woman, you become one. But her autobiography as a text also raises several question about women and gender roles, psychological conflicts and issues which had driven and challenged the narrator. Her four-volume autobiography gives us a picture of the writer with admirable honesty and precision. These are: *Memoirs of A Dutiful Daughter* (1959), *Prime of Life* (1963), *Force of Circumstance* (1965), *All Said and Done* (1974), collectively they offer an insight into the making of Simone de Beauvoir.

Born in Paris in 1908, she took a degree in Philosophy from Sorborne in 1928 and then onwards became a close friend of Jean Paul Sartre. She taught in Marseilles, Rouen, Paris from 1931 to 1943 and after war emerged as a strong force of the existential movement. She died in the year 1986.

Simone de Beauvoir's autobiography traces the progress and success of self in terms of intellectual and political achievements and also mirrors the history of the times. She chooses to call the first volume *Memoirs of a Dutiful Daughter* and hence it becomes imperative to distinguish this genre. The diary, journal, memoir, reminiscences and letters are all manifestations of the writer's self but each has a different perspective. Autobiography narrates the story of a person's unfolding a sense of identity, the process of becoming in the world. The account usually involves considerable self-analysis on the part of the author. The memoirs on the other hand focus on the outer world of people and events. The memoir writer's intention is not self-examination[1] (Pascal 5-6). Yet there is no autobiography that is not in some respects a memoir and no memoir which is without autobiographical context. There is a slender line dividing the two. The general difference is in emphasis. Memoirs are usually written by people who have either played a distinguished role in history and they concentrate on recording public events laying great stress on the 'self'. Memoirs differ from pure autobiography in its focussing point. The illumination of the self is but incidental. de Beauvoir's memoirs arise from personal experiences and follows a chronological order in the recording of the events. More often than not it tends to become reflective, wherein her attributes and feelings are revealed and also an account of the action and reaction of human relationship. *Memoirs of A Dutiful Daughter* projects the outside world refracted by her own self. She divides her life into segments whose principle of organization lies not alone with her but with others as well.

In this volume she struggles to piece together the progression of her self into an intellectual person and she devotes a considerable part of the autobiography to her depressing emotional life up to mid-twenties before her intellectual life took off. It covers the period of her birth from 1908 to completion of her studies in Sorbonne in 1929-30. Most significantly the autobiography makes an accurate psychological study of growing girls. V.S. Pritchett in his review in the "New Statesman" wrote "Mlle de Beauvoir is clear, honest and excellent psychologist and the central part of her book, which carefully takes the years between thirteen to seventeen to pieces is admirable".

The title of the autobiography is to an extent ironical because she displays her individuality within the confines of conventionality. Despite her social and psychological conflicts the narrative establishes a positive promise and strength of her conviction. Beauvoir's act of dependence and rebellion not only explains the shape her own search for identity and independence but also the strains and struggles of a feminine self. Her narrative strategy reveals both a female dilemma and a solution.

The *Memoirs* is divided into four books or sections to mark her gradual self-progression. It opens with Simone's birth, her childhood world and the perceptions and restrictions imposed upon her. She briefly mentions the war years, her schooling and her father's contribution to the World War. She describes the origin of her characters in the constellation of others who peopled her childhood. She identifies with people she is drawn towards and whom she rebels against. Her first affection is towards her sister Louise, a friend and an equal, on whom she asserts her personal identity and with whose help she moves out from the docile reflection of her parents' will. She has a strained relationship with her parents but she never rebels against them in her early years. She composes the personality of a good little girl because it brings her praise and a great satisfaction, also because it was her one reality. de Beauvoir dismisses her father in one statement "I found him amusing and I was pleased whenever he made a fuss of me, but he didn't play any well defined role in my life" (6). In fact, the parents represent the radically heterogeneous world of experience-spiritual and intellectual—without having anything in common with each other. The structure of power governing relationships between men and women continues to follow the pattern of subordination and domination as she writes that though her sister, mother and grandmother played the lead roles her father, uncles and grandfather were always superior to them. In section second and third she steps into an outer world of friends and teachers. Beneath the layers of oppressive social conditioning there exists an inner self which seeks fulfillment. Some major influences in her adolescent years together with her scholastic achievements gave her a sense of space. The close association she makes with friends like Elizabeth Mabille (Zaza) builds much of the narrative and others like Pradelle, Jacques and Stepha contribute to the growth of her personality. her need for identification with Zaza contains the need for an intellectually superior person who could direct her life to s brighter sphere. Later the need is manifested in her relationship with Sartre.

The book deals with the construction of a feminine self. The author honestly builds the young girl's adulation for Jacques, a close family friend with whom young Simone had the only serious affair of her adolescent years. Earlier, Louisa M. Alcott's *Good Wives*, a sequel to *Little Women* had disturbed her equanimity when Laurie marries Jo's younger sister, Amy. In Laurie she perceives a reflection of her childhood hero Jacques. The story finds parallel in her life as the affair ends in tragedy and Jacques moves away from her to make a wrong marriage, ruining himself and dying early at the age of forty-five because of malnutrition, while de Beauvoir like Jo finds a superior individual who becomes part of her life and this person comes in the incarnation of Sartre. Here she puts a question "What would I feel when I found myself face to face with my past?" (346) and disturbs the linear narrative to quickly summarize Jacques's life and clarify her relationship with him. The marginalised language of feeling swamps the distinction of an intellectual writer for she suddenly finds Jacques "idler, spendthrift, womanizer, drunkard, liar - to mention the least of his feelings. . ." (349). Shumaker's observation about the reticience of the female autobiographers to write about their partners or mates does not apply to her because de Beauvoir speaks at great length about her relationship with Sartre (Shumaker 24). The author's intellectual analysis of her life is almost like J.S. Mill's in depicting the extraordinary stimulation they received from intellectual coteries but she is also very much aware of her gender or infirmities and of her family configuration. As narrator her approach is both philosophic and emotionally emphatic.

The choice of her experiences is not just autobiographical but also psychological. She writes at length about the femaleness of her experience and the narrative is interrupted by detailed psychological study of her physical, emotional and mental growth. Her bourgeois upbringing forbade her from any sexual indulgences but as a growing teenager she is tormented by feelings of guilt, loneliness and anger. She feels bitter and alienated by the restraints imposed on her sexuality but ironically admits "Being a child filled me with passionate resentment; my feminine gender never" (55). The twin conflict of her personality is hinted at by her association with Mary Magdalene, Joan of Arc, Saint Blandine, and at a later stage to convert her passivity into active defiance she visits the "haunts of vice" (pubs, parties etc.) At the same time she foolishly confesses in her diary "There is within me I know what yearning - may be a monstrous lust - ever present for noise, fighting, savage violence and above all the gutter' (307). Probably her Catholic consciousness torments her for every unconventional action. The exchanges in the diaries are also the repository for emotion usually enclosed by conventions, the place to look for records for a person's secret doings. As a dutiful daughter she was compelled to extol the virtues of an existence that was noble, although it was not consistent with the nature and psychology of a growing girl and hence the split in her personality. Her self affirmation reverts back to anxiety and self castigation when she calls herself immoral. Ironically, her sexual initiation comes only from books and she discusses some of the books which unnerved her and one such was George Eliot's *Adam Bede*. In fact she is shocked by the violence and crudity of sex, almost eschewing and dismissing it from her life. Some restraint or fear prevents her from settling into any relationship during her growing years.

The *Memoirs* are also in a way psychological release of her self. In her psychological conflict, the imagery of the cage is sharply emphasized. Her loneliness, her alienation from her parents, her inability to release her from family ties and tradition had made her bitter, and she writes "Though this prison was one without bars, I couldn't see any way out of it" (175). de Beauvoir tries to rise above her bourgeois existence by seeking strength from the moral fable of the larvae who turns into a butterfly because she had wings and "She could fly under the sun's caressing rays, amongst hosts of marvelous flowers" (48). To exist happily in a conservative world requires an element of fantasy and make-belief. Sexual love, transitory and falsely constructed though it may be, seems a necessary step to female maturation. In fact like Harriet Martineau's autobiography, in de Beauvoir also "the pervading image is that of gradual ascent, from inside stultifying, paralyzing existence up and out to a wide, clear, far seeing view" (Myers 69). Beauvoir is never apologetic but always proudly defiant about her feminine self, though she camouflages it at times. Her singular individuality and release came in only one region in which she was free to venture—writing and literature. So she comes up in her autobiography not just as a woman or a feminist author but as a woman writer who traces the progression of her self into an intellectual person. There are lengthy narrative affirmations about her mission and vocation, about her need for writing this autobiography. de Beauvoir had always stated that she wrote her multiple volumes to show through her experiences and perceptions of the world, how she acquired and realized her "vocation in life" (*The Prime of Life* 10).

The need to write and communicate her experiences was fulfilled much later when Beauvoir found her mentor Jean Paul Sartre. In her memoirs she draws up her various similarities and differences with Sartre, and very modestly slips into a secondary position. Judging herself as an exceptional person, she subtly points out "I couldn't imagine living and not writing but he only lived in order to write" (341). She moved freely in the Parisian intellectual and literary society (dominated by men like Nizan, Herboud, Leibnez) but she considers them as comrades never as men or enemies. She also quietly enjoys the pseudonym 'Beauvoir' give to her by Herboud for "Beauvoir like company, they have a constructive bent". Beauvoir slightly hints at her androgynous vision when she feels flattered to possess "a woman's heart and a man's brain" (296). Beauvoir opposes an essential sexual ideology which would accept the complementarity of genders, instead sees women's psychic life sometimes as identical to men though distorted through systematic patriarchal inscription. Her feminist self struggles with moralized bastions of reason and feeling and ends with death of female pleasure.

The book has all the ingredients of a feminine text. It reveals the author's "girlhood crises" and how this awareness shaped her future. It also contains her individual views about love, marriage, about her man whom she wants "to be neither inferior nor different, nor outrageously superior, someone who would guarantee my existence without taking away my powers of self determination" (34). She emphasis the fact that women are not feminist by virtue of the fact that they are women but they become so by strength and commitment. They negotiate between experience and knowledge. The subjective experiences is recounted with such objectivity that the female self identifies closely with her experiences. While De Beauvoir is also defiant about her divergence from usual feminine roles and stresses her need to study and work for self assertion and not just for economic security. Only at times does she feel herself as an adjunct of her male, but otherwise there is seldom a lack of self esteem or the ability to feel herself as a sentient being. The narrative concludes with the death of her friend Zaza, her double self who exuded an aura of strength, beauty, integrity and independence, and projects a standard against which Beauvoir judges herself. Later Zaza becomes the locus of a sense of loss and pessimism and annihilates herself, giving way to de Beauvoir to escape from socially expected roles, from the bondage of tradition and prescription of behavior to her own freedom and certainty of vocation. The *Memoirs* contain not just the world of her own self but also of others. The narrative structure adopts various forms of presentation—diary, letters (specially Zaza's) and extracts. Despite the uni-dimensionality of her life, a progressive narrative is maintained, the letters and other reminiscences creep in when she arranges the diffusion and diversity of her existence and the fragmentation she experiences in her social, psychological and professional roles. It is also in a way a first person biography of Zaza and Sartre but chiefly as an autobiography it builds on her gradual progression from enslavement to freedom, from depressing emotional life to her fulfilling individual and intellectual life. Hers is a gender affirming narrative.

Memoirs of A Dutiful Daughter is, in fact, a kind of a sexual and literary odyssey of de Beauvoir, her rite of passage from childhood to maturity, to womanhood and finally to freedom. The conclusion has an openendedness about it, suggesting Simone's further journey and quest for freedom. The significance of the *Memoirs* lies in the fact that is not Beauvoir who comes first but our construction of her.

References

de Beauvoir, Simone. *Memoris of A Dutiful Daughter* trans. James Kirkup (1959). New York: Harper and Row, 1963.

de Beauvoir, Simone. *The Prime of Life* trans. Peter Green. New York: Harper and Row, 1962.

Myers, Mitzi. "Harriet Martineau's Autobiography: The Making of a Female Philosopher" in *Women's Autobiography*, ed. Estelle C. Jelinek. Indiana University Press, London, 1980.

Pascal, Roy. *Design and Truth in Autobiography.* London: Routledge and Kegan Paul, 1960.

Pritchett, V.S. *New Statesman* (from the blurb of the book).

Shumaker, Wayne. *English Autobiography: In Emergence Materials, and Form.* Berkeley: University of California Press, 1954.

16

Mythologising History: The Indo-British Experience

Jasbir Jain

Contemporary writing increasingly evinces a concern with the past, with the continuities and discontinuities of history and with the marginalized and peripheral voices and concerns hitherto neglected. Rewriting history with a view to unravelling the mysterious nature of reality is also a concern of postcolonial writing. Part of this concern is directed towards mythologising, which again is expressed in a variety of ways. Some writers have taken classical or existing myths and applied or parodied them, others have constructed new myths, at times by deconstructing existing ones. Traditionally myths have been used to explain origins and represent cultural realities, but myths also help to explain the resurfacing of the past, sometimes in totally unexpected ways. Negotiating the worlds of myth and history is the form of the novel. Michael Holquist in his "Introduction" to Bakhtin's *The Dialogic Imagination* points out that the form of the novel resists the "organizing categories" of history. While histories insist "on a homology between the sequence of their own following. . . and the sequence of what they tell on the other. . . . . The novel by contrast dramatises the gaps that always exist between what is told and the telling of it. . ." (xxviii).

In this paper my concern is with the narrative act of mythologising the past in Paul Scott's *The Jewel in the Crown* (1966) and Nayantara Sahgal's *Rich Like Us* (1985). Separated by nearly twenty years, cultural perspectives and historical locations these works have several things in common. They are about the Indo-British experience, are self-reflexive and selfcritical where cultural realities are concerned. They deal with metaphors of rape and of power structures; they project value-structures and create familiar worlds through fantasizing reality. Scott is concerned with defining Englishness and Sahgal's emphasis as on probing the Hindu mind.

Sahgal's *Rich Like Us* (1985) alongwith her other two novels of the eighties—*Plans For Departure* (1985) and *Mistaken Identity* (1988)—is a retrieval and a restatement of India's past. *Rich Like Us* is dedicated to the Indo-British experience and "what its sharers have learned from each other." *Plans For Departure* carries a blurb which highlights its historicity as a novel "set in a period when India was still the jewel in the Crown. . ." *Mistaken Identity* is about the "twilight years" of the Empire, and about a trial which never seems to be taking place. It brings in the princely states and looks at the confluence of ideological stances. Together the three act like a trilogy. In an earlier article I have examined *Rich Like Us* and *Plans for Departure* as political biographies.[1]

Paul Scott's *The Jewel in the Crown*, the first part of the Raj Quartet, opens with two accounts of violence against the white woman and symbolic of the double metaphor of colonial discourse—one where the colonisers rape the colonized culture and the other where the colonized rape the white woman.[2] The opening page describes it as the "story of a rape, of the events that led up to it and followed it and the place in which it happened" (9). It also draws a parallel between Edwina Crane and Daphne Manners, a parallel which is developed right to the end, establishes the two women as part of a continued symbol and embraces the span of history from Edwina's arrival in India to Parvati's birth and after. Both women have been subjected to group violence—one on 8 August as she is travelling back after inspecting a school, escorted by Mr. Choudhari who in order so save her becomes the target of mob fury. Choudhari's murder leaves Edwina Crane with mixed feelings of guilt and fear. The very next day, young Daphne Manners is raped by a bunch of hooligans when she has gone to Bibighar Gardens to meet Hari Kumar. Both the happenings are located within the matrix of the Quit India Movement and thus have sharp political nuances.

The political nuances in *Rich Like Us* are somewhat different. It begins with the declaration of the Emergency and the tightening of control, and part of this hegemonic control is in the hands of foreigners who still view India in the categories of "us" and "them". The desire to clamber into these power structures also leads to the duplicating of the same ruthlessness and brutality. Here also an English woman is placed in a position of subjugation and dependence, first through a bigamous marriage, then through the claims and *kirtans* of Mona, the first wife, still later through childlessness, Marcella and forgery. Finally she is sacrificed on the altar of power hunger, a modern version of sati.

Different as the two works are in their political thrust, their similarity is based on their working within postcolonial parameters. They seek to "disrupt European notions of history" (Ashcroft 34), and work towards a recognition and acceptance of cross-cultural relationships. Ashcroft, Griffiths and Tiffin define a postcolonial world as one "in which destructive cultural encounter is changing to an acceptance of difference on equal terms" (36).

Scott's work is very different from either E.M. Forster's or George Orwell's. Forster's *A Passage to India* while projecting liberal ideals is tentative about solutions and resolutions. It places its central characters in a triangular relationship with each other—finally each going his own way. The *Passage* is about uncertainties and suspicions, it is about the souring of the need to understand, and withdrawal on part of both Fielding and Adele.

Mrs Moore even abandons the will to live.[3] Orwell's *Burmese Days* is about exclusion and loneliness. Just as Fielding stands outside the charmed inner circle, Flory is an outcast, his redemption lies in his act of courage and the protection he extends to his own kind. Scott, as contrasted with these two earlier writers, is engaged in an analysis of the social structures which govern behaviour and of the psychological needs which determine decisions. Populated by childless women—Edwina Crane, Lili Chatterjee, Lady Manners, Shalini Gupta Sen, Anna Klaus and Sister Ludmila—it moves towards the birth of a child of mixed parentage and placed under the protection, first of Ethel Manners and then Lili Chatterjee, both women who have transcended cultural confines.

The India of *The Jewel in the Crown* is a mythical reality, it is created to convey meaning. The geographical location, the creation of space, the mixed landscape and the naming of people are an imaginary creation, removed from realistic structures and functioning in the nature of a collage. It is difficult to locate Mayapore on the map of India despite the several clues provided by the writer. It was once a native state, annexed by the British in 1814. A South Indian women married the King and it is in her honour that the Tirupati temple was built. (Scott is least concerned with the fact that in India temples are named after the dieties and not the names of places). Dibrapur is fairly close to Mayapore. It has mines which are administered from Aligarh. Jarhwar and Tanpur are nearby towns, the Grand Trunk road passes through it. At one time Lindsey believes it to be fairly close to Meerut. (Meerut, Aligarh and Pindi are real place names mentioned). Shalini Gupta Sen finally goes back to her home in U.P. (Does that mean that Mayapore is not in U.P.?) The vegetation is of stubbed banana trees and the soil is red. Anyone who knows India is all the time getting contrary signals. Then besides the echoes of Dibrugarh in Dibrapur and Kanpur in Tanpur, there are other echoes. Chillianwallah Bagh Extension named after a Parsee gentleman is closer to Jallianwallah Bagh of the Amritsar massacre than the name of any parsee gentleman. At one place it is juxtaposed with Chillingborough. Again Gupta

Sen is a distortion of Sen Gupta.

However, while place names and family names are removed from reality, dates and events are meticulously stated and the biographical details are systematically builtup and can be cross checked at various levels. Rushdie in his essay, " 'Errata': or Unreliable Narration in *Midnight's Children*" points out that unreliable narration might be due to either sloppy research on part of the writer or deliberate. When it is deliberate the "small errors can be read as clues" (*Imaginary Homelands* 24). History, Rushdie goes on to say, "is always ambiguous. Facts are hard to establish, and capable of being given many meanings. Reality is built on our prejudices, misconceptions and ignorances as well as our perceptiveness and knowledge" (25).

In Scott's case it is not the narrative which is unreliable but the context. On the very first page be refers to "the action, the place and the people." By projecting a place with vague, mixed bearings, the writer indicates his perception of the reality of India. Mayapore is, in many ways, a mini-India with people of different regions, religions and classes living there and having became part of its history. The different areas and movements are memorials to the past—the Chillianwallah Bagh Extension, the Sanctuary, the Bibighar Gardens, MacGregor House. People of different nationalities are clumped together, Edwina is British, born in 1885, she is now fifty seven and has lived in India for thirty-five years. Daughter of an alcoholic soldier father, Edwina had initially come to India as a governess. She preferred to stay on in India working in different capacities in search of independence and freedom and grows from ignorance to knowledge and finally commits "suttee" in her own back yard dressed for the first time in a white sari (145).

Another of nature's waifs is Sister Ludmila whose origins were obscure and who has been variously viewed as "a Hungarian peasant, a Russian spy, a German adventuress, a runaway French novice" (146) She recalls her childhood in Brussels, "We shall go back soon to St. Petersburg, my mother used to say, but at other times she said we would go back to Berlin and at others to Paris, where then, I wondered, did we really live, where did we belong? There was about our lives a temporary feeling" (153). The nun's habit she wears is of her own making, a protection against the heat and the sun and also a carryover from her childhood memories of nuns.

Others not so obscure in their origins, but equally mixed and ambiguous in their social standing are Anna Klaus, the doctor at the purdah hospital, and Lili Chatterjee. Lili is accepted by the British and plays hostess to them at MacGregor House. Her husband Nello had been knighted. Lili knows she is a living combination of contraries, "What an old mess I'm in with my Rajput blood, my off white skin, my oriental curiosity, my liking for the ways of your occidental civilization, and my funny old tongue that is only properly at home in English" (93). Lili Chatterjee and Ethel Manners are friends and as such it is this grey area that Daphne Manners occupies between the white and the black.

Daphne herself is an orphan having lost both her parents as well as her brother and is in India on the strength of her father's memories of the country. But the reality is far more engulfing and terrifying than she is prepared for; the India of her father's memories was very different. Her personal bereavement and sense of isolation are further deepened:

> I had what I can only describe now as a permanent sinking heart I hated everything, hated it because I was afraid of it. It was all so alien. . . . . I started to have awful dreams. . . They used to come out of nowhere. . . .
>
> (134)

Daphne's reaction to the blackness of colour is one of fear and repulsion. She realizes that people of the same nationality use a "kind of shorthand in conversation" (134-135). But having witnessed the discrimination against people of colour she is conscious of these differences and is motivated by a desire for wholeness. She realizes that bridges may take their own time to be built, it was no use waiting for that, one had to enter the flood.

Standing on dry land is like not living, one has to cross barriers:

> She did not divide conduct into parts. She was always attempting a wholeness. When there is a wholeness there are no causes. Only there is living. The contribution of the whole of one's life, the whole of one's resources, to the world at large.
>
> (179)

Sister Ludmila refers to Siva's dance of creation, preservation and destruction, "A complete cycle. A wholeness. It is a difficult concept" (179). Daphne in one of her letters to her aunt refers to this image of Siva dancing in a circle of cosmic fire and placed next to a framed Biblical text (492), projecting a wholeness of another kind. There is a third reference to it wherein the mobility and the movement of the Dancing Siva seems to absorb Daphne totally (517). In Sister Ludmila's view Daphne's child is Kumar's child, for—

> Why else should she look, carrying it, like a woman in a state of grace. Why else should she refuse to get rid, refuse to abort, to throw the disgusting embryo to the mongrels? Why else? Unless having leapt she accepted the logic of her action, and all its consequences? Including the assault in darkness by a gang of ruffians. And believed that from such an assault she carried India in her belly?
>
> (195)

Kumar who is suspected to be the rapist, but who is a young lover, is subjected to spiritual rape. In speech and thought he is English, in colour he is Indian (157), his speech is better accented than Merrick's (169) and he has internalized the English way of thinking, something his father had chased all his life. Duleep Kumar's pursuit of the English way of life and thought had alienated him from his family and country and had led to a self-imposed distancing from his son. Hari is as much alienated from India as Daphne or Colin, to him England is home (287), he doesn't know Hindi and he hated the black town as much as "any man fresh out from England would hate it" (191). Duleep Kumar had learnt it the hard way that more than speech it was the language which mattered. Language shaped thought and guided thinking patterns:

> Hindi, you see, is spare and beautiful. In it we can think thoughts that have the merit of simplicity and truth. . . . English is not spare. But it is beautiful. . . . . its subtleties are infinite. It is the language of the people who have probably earned their reputation for perfidy and hypocrisy because their language itself is so flexible. . . .
>
> (255)

Hari belongs nowhere, none of the two—the Indians or the British—trust him (308-309), Colin fails to recognize him and thus thrusts an anonymity and invisibility on him as if he doesn't exist (335).

The birth of their child, Daphne feels, has to be natural. She resists the idea of a Caesarian even when they find that the "pelvis was wrong, and the baby was the wrong way round." She is in labour for fortyeight hours. Finally it has to be a caesarian—like the partition of India. The proce: _, Ethel Manners feels, "seemed obscene, like opening a can—which isn't obscene but is when the can is a human abdomen. But then when the can was open and I saw what they were lifting out I felt I was being born again myself. It was a miracle. . . (566).

At the end, the balance sheet is against the British—their departure in haste, freedom for India to suit their own convenience (158) and loose ends and leftovers like Hari (570). On the Indian side is "a deep, lingering silence. Siva dances in it. Vishnu sleeps in it" (562).

Rich Like Us reflects a similar concern with the duality of experience and the double rape. India has been raped twice-over, first by the foreign rulers and then by the power structures. Spiritually India has been drained and sycophancy, servility, henchmanship, duplicity and self-deception have completely taken over. Power and greed have blinded them to all else. Like Gandhi's picture in Edwina Crane's house (*Jewel* 10-11), Indira Gandhi's picture in Kishori Lal's shop (*Rich* 167) becomes a symbol. If the first was a symbol of non-violence and the aspiration for freedom, of selflessness and sacrifice, the second was a symbol of power and control and aroused feelings of fear. There is also another rape, rape worked through seduction. Rose's marriage to Ram is a story of narrowing of choices, of closing structures and controlled exploitation. It is an unequal marriage like the unequal relationship between India and England, it is an account of yielding and succumbing to the unilateral demands of this relationship by Rose. There is first the cutting off from her past, a dislocation from her background, a sudden and a late revelation that Ram is married and already a father and then after entry into this bigamous relationship, a marriage not Christian-legal (40), she is treated as a usurper and an outcast. Mona is constantly present and is constantly interrupting Ram and Rose's relationship. Ram laughs off Rose's complaints and cites the example of Lord Krishna with his three hundred women, and points out that the "Hindu marriage is not a contract, it's a sacrament" (54). Epics like the *Ramayana* and *Mahabharata* are quoted in support of these shared relationships. Mythology, Ram believes, is "human behaviour in the raw" (55).

During the riots in the city Rose becomes conscious of a sense of fear, for she suddenly realizes how the colour of her skin renders her vulnerable for "what protection was a car if they smelled the blood of an Englishwoman?" Temporarily she feels isolated and abandoned and is ready to leave the country, "I've got to get away from things I don't understand. How can anyone live two lives, be on two sides without getting mad?" (59). Her childlessness also renders her vulnerable, without a child of her own she can never hope to be mistress of the house "not even half of it. She would pass through this family, this frightening unshakeable permanence, leaving not the shadowiest imprint of her own on it" (64).

There are other myths, myths which people feel will never come true, they belong to the hoary past. Zafar, who is Ram's alter ego, they are like blood brothers and "You couldn't put a grain of rice between them" (65) is of the view that Pakistan is "nowhere", it is a myth, unreal and fictitious but later he himself is serving a military government (191). Similarly the myth of

Ramayana of the twins being born in a hermit's forest is realized through the birth of Pakistan and of free India. But stories don't end with births; they end with deaths and suicides and murders. They end with murders disguised as suicides. Keshav's grandmother's act of committing sati (134) and Sita's prayer to the earth to open and receive her are acts of the same kind. Keshav views it as a community murder, a suicide engineered through social pressure for "why would a lovely princess cry out for the earth to swallow her if life hadn't become a wilderness?" (67). These events from the past, from the pages of history and the world of mythology are recurring images, forming a pattern which is reenacted in Rose's life when her body is found in a nearby well two days after Divali, murdered by two youth camp toughs but passed of as an accidental fall due to drunkenness. The past echoes through one's bones. Sonali intuitively feels this as she leaves Rose's house after having attended to her worldly possessions, "I drove out through the gates past the well. I had been here before, generations before, and I felt the enfolding chill of a death I knew to be murder." In her advice to Kumar to maintain his silence, and in her plans to take the cripple to a place of safety, she feels she is following the instincts of her great grandmother who had sent her son away to safety (226).

Myths are meant to convey messages. The myths of Draupadi and Sita also perform this role. Power had always been power; it was hardly a question of race or colour, it was always a question of power:

> The gods hurl a thunderbolt and it rains. He frowns his displeasure and his adversary is reduced to ashes. He comes to Draupadi's aid and her sari stays on. . . . Prahlad in the legend embraces a fiery pillar and remains unscathed. It all depends on whether you are on the right side of power and omnipotence. Sita wasn't and it was banishment to the wilderness for her. Smiles and frowns become the law of the land when power is arbitrary. . . .
>
> (198)

And arbitrary power creates many big and small tyrants, it leads to ruthlessness and brutality. It sniffs out life.

Sonali's discussions with her father Keshav, Kishorilal's gesture of solidarity towards his young co-prisoner, Ravi's confession of having fallen short of the ideals placed before him, are all of a pattern. They are voices in the wilderness like those of Sita and Rose. While projecting the wisdom of ancient myths, Sahgal is also engaged in deconstructing the myth of Hindu spirituality and selflessness. The marriage which is a sacrament, the supremacy of the male prerogative, are power structures. In a letter dated September 14, 1964, Sahgal describes her own marriage, the isolation and schizophrenia it forced upon her, and the realization of being cramped and stunted (*Relationship* 31-40).

There is a constant questioning of the characteristics of Hinduism (not only in *Rich Like Us* but almost in all her work, fiction or nonfiction).[4] The Hindu mind accepts contradictions and has internalized power structures in the name of religion. Women commit sati so that men may satisfy their greed, Ram marries Rose but does not promise her either fidelity, privacy or love, Ravi gives up Sonali apparently because of a disagreement over ideological interpretations but in reality because his ambitions needed the sacrifice of this relationship. There is a certain blindness in the Hindu attitude which permits it to see what it wants to see and ignore what it doesn't, whether it be Mona or the Emergency. The Emergency was not a state of control new to India but "a brilliant archaeological find, evidence of the early blossoms of our culture, institutions that had endured, proof that family counted" (82). In a letter belonging to an earlier period, (July 23, 1966), Sahgal describes an imaginary situation akin to the emergency and writes:

> Would I leave this country if there was a substantial change of regime? I don't think I would leave this country if there was any way of staying alive in it. . . .I don't know if I am capable of leaving this country in any circumstance whatsoever. The emotional surgery might be so great as not to leave much of a person to enjoy life anywhere else. I would be afraid to cut myself of from India. . . .I would be afraid without India.
>
> (*Relationship* 200)

The manuscript which Sonali inherits from her father and is written by her grandfather ends with the remarks, "So I cannot believe in Hinduism, whatsoever Hinduism might be. Not because of such evils as 'Sati' but because evil is not explained" (*Rich* 136).

The ending of *Rich Like Us* is too close to despair to promise hope. The escape of the cripple, the promise of artificial limbs is all there is in the way of hope—crutches and aids to life. Compared to this the ending of *Plans for Departure* and *Mistaken Identity* are more positive and hopeful. Anna Hansen's granddaughter in *Plans for Departure,* Gayatri, child of a mixed marriage is like Parvati Manners of Scott's novel a symbol of hope. The illiterate Ranee's marriage with Comrade Yusuf in *Mistaken Identity* is a coming together of opposities, signifying a crossing of barriers.

Rich Like Us like *The Jewel in the Crown* is strewn with dates and references helping one to build up biographical details, and like *The Jewel in the Crown* depends upon both personal narratives and written documents, and again both seek to project multiple perspectives. Scott's waifs and exiles match Sahgal's "failures" like Keshav and Kishorilal and the marginalised like the cripple and Rose. There are numerous suppressed voices seeking expression.[5] Through these narratives a decentring takes place, the ordinary idea of the heroic is turned inside out. The mirror-effect is created as a strategy of self-criticism and this is finally blanked out. Myths are used to infiltrate the language of power with the language of rebellion. Both writers bring in heteroglossia to orchestrate their themes in their totality. There are a number of narrators, sub-narrators, journals, manuscripts, newspaper reports and socially diverse speech styles, and "these distinctive links and interrelationships between utterances and languages, this movement of the theme through different languages and speech types, its dispersion into the rivulets and droplets of social heteroglossia" is its dialogization (Bakhtin 263).[6] Linguistic constructs are questioned, disrupted or transcended. The transcendence becomes possible through myth and metonymy, through repetition and counter-narrative. This helps evade censorship just as much as it helps in getting the meaning across. They are in themselves little acts of rebellion.

Notes

1. See "Sahgal: The Novel as Political Biography," *Recent Common wealth Literature 1* edited by R.K. Dhawan et al. 1989. "There are no protagonists in the conventional sense. The protagonist is India—and it provides a centre for different points of view to converge on" (142).
2. With woman being equated with nature/land, the retaliation to the occupation of land has often been the conquest of women. Cassandra is Agamemnon's prize in war. The Indian Mutiny of 1857 presented a concrete realization of this threat and the fear of the white man's woman being raped is present in most inter-racial situations. Also refer *The Empire Writes Back* p. 84 where Nkosi's novel *Mating Birds* is discussed. I also wish to stress here that the British are going through their own postcolonial period wherein they are questioning power structures whether they are political, social, racial or gender based. Scott's writing belongs to that category.
3. The power structures and the social discriminations and divisions are very concretely depicted in David Lean's film version of *A Passage*, where the stress is on the pageantry, servility and anarcly of India vis-a-vis the controlled structures of the British.
4. This questioning is most dominant in *The Day in Shadow* but is present in several of her newspaper articles as well. For detailed discussions see T.K. Thomas, "The Hindu Ethos A Novelist's Perspectives", *Religion and Society* Vol. xx. No. 4. December 1973 and Jasbir Jain, *Nayantara Sahgal* (1978) Printwell Publishers, 1994, Chap III.
5. For detailed discussion see Jain, "Postcolonial Realities: Women

Writing History', *Interrogating Postcolonialism*, IIAS, 1996.

6. Bakhtin uses these terms for describing the novelistic discourse, but they are, in fact, the basis of both postmodernism and postcolonialisin.

References

Ashcroft, Bill; Griffiths, Gareth and Tiffin, Helen. *The Empire Writes Back: Theory and Practice in Postcolonial Literatures*. London: Routledge. 1989.

Bakhtin, M.M. *The Dialogic Imagination*, edited by Michael Holquist, translated by Caryl Emerson and Michael Holquist. Austin: University of Texas Press, 1981.

Forster, E.M. *A Passage to India*, (1924). Harmondsworth: Penguin, 1989.

Holquist, Michael. "Introduction", *The Dialogic Imagination* by M.M. Bakhtin.

Jain, Jasbir. *Nayantara Sahgal* (1978), Revised edition with a postscript. Jaipur: Printwell Publishers, 1994.

—, "Postcolonial Realities: Women Writing History", *Interrogating Postcolonialism* edited by Harish Trivedi and Meenakshi Mukherjee. Shimla: Indian Institute of Advanced Study, 1996.

—, "Sahgal: The Novel as Political Biography", *Recent Commonwealth Literature 1* edited by R.K. Dhawan, P.V. Dhamija and A.K. Srivastava. New Delhi: Prestige, 1989.

Orwell, George. *Burmese Days* (1934). New York: Popular Library, 1957.

Rushdie, Salman, " 'Errata' or Unreliable Narration in *Midnight's Children*" *Imaginary Homelands*. London: Granta Books, 1991.

Sahgal, Nayantara. *Mistaken Identity*. London: Heinemann, 1988.

—, *Plans for Departure*. London: Heinemann, 1986

—, *Rich Like Us*. London: Heinemann, 1985.

Sahgal, Nayantara and Mangat Rai, E.N. *Relationship: Extracts from a Correspondences.* New Delhi: Kali for Women, 1994.

Scott, Paul. *The Jewel in the Crown* (1966). London, Pan Books, n.d.

17

Rich Like Us: Text, Context and Subtext

Viney Kirpal

In the first part of this paper, I ask whether gender has affected the representation of reality as constructed by Indian female and male writers. In the second Part, I examine Nayantara Sahgal's *Rich Like Us* (1985) as a feminist text.

Simone de Beauvoir in *The Second Sex* (1952), had concluded her examination of five male writers (Lawrence, Montherlant, Claudel, Breton and Stendhal) thus:

> We could multiply examples, but they would invariably lead us to the same conclusions. When he describes woman, each writer discloses his general ethics and the special idea of himself; and in her he often betrays also the gap between his world view and his egotistical dreams. The absence or insignificance of the feminine element throughout the work of an author is in its own way symptomatic; . . .
>
> (251-52)

Kate Millet in *Sexual Politics* (1970) had similarly criticized the male chauvinism of Norman Mailer, D.H. Lawrence and Henry Miller. These are judgments truer of the Euro-American novel (excluding the emerging feminist novel) than of the Indian novel. Generally speaking, male Indian English novelists have not portrayed women as adjuncts to the central quest of men heroes for selfhood (Although, Ramaswamy in Raja Rao's *The Serpent and the Rope* wants women to be his adjuncts in his metaphysical quest, he is to be distinguished from his creator). Rather, Indian writers have pictured women and their experiences in a male-dominated society, with deep understanding. Women in novels by Indian male writers have existed as protagonists and even as central voices. Consider, for example, the protagonists of Mulk Raj Anand's *Gauri*, R.K. Narayan's *The Dark Room*, and Salman Rushdie's *Shame*. Sensitively-portrayed women characters—individuals in their own right, although not protagonists—stand at the core of Vikram Seth's *The Golden Gate*, Amitav Ghosh's *The Shadow Lines* and Rushdie's *The Moor's Last Sigh*. In Raja Rao's *Kanthapura* and in K.S. Karanth's *Mookaji's Vision*, the narrators are elderly women.

The reasons for the difference between the portrayal of women in the novel in the West and the Indian novel, are not far to seek. Although the Indian novel began as an imitation of the novels of G.W.M. Reynolds, Dickens, Thackeray and Sir Walter Scott, the Indian novel soon evolved a distinctive character of its own. What gave the novel its unique character was perhaps the growing desire (since 1857) of the Indians to free themselves of the British yoke. Secondly, the nationalist movement which was both a quest for political freedom and social reform (including the emancipation and upliftment of women) left a major impact on the Indian mind. The Indian novelist, particularly since the 1930s (though earlier too its was evident in the novels of Bankim, Tagore and Saratchandra), had begun writing novels that reflected the changing needs, realities and aspirations of Indian society. Little attempt was made to write the Victorian type of romance where love, and personal relationships between men and women heroes were being explored. The general preoccupation in the Victorian novel had been with the eternal triangle of two suitors and a female character who got educated in the process of choosing the good and intelligent suitor over the sauve and evil one.[1] By contrast, the Indian novel has largely concentrated on the problems of the individual (male and female) vis-a-vis the family, community and even the entire society. In Indian literature, the absence of the theme of love and personal relationships has been remarked upon (Mukherjee 1-8). Always extremely responsive to social, political, economic changes in Indian society, our novelists—both male and female—have taken up the oppression and suppression not only of women but also of untouchables, factory workers, poor farmers, landless labourers, as themes.

Confining ourselves to the question of women, it can be seen that the marginalised condition of woman as girl, wife, mother, widow has been poignantly portrayed in the novels and short stories of Mulk Raj Anand, R.K. Narayan, Raja Rao, Rushdie, Rohinton Mistry, Amitav Ghosh, Amrita Pritam, Nayantara Sahgal, Shashi Deshpande, K.S. Karanth, Ismat Chugtai, Jayawant Dalvi, Rajinder Singh Bedi, Bhabani Bhattacharya, Anita Desai and many others. The sexual exploitation of a woman has been depicted in Anand's *Untouchable*, Dalvi's *Chakra*, Pritam's *The Skeleton* and Bhattacharya's *So Many Hungers*, Rushdie's *Shame*, Deshpande's short stories and her later novels *That Long Silence* and *The Binding Vine* to cite a few examples. Looking at male writers only, the subordinate social position of women in a patriarchal society is the theme of Narayan's *The Dark Room* and Anand's *Gauri*. Since the publication of *The Dark Room* (1938) many Indian housewives have written to Narayan to say that they can identify with the protagonist, Savithri, and relate to her dilemma very well. "It seems it is the pattern of the housewives", Narayan has said in an interview (1971: 82). The scene where Savithri asserts herself for the first time and tells her husband that a woman has nothing to call her own since everything belongs to her father, brother, husband, son is a scene that would do any modern day feminist proud (75). Again Savithri's realization that she should have asserted herself early in her marriage could be a statement straight out of Shashi Deshpande's *That Long Silence.*

The Dark Room is a re-writing of the Savithri-Satyavan story with Narayan's Savithri "returning" not to her husband but to her children.

Similarly, Anand's *Gauri* (1960) is a re-working of *The Ramayana* with Gauri shedding her Sita image to become a Kali (245). Unable to convince her husband of her purity, she decides not to be a Sita (In the epic she prefers death to a life of shame) but to stand on her feet, to work in Doctor Mahindra's hospital and to bring up her unborn child according to her newly acquired progressive ideas. If a feminist plot ending is one where the women walks out on the man to lead a life of dignity, then the conclusion of *Gauri* is a feminist one. Gauri shows the ability to take the initiative to reconstruct her life without dependence on a man's money. In the Indian context, Gauri's portrait may seem an implausible one (because she is an uneducated, village girl) but the point to remember is that in her, Anand, a male writer was suggesting a utopian, progressive future for the Indian women of the 1930s.

To sum up this section, as both *The Dark Room* and *Gauri* will have shown, gender has not generally affected the creative representation of women by Indian male writers. Some exceptions are Khushwant Singh, Chaman Nahal, Upamanyu Chatterjee, who focus on the sexuality of male characters usually with the object of reader titillation. But on the whole, it is only fair to say that our male writers have been very sensitive to women's issues and that they have tried to centralize her rather than marginalise her. The Indian women writers Amrita Pritam, Chugtai, Githa Hariharan, Sahgal, Shashi Deshpande have also worked towards the same end.

However, I would like to qualify this statement by adding that the portrayal of women and their experiences by some Indian women writers has undergone a significant change in the 1980s. Under the influence of the gender revolution of the 1970s, writing by women about women has become a political act. There is a strong element of protest in their novels now. Like their counterparts in the West, they question the oppressor or the social other. The other or the oppressor in the Indian context is not just the husband or lover but the entire family, and sometimes the whole society. This new writing by Indian women writers is feminist in character. It is a frontal attack on patriarchy and its tools—the processes of socialization, traditional myths, social customs, practices—that are responsible for the zero worth of women in our society. Women have always been told to conceal, edit, suppress the facts of their biological experiences such as menstruation, sex, pregnancy, childbirth. Like feminists in the West, some Indian women novelists have begun to speak uninhibitedly about their bodily experiences and to write as Mary Jacobus has said, "of what cannot be written" (in Abel, 9-36). So, Shashi Deshpande in *The Dark Holds No Terrors* describes her protagonist Saru's enjoyment of the sexual act with her husband on her wedding night. The intimate feelings and emotions of the women characters are caught in fine detail as if viewed under a high-powered microscope. Such writing shocks because, to quote Virginia Woolf, "a woman is saying what she feels (as Joyce does)," that is, she is writing without censoring, like a modernist, about everything her mind and body are experiencing (in Abel, 9-36).

Consider, for example, the occurrence of childbirth in novels until recently and its description in Sahgal's *Rich Like Us*. Before the advent of feminist writing, "When a baby arrive[d] in a novel it usually ha[d] the air of having been posted. . . Between Sterne and Joyce, scarcely any writer ha[d] tried to use the facts of birth. . . to work towards the psychology of the baby's mind and to utilize the literary wealth that must lie there. . ." (Forster 73-74). E.M. Forster, quoted above, still seems to concentrate on the exploitation of the act of childbirth for its psychological and literary value. He does not even imagine that it could be used in the novel to depict the woman's marginalized state of mind during childbirth. By contrast, the feminist writer would like to present the experience of childbirth entirely from the woman's point of view. She would like to focus on the maddening pain, the feeling of being left with a raw wound in her body, which everyone else seems to take for granted because that's how every baby is born. In *Rich Like Us*, Sahgal describes the rebellious feelings of Nishi at the time of childbirth. The account suggests both Nishi's silent revolt and her inability to protest the downside of the experience publicly because of the universal glorification of motherhood and the perpetuation of the human race:

> Her selves lay torn in jagged halves on the delivery table, under the masked indifferent scrutiny of strangers and their implements, ... It was night and a scientific light fell mercilessly on her exposed and wounded flesh, her cry deranging no one but herself. Their announcement of motherhood revived fresh raw protest . . . . A stranger laid the child she hadn't wanted, and next year the second child she did not want, like trophies beside her . . . . By morning, . . . a wall shutting out the memory of the night's violence had implacably, invisibly encircled her. Through slitted battlements,... she could smile and nod at telegrams, gifts and flowers. . . . Grappling with her selves was simple if she kept her inner and outer selves apart . . . .
>
> (234)

Subverting the social fiction that is the picture of contented, fulfilling motherhood, Sahgal foregrounds the intimate, secret, mutinous feelings of a woman in labour, feelings which were absent in earlier novels both by men and women writers. However, it is not the novelty of the experiences/feelings presented that alone gives feminist novels their worth or power but rather their ability to make the reader vicariously live the intensely private experiences narrated by women as insiders to those experiences, and the quality of art which increases the sensitivity of others towards a woman's world of feelings, emotions, even insecurities related to her biology.

Or consider, for instance, the way in which Sahgal challenges the dual standards, the gender roles and the processes of socialization in Indian society. In 1952, Simone de Beauvoir had made the seminal declaration in her introduction to *The Second Sex*: "One is not born, but rather becomes a woman" (xiii). In *Rich Like Us*, the feminist, Sonali's outburst centralizes the psychological gap in her's and Ravi's outlook by relating it to the difference in their socialization;

> I think he [Ravi] said that because he was a man. He had never fought a battle for freedom, never been patted down firmly when his sap was rising, never had a sari throttling his legs, making walking in the wind and running to catch a bus a threat to life and limb, never had his mother set up a howl when he went and got a haircut.
> (112)

At various places in the novel, Sahgal underlines the fact that the psychology of the girl child is shaped from childhood onwards with the straitjacket of restrictions, while the male child is indulged and spoilt no end because he must grow up to be a man; that is, one who is macho and sexually aggressive:

> But what troubled her [Rose] most was the sugarcoated glaze Ram had dropped over Dev. "My Son" had to be spoken in holy whisper. Never mind if he hijacked cars for fun, boys will be boys . . . . And when Dev and his picture-going, ice-cream guzzling gang took to abducting girls from Miranda House. . . these escapades were part of growing up. . . . A man has to get his experience somewhere. . . .
> (180-81)

In a novel dedicated to the "The Indo-British experience', Sahgal opposes the myths of both cultures because they create stereotypes and place women in a powerless situation. The story of Rose and Ram is a typical English fairytale, a Mills and Boon plot. Rose, the poor, pretty saleswomen/princess is rescued by the handsome, rich, Indian prince (Ram's eyes had the "power to open door sideways") and carried off to his kingdom/India. But unlike the everlasting happiness of fairytales, the modern day princess discovers that there is also a witch (Mona, the first wife of Ram) to reckon with, in the kingdom. The story of Rose and Ram is also the archetypal *Ramayana*. Ram (obviously named after the hero of the epic) is accompanied by Rose/Sita to India (Cythera, "her exile, her home", 74). Like Sita, Rose at the end of the novel "enters" the lap of the earth when she is murdered and her body dumped into a dry, unused well (251). Their story is also a re-writing of the *Ramayana* from a feminist angle. In this interpretation, injustice towards all women gets foregrounded. Mona suffers when she is discarded by Ram, in favour of Rose, only two years younger than Mona. In desperation, she tries to commit suicide but is saved. Rose is then cast aside by Ram when he has a four-month long affair with the sophisticated and intellectual Marcella. Thus, a fairytale within a fairytale is enacted: "The enchantress Marcella in the fairytale had let down her hair, and the candidate for bewitchment Ram had grasped the golden rope and climbed up into the tower" (104). Now it is Rose's turn to experience sleepless nights. It is her "trial by fire". In one scene, identifying with Sita, she wonders if after Rama had taken Sita back, wouldn't she sometime have asked him, "Why the hell did you have to put me through that grisly experience?" (215). Likewise, when Ram returns to her after Marcella's departure for England, she wants to give him a furious shaking and ask him what he means by his bland assumption that "they would go on exactly as before as though there had been no break in their married life. . ." (215). But surprisingly she doesn't. Having left her home, country, career, independence and not having had a formal education, she knows she had nowhere to go and she compromises.

Both Mona and Rose suffer intensely because of Ram's egotism and callousness. Both feel terribly lonely, anguished, helpless and oppressed. The real oppressor, Ram, goes scotfree, conveniently taking cover under the traditional sanction for bigamy, while life for the wives becomes increasingly unbearable:

> 'I don't think I can take much more of this, Ram."
> 'Of what'? he had temerity to ask.
> 'Your living with two wives.'
> He was stretched out on his bed too good-humoured and too lazy to quarrel. 'Lord Krishna had three hundred.'. . . .
> 'I can't go on like this.'
>
> (60)

The text "too good-humoured and too lazy to quarrel" suppresses the sub-text "You nagging, quarrelsome, mad woman, and I, the good-natured tolerant husband who puts up with you as no husband would". He silences her by asking her how the arrangement could hurt her when they live upstairs and Mona downstairs. Sahgal recreates in imaginative, aesthetic terms, the terrible fate of wives commonly trapped in polygamous marriages especially before the passage of the Hindu Code Bill in Parliament in 1955. Not that the law has put a complete end to bigamy in India (it continues clandestinely in a fairly large number of cases as reported recently in the newspapers) but at least the feeling that a man can keep more than one wife as a matter of right because the practice has the sanction of mythology or tradition no longer persists.

However, legislation alone can not change the status of women. In the novel, Sahgal moves from the particular to the general, from the feminist to the social to show for example, that despite the abolition of sati in 1829, several cases of sati continued to be reported in the nineteenth century (137-152). In almost all the instances, the satis were widows from the upper classes, who were burnt to deprive them or their minor dependents of their inheritance. In the author's view (expressed through Sonali, the protagonist), it is not just legislation but widespread social reform that alone can transform the evil attitude towards women:

> But what was needed was a crusade with all its passion and fever. Generations of lawyers will uphold generations of laws but the old evils will go on into the twentieth and twenty-first centuries because no torch has been lit. . . .
>
> (136)

And because "no torch has been lit", Sahgal shows that sati continues in post-independence India in the form of dowry deaths where brides are burnt for the sake of pelf. The earlier situation may have changed with new inheritance and property laws for women but the reasons for the destruction of or domination over women by men/society have remained very much the same—the greed for money and the need to demonstrate power. In the novel, the armless beggar, a friend of Rose, describes how eight policemen (keepers of the law!) sexually humiliate five women from his village to punish the male farm labourers for their "obstinacy" in defying the landowner:

> The landowner who owned most of the cultivable land in the village, and whom they worked for, had sent for the police at harvest time to make sure they didn't get off with their full share of the crop. . . . Feet marching in unison, scythes on shoulders and songs being sung in the fields made them jittery. The police plundered the stored grain . . . [and] made free and easy with the women, so lots of them had run away. . . . He [the beggar] found them, with eight policemen. Two of the men lay on their sides chewing blades of grass. The rest were in a circle with one woman in the centre. Through the shrubbery he saw the tip of a *lathi* raise the woman's sari above her waist, poke and prod her and turn her round and round like a marionette. Another *lathi* joined the first. She was the only one still clothed and standing. The others lay like overlapping corpses on the ground. He vomited into the bushes. . . .
>
> (246)

Thus, on the one hand, the book is about the unquenchable thirst for power that underscores all atrocities whether at the individual level (as in this case) or at the State level (as during the emergency, the focal theme of the novel).

On the other hand, the book is about the self-definition of Sonali, the Western-educated, strong, independent Indian woman. Averse from the start to prettying herself and becoming a sex object, she refuses to wear contact lenses and does not hesitate to conceal her lovely eyes behind a thick pair of glasses. Perhaps, modelling herself on Virginia Woolf, she makes a career for herself and has "a room of her own." "A bright young thing", she has a mind of her own and although not conservative, she does not feel the need to wear a soft, sexy look in her eyes as the dinner reaches the dessert stage of conversation as expected (by her date) of the woman in the West (170). She and Ravi Kachru had been in love during their student days in England but differences in the basic attitudes to life had driven them apart, although their paths cross repeatedly later on. It is Ravi who replaces her as Joint Secretary when, during the Emergency, she adheres to principles and annoys someone in power. Later, Ravi meets her when he is being similarly demoted for having displeased a Cabinet Minister and the circle comes complete. In an intimate conversation at that moment, Ravi tells her that he had always loved her but that she had been "too brave" and "too bright" for him. He asks her if she would ever want to do it all over again. She answers him tactfully that it had been was the happiest as well as the unhappiest time of her life (261). What she does not tell him is that she feels freer alone. This is the portrait of the WUPPIE, the women urban professional given by Sahgal in *Rich Like Us*. Such a woman is western-educated, economically independent, full of courage, self-respecting, dignified and capable of living by her own value system without compromising with State, society or a male. The portrait of Sonali is a progressive one; it spells hope for the upliftment of and emancipation of Indian women through education, economic freedom and self-determination. Like other Indian feminist writers, Sahgal has not addressed herself solely to anti-male issues. Like them, she seeks the transformation and reformation of Indian society and through that, the freedom of the woman.

The male Indian English novelists of the 1980s—Rushdie, Ghosh, Seth, Mistry—have also constructed women characters to foreground the hidden ideology of gender oppression but by focusing on the oppression/oppressor. Consider the exploitation and neglect of Sufiya Zenobia, Rani Harrappa, Bilquis, the Shakil sisters in Rushdie's *Shame*. The representation touches a raw nerve in the reader because the novel shows how ruthlessly their men—"modern", educated men—betray and oppress the women. The women's inability to checkmate their men lies not in the author's patriarchy (I disagree with Aijaz Ahmad's interpretation in *In Theory* 144) but in the paralyzed psyche of the women subjected to long spells of physical, mental and psychological decimation. The women characters in *Shame* are in themselves very strong, although not progressive or feminist—the way the 1980s women novelists' female characters are. Through their oppression, the novelist focuses on the unfairness of power structures within male-dominated societies. This is also true of the women characters of Seth, Ghosh and Mistry. While the women novelists have sought the transformation of the female characters into assertive human beings, the male novelists have indirectly sought the transformation of their male characters into kinder, humane partners. Thus, in different though complementary ways, both male and female Indian English novelists have sought "to light the torch" to extirpate existing gender inequalities and transform patriarchal societies.

Notes

1. In *Victims of Convention*, Jean E. Kernard has noted that a large number of Victorian and modern novelists have been unable to explore women's problems because of the two suitor convention, whereby the young woman is educated by the process of choosing between two young men, one good and intelligent and the other, evil. Cited from memory.
2. "I have not been able to find examples where love between man and woman preoccupies such a central position as, for instance, in many novels of D.H. Lawrence. Perhaps, our culture has not reached the point where individual men and women are driven to discover themselves and each other through love." Stated by Sujit Mukherjee in *The Indian P.E.N.* (1973).

References

Anand, Mulk Raj. *Gauri*. (1960) New Delhi: Orient Paperbacks, 1976.

de Beauvoir, Simone. *The Second Sex* (1952). Translated and edited H.M. Parshley, New York: Vintage Books, 1989.

Forster, E.M. *Aspects of the Novel* (1927). London: Edward Arnold and Co., 1945.

Jacobus, Mary. "The Difference of View" in *Women's Writing About Women* (12-13) quoted in Elaine Showalter, "Feminist Criticism in the Wilderness" in *Writing and Sexual Difference* ed. Elizabeth Abel. London: University of Chicago Press Ltd., 1982, 9-36.

Mukherjee, Sujit. "Love in Modern Indian Literature". *The Indian P.E.N.*, 39: 2 (1973): 1-8.

Narayan, R.K. Interview with V. Panduranga Rao., "Tea with R.K. Narayan," *The Journal of Commonwealth Literature*, VI: 1 (June 1971): 82.

—, *The Dark Room* (1938), New Delhi: Orient Paperbacks, 1976.

Sahgal, Nayantara. *Rich Like Us* (1985). London: William Heinemann Ltd., Sceptre edition, 1987.

Woolf Virginia, "Speech, Manuscript Notes", *The Pargiters*, ed. Mitchell A. Leaska (1978), 164. Quoted in *Writing and Sexual Difference*, 1982, 9-36.

18

Power Structure in Nayantara Sahgal's *Rich Like Us*

Mini Nanda

What we see in the novel is the play of power at various levels—political, physical, social, economic and domestic. The forces of darkness reflected in violence over the years and the forces of light emerging in the power of conviction, of integrity and compassion. The classic Marguerite/Mephistopheles situation is the timeless game of power politics.

The novel opens into a room with total anonymity, where there is no echo of things past or things to come. It is a strange vacuum, where nameless people flit among strong power symbols of imported cars and the delicate clink of Belgian crystal and Scotch whisky, "five times more expensive" than Indian whisky. The declaration of Emergency, witnesses the swift exchange of power from mother to the son, leading to the beautification of the "imperial" city by blowing up tenements, vasectomising the masses and setting up youth camps.

Sycophancy by any other name would really have no claim to individuality. The "nameless host" declares pompously to the "foreign guest", that Emergency has been a boon for the Country. The language sounds familiar to the reader, who is gripped by a strange sense of foreboding. The host continues effusively that the opposition has been wiped off and with power in the hands of one person, the country would move towards progress full steam. A well fortified structure of power emerges, no strikes, no meetings, creating an ambience of "sullenness" along the "heavily policed roads".

In this maze, the bureaucracy treads nimbly along, moving deeper into the labyrinth of power without glancing back. The distinction between politics and the service becomes blurred, with the two sides hopelessly mixed together and each taking part in the masquerade that the "Empress's new clothes were beautiful"(29). Ravi Kachru follows the rules of the game as if his life depended on it. Nayantara Sahgal uses the image, "bounding out like an alsatian" for Ravi. With glib professionalism he enlightens the 'masses' about the virtues of the emergency and the nationalisation of the banks. A contrasting picture emerges of Shivraj, the charismatic leader of *A Situation in New Delhi*. Shivraj had vehemently declared that he hated the word 'masses'. "It lumps humanness into a 'thing', like a mass of clay, for someone else's use" (*Situation* 51). History is a testimony to the fact that wherever power crosses the limits of democracy and rationality, it corrupts absolutely and reduces individuals to masses.

The novel offers two layers of narrative and two centres of interest—Rose and Sonali. Sonali, who topped the IAS, nevertheless finds herself an alien in this political circus. Very much like Nayantara Sahgal, she is nurtured on the values imbibed from her father, on non-violence and truth of the Mahatma. She cannot keep up the charade of the emergency and bluntly calls it a "fraud" and considers it an atrocity perpetrated on the people. Ravi Kachru and Sonali represent the polarities of the system. Both have had the same education abroad and are bureaucrats, but Kachru always manages to be on the right side of power, keeping out of controversies and avoiding wrong turns, and sailing smoothly with the current, "Kachru of course would get through any charade with finesses. It was the realities that floored him" (31).

At Oxford, both Ravi and Sonali were happy with all the 'unhaveable' things—the Sun, the Moon and the Stars. Sonali bubbling over her new found freedom, her escape from cumbersome saris and long plaits, into flouncing skirts and short hair falling all over her face and shoulders. On another level she is fascinated by the seduction of the powerful language of Marxism. "Expropriate the Expropriators", which seemed to open an unused attic window of her mind. Unlike Ravi she doesn't feel "committed" to the general humanity. With her there is the scratching of the inner surface of anxiety, a swirl of "conscience pricking images, mud-walled village classrooms and child brides taking their dolls to their husband's houses". This intuitive responsiveness to the Indian ethos made her sceptical about the Marxist credo. She hated dictatorship of any kind. Hadn't Gandhi taken human rights a hundred years ahead in two decades, without a glimmer of class war? What appealed to her was the new language of the new epic, 'Daridranarayan' and 'Harijan'. What was needed was an inventiveness that suited the Indian reality. Where freedom and dignity of the individual would percolate down to the grass-root level.

In the IAS, the reality was a travesty of that truth she had hoped for:

> Appealing images marched through my mind. The bride burnt to death by her in-laws. . .criminals blinded by the police. . . sharecroppers murdered. . . I must have been mad or so obsessed with my work that I would push accounts like these from my mind and forget them. . . !
>
> (34)

With Sonali there is the questioning and the guilt; hadn't she moved away in the closed security of her car, averting her face from the horror of the young boy, struggling without his spectacles and the baton-weilding police pulling him in the other direction? She defies compliance, refuses to be a party to the "conspiracy of silence", observed by the exclusive class of IAS officers so exclusive that they formed a club. On receiving the "midnight knock" in the afternoon, in a symbolic gesture opts out of the situation.

In an interview with Jasbir Jain in 1990, Nayantara Sahgal, has spoken about the play of power in interpersonal relationship, between husband and wife, parent and child, between lovers, "I think of politics not as a leading the country—but politics as the use of power. And also the abuse of power—it happens at so many levels"—(Jain 186).

With the decline of moral values in pubic life, we see the break-up of family values. Marriage becomes a move for power and possession. Ram, the suave, glib businessman, wonders about Rose the Cockney girl: "a chocolate shop pick-up talking to him like an equal" (41). For Rose, Ram was not a person but a magnetic pull, luring her away from the counter in London and she had never looked back. "She had entered an emotional labyrinth and she was drawn magnetically on . . . . She was out in a strange territory and had lost her way home" (44). Resigned to the fact of being a second wife, Rose is later displaced as a threesome to Ram and Marcella's twosome. Discarded for five years as Ram callously puts her away on the shelf like a pumpkin, when he goes off in search of a Cinderella. After this amnesia of separation lasting five years, with equal nonchalance Ram brings the whole family back under one roof.

Lorna Sage in her perceptive article, "Available Space", speaks about women on the margins of society, attempting to create their own space. There is the appropriation of Rose's mental, emotional, physical and economic space. The narrative structure shifts in the novels not just in terms of political dates, but in economic and social terms also. In the Second World War, the entire street in London is destroyed, in an air-raid killing her parents, "Not just two people she dearly loved had perished. . . but there was not a brick or a pebble now to connect her with her past" (199). Her room in the new house is an island off the mainland creating its own ambience and rhythm. A room to live of what was left of her life. With Ram in a state of comatose, Rose is left a destitute, with no legal rights and no money.

Rose's marginalisation brings to our mind a montage of several other haunting images of child-widows wrapped in grimy saris, made to suffer for their "Karma", living like beasts with food thrown at them from the "Saint's Kitchen". There is also Sonali's great grandmother forced to commit sati as part of a bargain that her son would come into inheritance before age and he would be given the money to go abroad for his studies.

Sonali's father recalls with anguish a painting he had seen in an art gallery in England. A group of cowled head monks, dressed in thick black clothes, sitting in a stark room with stone walls, a high circular window in the wall, reflecting light on their impassive faces their eyes intent on a single person whose eyes are lowered. An intense moment captured on the canvas, a structural claustrophobia powerfully conveying the terror and the plight of the victim anywhere and everywhere, surrounded by the forces of darkness. Sonali's father who was a student of law saw the ineffectiveness of the law which had banned sati, but it was still going on "openly or clandestinely in parts of the country". The harrowing soul-wrenching accounts of women forced to perform sati, make him sum up the age old drama of violence, "You are not paralyzed by the legalities when it suits you to set them aside"(135). The relatives who had pushed Sonali's great grandmother into the pyre had built a shrine on the spot, turned it into a pilgrimage centre and there was nothing but a document at the bottom of her father's trunk to prove that it was murder.

Sudhir Kakar in his book, *The Inner World* makes a very fine point when he says, "in daughterhood an Indian girl is a sojourner in her own family and with marriage she becomes less a wife than a daughter-in-law. It is only with motherhood that she comes into her own as a woman and she can make a place for herself in the family, in the community and in her life circle"(52). Rose is truly isolated and like her room in the house she is cornered. A Ruth among the alien corn. Mona seeks her escape through her *kirtans* and has a stronger status for she is the mother of a son, however wayward, good for nothing he may be. With Mona, Rose bridges the gap of hate and isolation, by saving her life and the two come together as friends. Rose reconstructs her childhood with reminiscences captured for Mona.

Nishi the daughter-in-law is also reduced to be a social butterfly, a puppet dancing to the tune of her husband, "Yes Devikins" and "No Devikins". Unlike Sonali, Nishi is not touched by her father's values. Nishi finds the emergency safe, giving her a sense of purpose, a chance to poor "Devikins" to come into his own with the Happyola factory. She addresses exotic meetings in five star hotels, discussing the important agenda of vasectomising the masses in kitty party settings, among skin fragrances, sheer cotton sarees and mouth melting samosas. All this is heady stuff for her, away from the childhood memory of sharing bed and clothes with four other sisters. Nishi loses all contact with ground reality, as she drags Kumar the old servant and the cripple in the biscuit factory van for vasectomy. It is Rose who restrains her frenzied action pointing to her that Kumar is old enough to be her father and the cripple not being a whole man wouldn't even count. Nishi symbolises the total alienation of a native, blind to the reality around her, signifying the journey from Mahatma to Madam.

Rose, the outsider, symbolises the benign colonial situation, alienated from her husband and family she creates her mental and emotional space with Sonali and the cripple, there forms an intangible link between the three. A seven-year old Sonali had chimed gaily on meeting Rose for the first time, "Is that her name or is she one?"(255). In fact Rose and Sonali are the only two people with whom the armless person communicates. To Rose the cripple recounts his story, his anguish. The forces of darkness wrecking havoc on his life and limb, also the age old subjugation of women in brick kilns, where his wife like many before and after had just disappeared finds an echo in Rose's heart, "And the beggar was a sight to match the story, a man who couldn't even wipe away his tears" (75). Now she understands the essence of the

Mahatma's hymn to wipe the tear from every eye. Rose who usually struggled with words, the right ones always seemed to elude her, arranges for artificial limbs for the cripple, she is rich in her dreams and aspirations for him, "she could picture him healed and whole. . . exultantly whole once again by the light of the stars" (90).

Rich in their conviction and their perseverance are Lalaji and Kishori Lal. Lalaji who is whipped for he refuses to crawl through the street is a disciple of Gandhi. He throws away every foreign article from his shop, and holds prayer meetings, long before the call of Quit India in 1942. Similarly Kishori Lal refuses to be released from the jail, until the release for the innocent boy is also arranged. He does not see his release as a 'Lifeline', his pull is in the other direction. The prison cell had left him with a mission. On the hard prison floor his dream is reminiscent of the whisky priest in Graham Greene's, *The Power and the Glory*, where the prison cell signifies the microcosmic world. Kishori Lal dreams of addressing the multitudes, Muslims, Sikhs, Hindus and Christians, all of whom form a unified sea of humanity, discarding in union, home, food and shelter for freedom and dignity. In his business he felt he had completed the crusade against untouchability started by Gandhi, "I like to think of myself as an honorary, transmuted, transposed and transfigured Harijan. . .I am carrying out the commandment as it relates to our times" (192). From a cosmic perception his bathroom paraphernalias had restored the balance and done away with the injustice, "Chi-Chi-Chi move away son. . ." (192), with the passage of time the menstrual rags were as clean and full of sunshine as the rest of the laundry.

Integral to the text is the symbol of the tomb. Rose taking a walk into the tomb, signifies a voyage into the self, a questioning and probing, "Why was I born? Why am I living, What do I get? What am I giving?"(219). The architecture symbolizing the rich heritage lying in ruins, the moral values declining and becoming defunct. The tomb also symbolizes the darkness within, the naked lust for power. In her questioning, perhaps Rose finds her purpose in the cripple who has made the tomb his home. It becomes a reaching across, a silent communion, a pledge to restore his lost dignity. In the stillness of the tomb, she hears the echo of the timeless quality of human actions and memory, "No good or evil deed, nothing—great or small was ever wiped out. . .!" (115). This feeling cuts across class, culture, and race.

Hidden within the tomb are the dark, secret, forces of evil at work in every century. Rose had wondered about Sita's second banishment and queried, if that was the fate of a princess what about ordinary women? There is a dramatic and tragic shift in narration as history repeats itself in Ram's house, Rose's body is found in the well two days after Diwali. We have a macabre sense of *deja vu* in Sonali's apprehensions, "It was plain she had been killed and plainer still that Rose's killers would never be brought to justice. They would live their comfortable lives and die patriotic citizens"(253). All democratic norms, the Mahatma's life and its message are cremated in the ovens of power and decadence.

But the ending of the novel offers hope and a certain confidence, and affirmation. The intangible link between Rose, Sonali and the cripple becomes a bond of togetherness. "There had to be a special grace and favour reserved for people like her who loved and cherished strangers"(259). A Rose by any other name would smell as sweet. The legacy of her love and compassion that she leaves behind would continue, the cripple would learn to live with dignity. There would be the continuance of friendly relations with goodness with Brian and Marcella mounting an exhibition on ancient Indian Art and Sonali, their researcher. Perhaps the pristine architectural beauty of the Tomb would emerge resurrected.

References

Jain, Jasbir. *Nayantara Sahagal*, 1978, revised ed., with Postcript and Interview, Jaipur: Printwell Publisher, 1994.

Kakar, Sudhir. *The Inner World. A Psycho-Analytic Study of Childhood and Society in India*, 1981. Delhi: Oxford University Press, 1991.

Sage, Lorna. "The Available Space", *Women's Writing*, ed Moira Monteith. Harvester Press, 1986.

Sahgal, Nayantara. *A Situation in New Delhi*. London: London Magazine Edition, 1977.

Sahgal, Nayantara. *Rich Like Us*. (1985) London: Sceptre, Hodder and Stoughton Lt. 1993.

19

Nayantara Sahgal's *Rich Like Us*: The Discourses of the Political Novel

Sudha Rai

In an interview given in 1990, Nayantara Sahgal defined what politics signified for her, and also offered a definition of the political novel. If politics was "the use of power" and "the abuse of power", a political novel "would be an awareness of the use of power whether it is directly in politics or reflected in domestic life or other aspects of it" (Jain 1986).

My reading of *Rich Like Us* (1985) opens up the novel through two types of discourses—one postcolonial and the other feminist. While the postcolonial discourse of the political novel foregrounds a nation's cultural and historical past, liberating itself from Eurocentric perspectives and confronting its present social and political realities feminist discourse decentres patriarchal power structures, writing *in* a woman's body, perspectives, struggle and value. Both discourses reject manipulative power structures and speak for a renewal of human relationships based on reason, equality and love (Ashcroft et al 1989: 166-176).

The use of postcolonial and feminist discourses serves to

demonstrate how the ideological components of this text are represented at the levels of narrative with an emphasis on multiple voices, and, stylistically, the privileging of selected structural motifs and patterns. Both discourses advocate the expression of the subjectivity of the self (as cultural insider/as female) standing in opposition to the autocracy of "the other". Both discourses again posit a liberating movement out of inarticulation into speech, through interrogation of stereotypes, roles and conditioning. Violence upon the body and suspension of legal processes and civic rights, claiming victims, connect both discourses. Working through the problems of the states of postcoloniality and female being, Sahgal offers resolutions springing from a true humanitarian discourse resulting in positive action.

The opening chapter of *Rich Like Us* creates a focus around the "shambling bureaucracies" of postcolonial nations, in this case India. The "host" Dev is justifying to the foreign business contact Neuman, the declaration of an Emergency in India (26th June 1975) which has also paved the way for ventures such as the opening of a new factory, ostensibly for the production of a fizzy drink Happyola. The omniscient narrative voice dissociates itself from the "fat, sleek" cheeks of Dev, allowing the critical no-nonsense voice of Rose, Cockney wife of Ram, to dominate. Rose rejects the primacy of money - "compensation" which will be paid to the villagers whose homes will be uprooted when the factory comes up. The discourse polarises around the new business ethic which gains support from blind supporters of the Emergency like Dev, and the Joint Secretary, Ministry for Industry, Ravi Kachru, who is the perfect liaison man. The perils of a postcoloniality which has bartered away its newly-won freedom, placing itself for sale in a context of relations where money, gold and riches are prime values—are sounded out in the very first chapter. Neuman is a believer in only "the financial basis of his happiness". Significantly, he has discarded his interest in history and archaeology, arriving at a formulaic approach to work and relationships, shunning the reality of the crippled, deformed beggar without arms, whom he spots as he leaves Dev's house after the business deal. The beggar is "the other" whom he nullifies, satisfied only when he has been able to appropriate the Indian in a Eurocentric discourse of "riches". Neuman accepts unquestioningly, the truth of his briefing before leaving for India—"If they'd do like we do, they'd be rich like us"(16).

Sahgal explores the theme of decline, deterioration and disorder in the post-independence scenario of former colonies through the narrative consciousness of Sonali, ICS officer, recently transferred and humiliated because of her fidelity to truth and standards of work. She opposes the dehumanizing values of the Emergency, the sychophancy before Madam, and the culture of money which informs politics and erodes the bureaucracy. Sonali is disillusioned by the current state of affairs: "The emergency had given all kinds of new twists and turns to policy and the world's largest democracy was looking like nothing so much as one of the two-bit dictatorships we had loftily looked down upon. The things that had set us apart were not very clear to me any more"(31).

Sahgal's postcolonial discourse conducted through Sonali's investigative consciousness, does not indulge in the glorification of a pre-colonial past in Indian history. The discovered "text" of Sonali's grandfather's diary written in 1915, illuminates the barbarism of practices like the 'Sati' of her great-grandmother. The discourse of the diary examines the complexity of Hinduism, the status of a Hindu woman as wife and widow, and the patronizing attitude of British policy which its administrators implement. The 'pitfalls' of the Indo-British encounter as well as the possibility of the meeting of diverse racial minds through debate and discussion, are presented in the friendship between Sonali's great-grandfather and Mr. Timmons, the British resident. The ineffectiveness of British law in responding to the horrors of "Sati" are confirmed as it were, when Sonali's great-grandfather, a lawyer, dies suddenly at the age of fifty and his wife is forced to commit Sati. Ironically, Mr. Timmons is away on leave in England when the incident occurs and apart from looking after the boy and ensuring his sanity by making arrangements for his safe passage and education in England, Mr. Timmons is left to struggle with a question as to why his lawyer friend's 'enlightened' wife actually committed sati.

Sonali's interrogation of her country's past, precipitated by the crisis of the Emergency, leads to an initial act of negation, where she disowns the idealism she has been endowed with in her father's tradition, an idealism which celebrates the fact that Indians "were moderate, tolerant people, steeped in civilized ways" (35). Sonali, refuses to take refuge in "monumental lies" and commences her journey of truthful, individualistic evaluation of self and country, resisting the commodification of both.

As feminist discourse, Sahgal's novel charts out first of all, Sonali's interrogation of gender and her protest against her Kashmiri mother's pressures upon her to make her romanticize marriage and wedded bliss, status, and the snobbery of state and region (Kashmiri). Unlike her sister Kiran who has opted for a safe and complacent marriage to Neel, Sonali takes pleasure in being different and therefore herself. This is captured in references to her persistent fondness for wearing spectacles though she is told they obstruct her beauty. She enters into a close relationship with her childhood friend Ravi Kachru, but gradually perceives that her intellectual direction is separate from his "straight and narrow doctrine" of Marxism. Predictably, Ravi joins the ICS and becomes a true bureaucrat, toeing fashionable and practical policy lines. Sonali herself, during her Oxford years has begun questioning the influence of a heavy dose of Westernization on the Indian mind. As she puts it:

> But I couldn't understand why we had to keep cutting and pasting Western concepts together and tying ourselves to them for ever as if Europe were the centre of the universe, and the Bible and Marx were the last word on mankind.
>
> (113)

Though Ravi is her 'intended' husband, the relationship withers away and the rightness of Sonali's instinct is borne out when Ravi gets her job in the Ministry of Industry and rides along the crest of the Emergency, until experience and a revival of conscience steer him back to Sonali. Sonali fights her battle determinedly, as woman, as citizen of a free country, proud to be Indian, and as an intellectual concerned with the preservation of human rights and her country's future: "For me this was the world's most interesting country with life's biggest challenges to be met" (170).

Sonali shares her emotional conflicts with Rose, turning to her for womanly sympathy and support and clarity of advice. Both women scorn materialism, keeping alive channels of honest communication and concern for the suffering and downtrodden. Rose hands over her "legacy—humanitarian and optimistic to Sonali, making non-existent the cultural divide."

Rich Like Us presents other women's voices besides that of Sonali and Rose. Sahgal gives us a portrait of Nishi, Dev's wife, who has accepted the roles of loyal daughter to her father Kishori Lal who is in prison, because of his supposed connections with the RSS. Nishi is adept at her social role, the perfect, restrained hostess who asks no questions and does not look beyond the veneer of Dev's contacts. Coming from a lower middle-class socio-economic background and seeing her mother overburdened with too many children, Nishi apparently has opted for the order created by "riches". Sahgal's ironies pick up Nishi's misjudgements and acceptances, born of class and poverty, which imprison her being: "The idea of a Leader, someone to look up to, made her pulse beat faster, fulfilled a yearning for tidiness, and a woman in command put at least one woman beyond the furies all others face"(81). Nishi opts for "silence, constraint, dignity" in meeting her husband Dev's denigration of her father. Unlike Sonali, she opts to live with the tragedy of her divided being, knowing her need as woman, yet screening herself: "Grappling with her selves was simple if she kept her inner and outer selves apart. Pulling them together showed her the world as it was, and her single will, defiant, disobedient and distraught, confronted it"(234).

Sahgal's characterization of Rose, conveys that Rose's relationship with Ram is made and cherished because of her own individual act of choice. Knowing Ram is married and has an infant son, Rose bows before the dictates of her heart. Shaken by Ram's wife Mona's suffering because of his second marriage, she accepts her in-between status, gradually cementing a new relationship with Mona. Sahgal depicts the "sisterhood" which nourishes the relationships between the two wives—Mona explains Indian myths to Rose and begins to consult her on important matters like Dev's marriage. While Ram is shown as impervious to Mona's pain—psychological initially and later a physical one when she succumbs to cancer, Rose pleads for his greater attention to Mona. Surmounting patriarchy, "within those walls they had adventured over hills and woods into another pasture, into friendship, and one fine morning, into love"(185). Sahgal counterpoints 'stories' of four women-Sonali, Nishi, Rose and Mona in modern India and the intersecting arcs of their experience apart from articulating a feminist discourse of subjugations of self and attempts to counter male power-structures, bring forward the positive role of women in stabilizing relationships and making for a better society.

The narrative structures and metaphoric patterns of *Rich Like Us* enact the interconnectedness of postcolonial and feminist discourse, converging on the distinction between the "real" and the "role". Both discourses attempt to make a successful passage from the latter to the former.

Sahgal presents the emergency as theatre, a counterfeiting of reality where the performers through their pretence, create the illusion of a reality that is non-existent: "We were all taking part in a thinly disguised masquerade, preparing the stage for family rule", says Sonali. The public is deluded into thinking that "the Empress's new clothes were beautiful." Kachru is a lead performer, excelling at the game of "charades". There are other references to "pantomines" and "masks" which identify the collaborators of the Emergency and distance us as readers from them. We dissociate from Dev, forger of his father's signature, who has been appointed Cabinet Minister, having played his role in supporting the Emergency, to perfection.

The language of *Rich Like Us* alerts us to various categories of lies, false reports, justifications and twisted uses of language which the supporters of autocratic structures adhere to, to strengthen their sway. The very idea of the Emergency being beneficial and necessary for India's betterment, is a political falsification. The Happyola factory is only ostensibly being set up for the production of a fizzy drink; it is actually a cover for the manufacture of the people's car which is Madam's son's enterprise.

Rose's drunkenness is held responsible for her "accidental" death in the well, though the beggar's eye-witness account confirms Sonali's suspicion that it was a murder. Nishi deliberately misinterprets Rose's death, claiming that Ram's illness was the reason why Rose lost interest in living. Sonali's greatgrandmother's "Sati" is explained away as an act which she underwent willingly, as it would ensure her son's education and future.

Sahgal sets up a counter-discourse to such lies by bringing in, through various individuals and sources, the discovery of authentic news, fact and truth. Channels of communication between individuals must be courageously kept open. The conversation between Rose and Sonali at the Happyola foundation ceremony exposes the suitcase-corruption of the Minister and his Collector daughter. On another occasion, Rose overhears a conversation (at one of Dev's parties which punctuate his rise to power) between Dev and a doctor friend where she learns that the "doctor-butcher" is proposing a method for killing off an old freedom fighter in jail during the Emergency, through an overdose of salt. Again, Nishi innocently reveals to Rose that the underground shelter in their house is actually being used, secretly, to store spare imported parts for the production of an all-Indian car. The car has been approved even before production!

Those who reject the lies of the given, sanctioned discourse defend, through their questioning, articulation and talkativeness, human values.

Sahgal uses silence very powerfully as a descriptive device leading to deeper connotations. The silence of Sita in the face of her trial by fire drives home a feminist point about the meaning, and the dangers of inarticulation. Sonali's grandfather's record in his diary about the day his mother was forced to commit sati says: "No house is ever that silent, as though every single person in it has gone on a journey. I had an instant's forewarning of disaster" (149). The Emergency is an "artificial silence", censoring news and silencing tongues forcibly. A veil of silence shrouds the death of Rose—the latent power of her honest, talkative voice has led to its being silenced at the bottom of the well. Silence is usually menacing in *Rich Like Us*—Ram's sudden infatuation and affair with Marcella which usurps Rose's claim on him, develops in silence and communicates in silence. It is the rare moment when the silence is a silence of love, which creates communion between Rose and Ram, as he lies paralysed.

The twisting of language and its unnatural simplification produced in authoritarian contexts is a theme George Orwell has developed in "Politics and the English Language", and Sahgal uses this essentialism in language styles to categorise the power-mongers. Dev's formulation for Mr. Neuman that "business is business" has a glib formulaic reductivity which Rose rejects. On the other hand, there are styles which are excessively rhetorical as can be heard in the Minister's speech at the Happyola ceremony, which is an outpouring that combines a Gandhianisation of language with a reverence for Madam, emphasising the right chords such as the country's golden future and the opportunities for the poor. Sahgal exposes both styles, the essentialist and the rhetorical, as styles to beware of.

By contrast, there is stress on the reflective, individual and interrogative uses of language which is the discourse of free individuals. Such uses of language acknowledge that the truth of any situation is "complex". Rose interrogates the beggar to probe one power-structure rooted in class—his hands have been sliced off because he dared to take what was his sharecropper's due and "they" did not want power-distinctions to be obliterated. Other probing questions of hers reveal the atrocity of rape, where the beggar's wife has been raped by kiln owners, with whom it is a habitual practice.

Rich Like Us gathers together realities and metaphors pertaining to sickness and illness, the crisis of moral being the country is in the grip of. Sonali's hepatitis is a reaction to a nation gone wrong. Ram's paralysis speaks eloquently of the state of Ram-Rajya. Mona's cancer underlines the passive suffering of women in a patriarchal structure. The handicapped beggar communicates the marginalisation of the have-nots by their economic overlords. Above all, the forced sterilizations which were one of the most demeaning aspects of the Emergency, proclaim the State's intent to throttle all possibilities of new life and hence new alternatives.

Rich Like Us interrogates old cultural myths and Sonali muses that even myths contain the structures of power: "It all depends on whether you are on the right side of power and ominipotence. Sita wasn't and it was banishment to the wilderness for her."(224) Keshav, friend of Ram, a feminist by orientation, also questions the Sita story arguing that she was "murdered by society".

Doing some hard thinking during her illness, Sonali asks a question:

> What if there was a collective will to cowardice, when men and women in their millions, a whole nationful, did cowardly deeds? Was there a way out of that?
>
> (35)

Yes, says Sahgal, illuminating Rose's way. Unsophisticated and perceptive Rose who dares to speak the language of love in a context where relationships are sacrificed at the altar of money and power, expresses her love as humanitarian action, worrying till her end about a pair of artificial hands for the cripple. Sonali's tribute to Rose affirms that "there had to be a special grace and favour reserved for people like her who loved and cherished strangers"(259).

It is a Britisher's transcending of race, a woman's profusion of love, a dreamer's commitment to a mythical Cytherea which makes Rose a free individual. Staunchly clinging to a discourse of her woman's imagination, and rejecting all discourses of power, she impels young Sonali into a richer relationship with her own country, India.

References

Ashcroft, Bill. Griffiths, Gareth and Tiffin, Helen. *The Empire Writes Back: Theory and Practice in Post-colonial Literatures*. London: Routledge, 1989.

Jain, Jasbir. *Nayantara Sahgal* (1978). revised ed. Jaipur: Printwell, 1994.

Orwell, George. "Politics and the English Language", *Inside the Whale and other Essays*. Harmondsworth: Penguin 1979.

Sahgal, Nayantara. *Rich Like Us* (1985). London: Sceptre Edition, 1993.

20

Autobiography: A Literary Genre

Sarojini

All art involves self-projection in some measure. In literature, the writer who chooses the objective form to create new worlds merges his self so thoroughly in the objective form that the self is no longer discernible. In the novel or the drama, the writer's self merges with the characters he creates. Everything in him leads to the universal reality of the world he creates. His gaze is fixed on the outer world. The subjective writer whose gaze is turned inward, makes everything in the real world lead back into his own personality. His writings tend to be expositions of his own ego. No matter what form he may choose—drama, epic, lyric or autobiography—he will unawares make his own self the medium and the centre of all his works. Hence self-portraiture is inevitable in all types of literature. In autobiography it takes a peculiar, deliberate form, where in the very aim of the writer is to reveal himself from all angles.

Self-portraiture has fascinated man for centuries. Every age has produced some form of autobiographical literature, which is generally confused with the distinctive genre of autobiography.

Diary, memoir, reminiscences and letters are all manifestations of the writer's self but each has a different perspective.

A diary deals with the day-to-day record of a person's life. The advantage of this characteristic quality is that nothing gets left out. The disadvantage lies in the overabundance of such jottings, and their lack of arrangement. The diary is characterized by uncertainties, false starts and momentariness. The reader can gauge the tastes, aptitudes and the sensitivity of the author but there is no conscious attempt at a coherent shaping of his life. The diarist moves through a series of moments in time; recording his feelings and reactions. The mode of presentation of the diarist differs from that of the autobiographer. The one lives from moment to moment, the other builds up his life by looking back from a certain point in time. The diary, therefore, retains the freshness of feeling and emotion of a particular moment, but it lacks the long-range perspective, which only time can bring. A journal is usually more elaborate than a diary but the crux of the difference between them is in the matters of formality and personality. A journal is usually written to a plan. The writer sets out to record certain types of occurrences or experiences in regular fashion and usually he has from the beginning an idea of what use will be made of his record. Unlike journals, which usually have specific objectives, diaries normally mirror the attitudes, feelings, and thoughts of individual days and moments without regard to what has gone before and obviously without knowledge of what is to come. Mathews observes, "The striking result is that better than any other kind of personal document, he diary reflects the shift and inconsistencies of ordinary human ehaviour" (288).

Diaries and journals are interesting due to the wealth of detail they provide about their times. Reflections of the writer on the incidents, supplemented with anecdotes make such works pleasant reac ng. Some diaries are an intimate record of the writer's moods and thoughts, like the one's written by Katherine Mansfield and Andre Gide. In theory, diaries are not written for publication. Hence there is no attempt at wilful distortion or camouflage by the writer. However in diaries and journals we usually feel the lack of two elements which are essential to the narrative act, selectivity and movement. The two are interrelated, the lack of selectivity impedes movement and inhibits the growth of anything like a plot.

Memoirs, confessions and reminiscences are so closely related to autobiography that it is sometimes difficult to draw a line of separation. There is no autobiography that is not in some respect a memoir, and no memoir which is without autobiographical content. There is a very slender line dividing the two. Both are based on personal experience, but there is a general difference in emphasis. The memoirist concentrates on recording public events and lays but little stress on the 'self'. Memoirs are usually written by a person who has either played a distinguished role in public life or has had the opportunity to observe, at close quarters, history in the making. He is, therefore primarily, concerned, with public men and matters—the political luminaries and social winds of change. It differs from pure autobiography in its focusing point. The illumination of the self is but incidental. Basically the memoir arises from personal experiences and follows a chronological order in the recording of events. More often than not it tends to become reflective when the writer's attitudes and feelings are revealed. But his searchlight is meant to penetrate his public life, not his private self. In this respect, the art of the memoirist is not a self-conscious art, nor does it require any act of introspection. He is merely expected to give a running commentary on his life and times as he witnessed it, enriching his account by his personal reactions. He must, however, never be confused with the historian, who deals with facts in the objective manner from the point of view of an anonymous, impartial observer.

Writing about one's times, one reveals a lot about one's personality. Consciously or unconsciously the memoirist weaves his own life-story in the web, for it is difficult to distinguish the individual from his times. The reader can easily deduce the outlines of the writer's life and mistake this account for his autobiography. The essential difference between the two genres lies in the amount of external life that is described. The memoirist makes it his intent and purpose; the autobiographer uses descriptions of external life to illumine his inner self. A happy balance between the outside world and the inner life distinguishes autobiography from memoirs.

The memoirist concentrates attention on public events, the writer of the reminiscences penetrates personal relationships. There is a light shift of emphasis. The focus is still on the outside world, not the inner self. It is an account of action and reaction of human relationships. The confession too, is an account of a man's private life, centering on his emotions, feelings, secrets and frustrations. The writer deals essentially with his private world. The memoir is more like a chronicle, relating the individual with history; the confession is meant to bare the inner thoughts and chronicle the history of the mind. Autobiography is a blend of both confession and memoir. In fact the term autobiography was coined only in 1809, according to Oxford English Dictionary, when Robert Southey commented on a life of the Portuguese painter, Francisco Vierira in the *Quarterly Review*. Since then autobiography has gained popularity as it is the most democratic form open to all.

The preservation and publication of the letters of great men and women is a practice that goes back to antiquity. Yet no writer writes them with that aim, letters are a purely personal, informal, intimate and spontaneous form of writing. We get to see the writer in his undisguised and natural self, for in correspondence with a friend, doubt and distrust have no place. The reader is immediately admitted to the writer's confidence and rapport of intimacy is established.

Although letters reveal a great deal of their authors personality, yet they are different from pure autobiography. There is no attempt at conscious, retrospective recollection and an ordered narration of the author's life, which is the main feature of the autobiographical genre. What is common in letters and autobiography is that both keep a delicate image of the writer alive and present a subtle likeness of the author.

Autobiography is the hardest of all forms of literary art. What makes it unique is that it is a retrospective account of the autobiographer's life, (if not the whole life, at least a significant part of it), written with avowed fidelity. The generic characteristics determine the content and form of autobiography—the material must be restricted to the content of the autobiographer's life. It should be a retrospective account of his life. This involves a cool consideration of the past at a different level of awareness and an interpretation of facts in a specific perspective. The account should be written with complete honesty. Like the sculptor, the autobiographer is not free to choose his material. The novelist and the painter have much more freedom in this respect. Hence a greater inventive element in their works. As Mandel points out: while a writer is free to create a world of the future (*Nineteen Eighty Four*, the various worlds of Dickens), the autobiographer must feel himself committed to casting his glance back over real history. He need not treat it factually, but he cannot avoid creating his autobiographical world as an imitation of the actual past, as he understands it (219). Since the autobiographer has all the facts of his life with him, he can see the end in his beginning. As the past is reactivated in the present he must discover a "Structure" for his life. If he is to achieve coherence, he must take a stand point, and that stand point will naturally be of the moment at which he reviews and interprets his life. It is from this position that he can see a unity which can be reduced to order. For Mandel, the motivation of the autobiographer determines his self-view that emerges in the work, and is as a matter of fact, the "Organizing Principle", of the work. Hence, "the critic's first responsibility is to ascertain what the organizing principle of the work is, for not until the purpose is clear to the critic can be sure whether the materials have been selected and arranged in a meaningful way" (221).

The autobiographer may not realize what his real motivation is. His desire to write his life may arise from a need to clear certain misunderstandings and justify his past actions, he may wish to confess his misdeeds and seek to communicate the essential nature and the truth of his "self" For some it might be an urge to articulate the historicity of the self, demonstrating their place in the cultural milieu, while for others self-portraiture might be an aesthetic artifact, or a personal account intended to convey a moral or leave a record for posterity. There can be innumerable reasons for writing one's life. Autobiographical intention may not always be consistent. It may evolve and fluctuate or refocus and redefine. It cannot be presumed that autobiographical intention will always be explicit. This means, as Francis R. Hart suggests, "recognizing distinct intentions for what they are and proceeding to identify and interpret their correlations and fluctuations predominant in individual autobiographical works" (491). Hence every autobiography is unique in its formal aspects.

The nature of truth in autobiography is another major issue of the genre. Most critics concede that "truth" established in autobiography is not one that is objectively verifiable, for the autobiographer presents himself not as he really was but as he thinks he was and as he would like to have been. Truth in autobiography is a very complex question. The autobiographer presents the truth of life seen from inside. Hence it is more subjective then objective:

> The story structure of autobiography is its mode of presenting truth—truth as process drama, image, symbolic form: Truth in autobiography is not merely fidelity to fact of conformity to 'Likeness', to the way one appears to others, but rather the projection of a story of successive self images and recognition or distortions of these self-images by the world; it is the story of identity of the tension between self image and social recognition.
>
> (Shapiro 426)

Shumaker and Pascal too see the problem of truth in autobiography as one of a particular literary form. We are more concerned with truthful portrayal of autobiographer's relation to himself and to other people—the truth of belief, the truth of his outlook and the truth of his facts. Mandel accedes to the fact that the concept of absolute truth has ceased to have much meaning in the 20th century (219). In modern autobiography the emphasis is not on accuracy of facts. That is the biographer's domain for he is dependent on recorded data. The autobiographer actually depends entirely on his memory which apart from being inaccurate, is highly treacherous and often misleading. The autobiographer has no control on his memory. Apart from his own selection, his memory too selects for him. but sometimes memory is tricky and perverse. It may retain unimportant details and drop the all-important entirely. In some it smothers the unpleasant and in others gives them an undue dominance. Besides being forgetful and selective, memory is also creative. After some lapse of time, memory often fills in the gaps with imaginative addition. It is probably an artistic instinct to improve highlight and adjust the details. There is also a rationalizing tendency of memory. After the event it "creates" feelings or ideas which might have been the cause of the event. The mind discovers motives for actions which we have performed unwittingly. Hence there is evidently a dual element of fact and fiction in autobiography.

There is nothing in an autobiographical passage itself to distinguish fact from fiction. A careful arrangement of incidents from one's life into a narrative may result either in a work of fiction, or an autobiography. Neither the technique nor the contents are the distinguishing determinants. It is the signals that the writer sends about the nature of his narrative. Couser rightly observes, "The meaning of a literary work is, to some extent, genre-bound, and the writer's signals rightly determine the way a reader will take the text" (7). Many skilful autobiographers tend to subordinate historical documentation to aesthetic values.

The relativists seek to evaluate the autobiographical genre by recognizing its affinity to fiction. They are inspired by the disappearing boundaries of the novel. Wayne Shumaker, towards the end of his survey of English Autobiography concludes that "the novel, and autobiography are moving toward closer similarity, the novel is becoming highly personal, autobiography is adopting more of the techniques and tone of fiction" (118).

Critics of fiction too have noticed the dissolution of traditional boundaries. The novel is becoming more autobiographical and autobiography giving in to the fictional impulse. Northrop Frye notes, "After Rousseau—in fact in Rousseau, the confession flows into the novel, and the mixture produces the fictional autobiography, the *Kunstler roman*, and kindred types" (307). Although autobiography by definition is restricted in its contents (it deals with the central facts of the author's personal history) yet this may not refer either to the manner of treatment or to the angle of perception. Autobiography is more than just a retrospective account of one's life. It involves the shaping of the past and imposing and pattern on a life to construct a coherent story of individual experience. Frye comments, "Autobiographers are inspired by a . . . fictional impulse to select only those events and experiences in the writer's life that go to build up an integrated pattern" (307). Relativists like Alfred Kazin therefore hold that autobiography is another form of story-telling. Many great autobiographers have utilized all the rhetorical resources of fiction. Hence it is indistinguishable from the novel and is comparable to fiction. But there is one limitation. Alfred Kazin rightly observes that—"Autobiography as narrative obviously seeks the effects of fiction, and cannot use basic resources of fiction like dialogue, without becoming fiction" (185). The subtle difference between autobiography and fiction lies in that autobiography uses facts as a strategy to tell another kind of story—a story of the writer's turning toward himself for the new vision of reality. Scholes and Kellogg are of the view:

> The raw material of human existence remains ever the same, the moulds by which it is given significance and recognizable/shape are forever being recreated by the writers of empirical narrative and drama. The new in empirical narrative depends upon an originality of vision, a creation of new types of actuality, and not upon a flight of the imagination away from the actual. If any distinction can be said to exist between the autobiography and the autobiographical novel it resides not in their respective fidelity to facts but rather in their respective originality in perceiving and telling the facts. It is in

the knowing and in the telling and not in the facts, that the art is to be found.

(156)

A clear distinction between novel and autobiography, however cannot be sustained for too long. The convergence of autobiography with the novel is visible in the themes and techniques shared alike by autobiographers and novelists. Autobiographers use many devices of compression and clarification to order the chaotic experience of their lives. Apart from the interweaving of dramatic presentation and reflection, turning points, letters, dramatic scenes, self images etc., are used in the narration. Sometimes years are compressed into the formula of a typical day and at times the experience of a brief moment becomes a symbol. Shapiro is of the view that "The autobiographer must know when to dramatise and when to summarize. He must be master of the art of anticipation" (439). Within his scope the autobiographer realizes immense possibilities of ordering his material imaginatively. Autobiography is primarily an art of juxtaposed perspectives of past and present. Moreover in autobiography, the subject and the narrator are literally the same person. Scholes and Kellogg perceptively observe that Rouseau, the father of European autobiography, taught future novelists that even when the subject and narrator are identical different points of view in time allow for ironic distance and also for multiple perspectives upon the same set of facts (157). Hence time became a significant dimension in the conception of character in the novel as it was in autobiography. The ultimate aim of every autobiography is to tell a story of recognition and attempt to align the private and the public man, the autobiographer's idea of himself and his social image by which he is recognized. Roy Pascal calls this the "contrast between the meaning of a man's work and life for us, the 'Likeness' we make and his own image or idea of himself (Preface vii) which he calls the 'Life Illusion'."

The interdisciplinary aspect of autobiography can hardly be overestimated. If there as a generic affinity of autobiography with fiction, it has many similarities with history, anthropology and psychology as well. Historians consider it to be a cultural document. This democratic literary genre has much closer links with political and historical events as do fiction, poetry and even drama. Cox asserts that the very idea of autobiography has grown out of the political necessities and discoveries of the American and French revolutions (114). Cox's thesis is based on the hypothesis that in time of wars, revolutions and social turmoils, "remind us that autobiography becomes more possible when history and politics seem to possess the very drama we seek for on stage and fictive experience in periods of equanimity and peace" (156). Hence he links all autobiographical interpretations with historical events and social change.

The anthropologists, however, assert that the use of autobiography is mythic for the writer explains his life by depicting himself according to culturally evaluated images of character. As he turns his private experience into language he assumes one of the many identities outlined in the myth and so asserts his connection with his culture. Spengemann and Lundguist explain:

> The language of autobiography stands in symbolic relation to both author and subject. As an author translates his life into language he creates for himself a symbolic identity and sees himself through the focusing glass of language. Since the language of the autobiographer is the common possession of his culture, it is not only subject to his personal manipulation, but it is filled with the assumed values of society. The act of writing about oneself brings together the personal, unassimilated experiences of the writer and the shared values of his culture.
>
> (502)

As the autobiographer turns his private experiences into language, he assumes one of the many identities outlined in the myth and so asserts his connection with his culture.

The American myth, according to Spengemann and Lundquist, describes human history as a pilgrimage from imperfection to perfection—an adaptation of Christian mythology to the challenging problems and possibilities of American life. This challenging thesis rests upon the prescriptively narrow assumption that all autobiographers settle upon an accepted role of the prophet, the hero, the villian, the outcast, or the disenchanted. The autobiographical act is far more protean than this 'cultural' theory makes it out to be. There are many autobiographies that display the fragmentation of self and society more clearly than consistent identities and clearly defined roles like that of Robert Graves's *Goodbye to All That* or Andre Malraux's *Anti-Memoirs.*

However, despite all controversies, autobiography has become one of the dominant forms in the present century. Under the stimulus of the first World War a new trend in autobiography set in. Violence, horror, and the inhumanity of man on man, the continuation of slavery and human bondage gave rise to various forms of protest. Black autobiography in America is one such example. In most black autobiographies, protest against cruelty and injustice imposed upon the black and their personal inability to handle their hatred for the whites is an of trecurring theme. All black self-portraits focus first on the reciprocal relations between the blacks and the whites based on hatred and on the persistence of white superiority. James Baldwin's *Notes of a Native Son* (1955), W.E.B. Dubois's *Dusk of Dawn, an Essay Towards an Autobiography of a Race Concept* (1968) and the *Autobiography of Malcolm* X (1965) are examples of black protest in literature. These writers interpret their lives in the context of exploitation and suppression of an entire race.

Women too have been suppressed for ages. The public sphere has been dominated by man. Women have always been taught to put a man at the centre of their lives. Thus marginalised, they are prohibited to express their anger, or even to recognize it within themselves. By simple extension, they have been refused both power and control. The women's movement, in fact, began with a discussion of power, powerlessness and the women's right of power on her own life. Most women therefore rarely emphasize the public aspect of their lives, or for that matter their careers. Instead, they focus on their personal lives. domestic detail, family difficulties, close friends and people who have influenced them. Even in the life-stories of women whose professional work is their claim to fame, one finds them either omitting their work-life or referring to their careers obliquely. Gertrude Stein in *The Autobiography of Alice B. Tok las* places her concern for her work in the background by camouflaging it behind humorous anecdotes about others. Allusions to her actual writings are interespersed among her entertaining stories. Edith Wharton too, does not tell us much about the writing of her successful novels in her *A Backward Glance* (1934).

In consideration of his life and in order to impose a coherence on the narrative, a chronological, linear account has emerged in the male tradition of the genre in which the autobiographer concentrates on one particular period of his life, one theme or one characteristic of his personality. It is not surprising that with persistent social conditioning men pursue the one and only single goal of a successful career which orders and harmonises their autobiographies. However, the form that women ordinarily choose for their self-portraits is neither chronological nor linear but fragmentary, disconnected or one that is organized into self-sustained units. Mary McCarthy's memoirs are a collection of eight essays. The pattern of diffusion and diversity in the self-portraits of women is, I guess, due to the multi-dimensional roles they have to play in their lives. Hence the criterion of wholeness or a harmonious shaping of the past is seldom applicable to women's autobiography.

Most autobiographers describe their childhood. Men tend to idealize their lives to cast them into a heroic mould, or to project their universal importance. Hence they exaggerate, mythologise or monumentalize their boyhood. The view of childhood as idylls of innocence and adulthood as heroic is a male literary tradition. This is contrary to the self-image projected by women's autobiographies. What their life stories reveal is a self-consciousness and a need to sift through their lives for explanations and understanding. The autobiographical intention is often propelled by the motive to convince readers of their self-worth, to clarify, to affirm and to authenticate their self-image. Instead of sentimentalizing and glorifying their narrative, women tend to write in straightforward objective manner about their girlhood and adult experience. They resort to strategies of understatement, reportage or humour when they choose to camouflage their feelings of discrimination in their girlhood. Childhood accounts of most women often lack that nostalgia so common in men's accounts, perhaps because it is more usually the savagery of girlhood that is most remembered.

In the late twentieth century the autobiographical mode has been undergoing considerable experimentation. While linear, detached autobiographies by people who concentrate on their professional lives still dominate, more men are setting out to write in more irregular forms, including more personal subjects. The complexity of the atomic era has made a holistic view of life impossible. This affects the form and content of autobiography. However, what distinguishes autobiography as a literary enterprise is the particular manner in which each autobiographer expresses his selfhood. That there can be such varied forms of expression as the autobiographers have discovered for giving meaning to their experiences implies that each autobiographer creates a unique manner with which to conceptualize his selfhood. This is what characterizes the inherent fascination of autobiography.

References

Couser, Thomas C. *American Autobiography, The Prophetic Mode.* Amherst: University of Mass, Press, 1979.

Cox, James M. "Autobiography and America", *Aspects of Narrative*, ed J. Hillis Miller. New York: Columbia University Press, 1971.

Frye, Northope. *Anatomy of Criticism.* Princeton: New Jersey, 1957.

Hart, Francis. "An Anatomy of Modern Autobiography", '*New Liter-*

ary History, Spring 1970.

Kazin, Alfred. "Autobiography as Narrative", *To the Young Writer*, Hapgood Lectures, 2nd Series, ed. A.L. Bader. Ann Arbor Paperback: University of Michigan Press, 1965.

Mandel, Barret John. "The Autobiographers Art". *Journal of Aesthetics and Art Criticism*, 27, Winter, 1968.

Mathews, William. "The Diary: A Neglected Genre". *The Sewanee Review*, Spring, 1977.

Pascal, Roy. *Design and Truth in Autobiography*. London: Routledge and Kegan Paul, 1960.

Scholes, Robert and Kellogg, Robert. *The Nature of Narrative*. Oxford University Press: New York, 1966.

Shapiro, Stephen A. "The Dark Continent of Literature: Autobiography", *Comparative Literature Studies*, V. 4, December 1968.

Shumaker, Wayne. *English Autobiography: Its Emergence, Material and Form*. California, Berkeley and Los Angeles: University of California Press. 1954.

Spengemann, WMC and L.R. Lundquist. "Autobiography, and the American Myth", *American Quarterly*, Vol. XVII, Fall. 1955.

21

My Story

Ranjana Harish

> This book has cost me many things that I held dear, but I do not for a moment regret having written it. I have written several books in my life time, but none of them provided the pleasure the writing of *My Story* has given me. I have nothing more to say.
>
> (Preface)

In Virginia Woolf's view any woman who sets her pen to paper and adopts the writer's profession, like her, has to undertake two enterprises: "killing the 'Angel in the House' in her and 'telling the truth about (her) own experience as a body' ". She describes an Angel in the House as an "intensely sympathetic, immensely charming and utterly unselfish" woman who "never had mind or a wish of her own, but preferred to sympathize always with the minds and wishes of others." Killing this angel within one is no doubt difficult enough but telling the truth about one's body is perhaps the most difficult. Virginia Woolf herself succeeded at the first but, by her own admission, failed at the second. "The first - killing the Angel in the House—I think I solved. She died. But the second, telling the truth about my own experiences as a body, I do not think I solved. I doubt that any woman has solved it yet" (Woolf 538). In her view, what man will say of a woman who tells the truth about her passion always hampers the creativity of a woman writer.

My Story is the only attempt of its kind among Indian women autobiographers in English to tread the untrodden challenging area of exploring and sharing one's experience as a body which serves as the foundation of her sociological, psychological and even spiritual development. Discarding the superficial way of the fellow women autobiographers, who try to grapple with the acute problems of their existence avoiding any talk about their bodies, she confronts her body with unparalleled frankness and honesty. But the most noticeable fact about her bold attempt is that, in spite of trying hard to kill the "Angel in the house" within herself and throwing the traditional Indian morality to winds in her love-life Kamala Das constantly remains aware of her deviation from the accepted norms. The awareness of the culturally defined category 'woman' looms over her existence. Time and again she tries to return to her culturally defined self and then discards it realizing that it is not meant for her, that she cannot live her life in accordance with the cultural prescription.

From such a vacillation between the traditionally defined role model and her personal yearning to carve out an undefined, independent role for herself springs an apparent inconsistency in her narrative, for which she has often been blamed. At times, when the super ego of the Angel within dominates her self, she behaves as a traditional Hindu woman with a deep-seated fear of sex and with a deep love for her feminine role. But even this inconsistency has its justification in the context of her autobiography; that is what she has been. Like a true autobiographer she just projects herself honestly as she really has been, leaving it for her readers to pass their final judgement on her personality; they may brush it aside as a sheer inconsistent or try to delve deep into the psyche of the person to get at the roots of the apparent inconsistency. Any such attempt would lead them to the surprising realization that deep down the apparent inconsistency there lies an inherent consistency.

To a sympathetic reader who looks upon the writer as a fellow human being and not as an accused on whom he is required to pass his moral judgement, Kamala's case provides an excellent opportunity for a psychological study of the loveless and emotionally deprived life of an imaginative romantic being who could not get what she desired out of any of her usual, socially recognized relationships. The lack of security and love in her well-to-do parents', as well as her husband's family made her whatever she became. 'Women are not born; they are made', said the great French feminist Simone de Beauvoir in her thought-provoking book *The Second Sex* (683). In her view it is the socialization of women as women which makes them what they become. Kamala's case convincingly demonstrates the truth of this observation. She was an ordinary girl, a 'good' girl from society's standard, whom her deprivation and psychological needs turned into a rebel. Circumstances made her what she became. With an understanding husband she would have been a happy wife and would have made a success of her marriage. But her husband's aggressive, assertive approach to sex and her, as yet, immature body at the time of their marriage, resulted in her being labelled as frigid, an adjective that comes in handy to any man, who, as a member of the dominant group, readily uses it for woman who fails to boost his ego or play up to him in such a way as to confirm and enhance his feeling of being a real "man". How strange it is that even in the context of this most intimate relationship between man and woman, in which they both ought to be equal partners giving and receiving pleasure from each other, women are looked upon as mere instruments of joy, judged solely on the basis of the extent to which they satisfy the men and are readily labelled as cold or frigid when they fail to do so, while in fact the poor ones do not even know what frigidity is; for more often than not, as Nancy Friday points out in her book *My Mother My Self*, they are strangers to their own bodies.

Later, when Kamala had physically matured, her husband lost

interest in her after the birth of their first son, and resumed his flirtatious relations with his cousins. Driven by sheer indignation Kamala now made up her mind to be "unfaithful to him, at least physically" (95). Feeling as if her love were alms meant for general distribution, she started looking for the "begging bowls" needless to say there was no dearth of such begging bowls to come across. In those relationships she was no more passive. She discusses a number of affairs she had. Unlike any other woman autobiographer she makes an open confession of her sins, if sins they are to be called.

What an irony of fate it is that Kamala, who was condemned by her husband as frigid, who herself accepted the label saying, "Sex did not interest me except as a gift I could grant to my husband to make him happy", should now, out of sheer disgust and a burning desire for revenge, step outside the sacrosanct orbit of marriage and send for the handsome bricklayer working across the street in order to gratify her own desire! But this was only her first transgression and "was to be followed by many more".

Back in Bombay, again the same old routine life was resumed; the days were for child care and house work and the nights for the silent surrender to the cruel tax collector's brutal handling. At times she would just helplessly go on listening to the poor hungry child crying in the next room while her body tried to please its owner. Once when the child was just two years old the cruel father had locked him in the kitchen so that he would not come to their door crying. The poor child had cried himself to sleep on the cold bare floor of the kitchen. This incident made her lose whatever little love she had for the man. She often felt like committing suicide or taking a divorce; but neither course was open to her because after all she was a daughter of the famous Nalapat House. She silently continued her drab, dreary existence.

When her second son fell seriously ill, the suppressed thoughts of suicide once again came to the surface, this time with greater intensity because her husband had now, in the face of the crisis, sought comfort in a homosexual relationship with one of his friends. "They behaved like lovers in my presence", writes Kamala (104). Driven to despair by sad circumstances she once made up her mind to jump from the terrace of their multi-storeyed building and end her life. But during that dark moment of desolate desperation she had a rare experience; out of her agony sprang a poem. What a miracle! She was not meant to die in defeat. She must live to face the cruelties of the world and express her pain in poetry, returning beauty for ugliness, pleasure for pain. Climbing down from the terrace she sat at the writing table and penned her first poem, beginning:

> Wipe out the paints, unmould the clay.
> Let nothing remain of that yesterday. . .

It was printed in the journal of the Indian P.E.N. of the next month. Now her sorrow was not hers alone; it was shared among many and so less severe and more bearable.

Kamala was now determined not to let anything from her yester-years shadow her present life. As promised in her first poem she did wipe out the old paints and unmould the old clay to mould her new self. But before she could begin afresh the great strain of all these years of married life and of her body's sickness made her suffer a nervous breakdown. Recovering from the breakdown she steadily and resolutely marched on the new course she had set for herself.

Now she was a new self, determined not to live a loveless, miserable life of a timid frigid woman, "ripe for the sexual banquet" she looked for the right man. And she writes, "At the hour of worship even a stone becomes an idol" (118). Yes, her love turned many a stone into idols—men from different walks of life and of different ages, some even old enough to be her father. They loved her for different reasons; some to fill their own inner void, some to enjoy her poetic company, some to satisfy their needs, some to worship her while some like Carlo, her white pen-friend-turned-lover, to marry her. But she was not "the divorcing kind". She may love them, may lie in their strong arms for some time; but she must return to her sons and husband.

Carlo was not mistaken in believing that he was like a waiting room between trains in her life.

With so many lovers and admirers around, life for Kamala was a wonderful experience. Recalling that happy feeling she writes, "I was like a poor girl who found herself rich all of a sudden. I was drunk with power" (145). For the first time in her life, now, she had the feminine urge to look beautiful. She visited beauty parlours, changed her hair style and tried to look modern. At last her cup of life was overflowing with love. She was in love with life itself.

It was just as this most blissful juncture of her life when her euphoria was at the highest that she was suddenly and dramatically reminded of the mortality of the human body. She had a bout of serious sickness followed by a long period of hospitalization during which she promised God that she would live an acceptable, respectable life if she survived. But on her recovery she was once again charmed by the magic of love, she yearned for an ideal lover.

By now she was well recognized as a poet whose personal life had public significance. Her notoriety preceeded her wherever she went making people wonder why she lived her life the way she did when she had "everything" that a woman looks for. What and how could Kamala explain to them? "Even birds have their own particular heights. The land birds who do not rise far into the lonely sky, often wonder why the eagles fly high, why they go round and round like ballerinas", she says (175). Despite being surrounded by relatives, friends and admirers she became increasingly lonelier and finally withdrew into the cave of the self.

This lonely phase of her life co-incided with her middle age, the time which fills most women's hearts with the fear of old age. Simone de Beauvoir's creative output of her middle age clearly and indubitably demonstrates the validity of this observation by providing ample evidence of her deepseated fear of old age and the consequent loss of youth, beauty and love. Kamala, too, was now beset by the same fears. Looking at the mirror, during that lonely phase of her life she would ponder over what was happening to her thus:

> Was it no longer possible to lure a charming male into complicated and satisfying love affair with the right words, the right glances, the right gestures? Was I finished as a charmer?
>
> (177)

It was at this critical period of her life that Kamala, as if to reassure herself of her own charm, embarked upon a love affair with an elderly man known for his "fabulous lust"; it turned out to be her most satisfying relationship as the dark, tall man gave her the sense of security she had longed for all her life. With his soothing arms encircling her body in a warm, loving embrace, she felt as if she were a child again, bathing in the pond at her Nalapat House. The eighteen mirrors in his room too reminded her of the same pond. Her love for this man was so deep that she confides to her readers that she "wanted to grow in him like cancer", wanting him "to suffer from incurable love" (184). Drunk with the euphoria of such a fulfilling experience of love Kamala makes an open declaration of her sin thus:

> City fathers, friends and moralists, if I were a sinner, do not forgive my sins. If I were innocent do not forgive my innocence. Burn me with torches blood-red in the night. . . . Or, bury me in your back garden, fill my crevices with the red dust of Bombay, plant gentle saplings on my belly, for, he and I met too late, we could get no child of our own, my love for him was just the writing of the sea, just a song borne by the wind. . . .
>
> (184)

This is just a specimen of her open, candid writing which earned her considerable notoriety and the wrath of the conservatives. They disliked her for being bold enough to tell her experience as a body so honestly, so articulately, though she was a member of the muted group.

This most satisfying relationship with the dark, elderly man gave her a sense of satiety that her love-starved heart had never experienced before. As a result her carnal desires died a natural death. Using her favourite images of lotuses and the pond she records her experience of shedding her desire like a snake shedding his skin as under:

> If my desires were lotuses in a pond, closing their petals at dusk and opening out at dawn once upon a time, they were totally dead, rotted and dissolved and for them there was no more to be a re-spouting. The pond had cleared itself of all growth. It was placid. (209)

She returned to Kerala to lead a simple life. However, on reaching there she found that she was not a welcome member of the family. Her people, scandalized by the salacious stories of her immoral escapades that had reached them, looked upon her as the black sheep who had brought disgrace and dishonour to the family name. They burned with indignation and rage. How dare she ever live her life in such a way; and even if she had to do those things, how could she, being a woman of their family, ever make it public? But what could Kamala do? She couldn't help the situation, as everything she did automatically became public. After all she was a writer, and as such, in her own words like a "goldfish in a well-lit bowl whose movements are never kept concealed" (206). Being a bold person with a convition of her own she had lived her life in her own way, "never hanging it on the pegs of quotation for safety" and burning all the boats that would take her to security. Without entering into any dialogue with them she quietly settled down there to pass her old age in her native place. The end of her autobiography presents her as a happy, contented woman who has accepted death as the ultimate reality of life, "ready to depart when the time came, with a scrubbed-out conscience", having emptied herself of all the secrets in her autobiography (Preface).

Lately Kamala Das has been expressing some regret for having written her autobiography. After the *Time* magazine printed a full page piece on Kamala Das describing her as the queen of Erotica, she has been more cautious in her public utterances. Indeed, she has gone to the extent of saying that the book was deliberately made sensational at her husband's insistence as they needed the money to pay the hospital bills, and adding that a woman-writer fulfills her unfulfilled desires of real life in her writing, has tried to suggest that whatever she wrote in her autobiography was not all true. Such statements of hers would naturally make an average reader doubt her honesty as an autobiographer. But a discerning reader knows what these statements mean, especially when they come from a member of women's subculture. They do not mean what they say; the real meaning is to be found in what remains unsaid, to be understood without words. They say that a woman has to pay a heavy price for being a woman, she must deny her real self, which might be that of a declared non-conformist in order to win back her people's so-called love and respect. She might have acquired a room of her own but it is still the society who decides with whom the room is to be shared. It will still take many more years for woman to be powerful enough to take such decisions herself.

Kamala Das succeeds admirably at the task of narrating her experience as a body—a task which even the great Virginia Woolf found herself facing diffidently. However, even the staunchest admirer of Kamala Das will have to agree that in her attempt to share the truth of her bodily experience her pen sometimes becomes too bold; crossing the age-old barriers of the feminine culture of modesty and propriety, it verges on vulgarity. So much so, that just the titles of many of her chapters would suffice to shock many a conservative soul among her readers.

As all novels written by women are not feminist novels, in the same way this autobiography written by a woman is definitely not a feminist autobiography. Nowhere in the book do we come across even a faint suggestion of the feminist commitment with correcting, modifying, supplementing or attacking the male culture; but one may definitely trace the positive side of the feminist enterprise in it, namely, an attempt to create a woman's text. Kamala Das could be good subject for gynocritical study which, according to the famous feminist critic Showalter, who coined the very term 'gynocritique' in 1979, is the study of 'woman as the producer of textual meaning'.(25). In spite of various ideological rifts among critics about 'woman's writing' Kamala Das's rightful place among the producers of women's text can never be doubted.

Notes

1. See *Udit: The Airport Magazine*, Mar-April 1989 pp. 28-33 and *Savvy* December 1990 pp. 11-30.

References

Das, Kamala. *My Story*. New Delhi: Sterling Publishers Pvt. Ltd. (1976), 1988.

Das, Kamala. Article in *Savvy*, December, 1990.

de Beauvoir, Simone. *The Second Sex*. trans. H.M. Parshley New York: Bantam 1964.

Showalter, Elaine. "Towards a Feminist Poetics", *Women Writing and Writing About Women*, ed *Mary Jacobus*. London: 1979.

Woolf, Virginia. "Professions for Women", *The Dolphin Reader*, ed Douglas Hunt. Boston: Houghton Miffin Company, 1990.

22

Protest Against Sexual Colonialism: Kamala Das's *My Story*

Iqbal Kaur

Sexual colonialism refers to the relationship between the sexes which is 'a relationship of dominance and subservience'. It refers to the relationship between sex and power and as Kate Millett puts it "Through this system a most ingenious form of 'interior colonization' has been achieved". Men are the colonizers, the women colonized and as Simone de Beauvoir perceives it, the position that women occupy in the society is "comparable in many respects to that of racial minorities in spite of the fact that women constitute numerically at least half of the human race" (Parshley 9). She argues that "this secondary standing is not imposed of necessity by natural 'feminine' characteristics but rather by strong environmental forces of education and social tradition under the purposeful control of men. This. . . has resulted in the general failure of women to take a place of human dignity as free and independent existents associated with men on a plane of intellectual and professional equality, a condition that not only has limited their achievement in many fields but also has given rise to pervasive social evils and has a particularly vitiating effect on the sexual relations between men and women." Sexual colonialism, thus, has a reference to the imbalance of power between the two sexes.

This paper deals with protest against colonialism as voiced by Kamala Das in her autobiography *My Story*. She finds it intolerable that woman be assigned the status of the colonized and that she be the victim of the colonizer's 'brutal indifference' to her. She protests against women's socialization into an unquestioning acceptance of their destiny as inferiority, passivity, submissiveness and dependence; against society's expectations that a woman should conform to her 'Angel in the House' image. Revolting against the rigid gender divisions that a sexist culture wishes to establish—divisions according to which men are superior, God-like, while women are inferior, inert, "afflicted with a natural defectiveness", Das has voiced, without any inhibition, her restlessness with the fact that the sex-roles, as perpetrated by a society ruled and governed by men, trap women in wifehood, and motherhood and do not allow them any freedom for self-actualization. Marriage as an institution nauseates Kamala Das because it legitimizes violence on women and gives men a legal control on women's bodies.

Kamala Das condemns the gender divisions created by the male dominated society and pities the lot of women because they have been losers in the war of the sexes. The male desire to relegate women to margins suffocates her. She writes:

> Even the air-conditioner helps so little,
> All pervasive is the male scent of your breath.
>
> (*My Story* 192)

Kamala Das finds it difficult to reconcile with man-woman relationship as a relationship in which man is the 'Subject', the 'Absolute' and woman is the 'Object', the 'Other'.

Interestingly enough, the society that Kamala Das belongs to and which she is grappling with in *My Story* is a matriarchal one. But, unfortunately it is as much obsessed with the myth of male sovereignty as any patriarchal society. Kamala Das was disturbed by the fact that women had been trivialised and marginalised but more disturbing than this was the fact that even the matriarchs had accepted their biology as destiny and did not revolt against their colonization by men. A society in "which being female and being fully human were mutually exclusive" nauseated her. Since she had an acute consciousness of the fact that the society tried to trap women in their biology, she came to hate her female body. She writes:

> I felt then a revulsion for my womanliness. The weight of my breasts seemed to be crushing me. My private part was only a wound, the soul's wound showing through.
>
> (110)

She defined female body as the "silly female shape", "the clumsy gadgetry" that "ruined a beautiful relationship" and "always, always damaged bonds" (193).

Even as a child Kamala Das had an overwhelming awareness of victim-victimizer relationships that exist between men and women as well as an awareness of the adverse effects of sexist culture on female psyche. Her father, who thought himself sovereign, expected total submission from his wife and she did display a passive acceptance of the scheme of things which negated women. As soon as he got engaged to her mother, he "stipulated" and that too "firmly" what all she was to wear and what all she "was not to wear" (4). He announced "that his wife was not to wear anything but khaddar and preferably white or off-white" and "After the wedding he made her remove all the gold ornaments from her person, all except the 'mangal sutra'." Kamala Das imagines that to her mother "it must have seemed like taking to widow's weeds" but the inner experiences of woman in the over-masculinized culture are insignificant and are not taken into consideration. Kamala Das voices her restlessness with the fetters of femininity in *My Story* as well as in her poetry. In one of her poems entitled "Suicide" she writes:

> But,
> I must pose.

I must pretend,
I must act the role
Of happy woman,
Happy wife.

Thus, the male-governed society leaves a woman no choice so far as acting her satisfaction with her position as the inessential is concerned. In the society to which Kamala Das belongs, it was impossible for a woman to rebel against the masculine yoke, against a male's overwhelming sense of superiority because a male, she was given to understand, was no less than a god. She narrates that her granduncle "did not have enough money even to buy the books that he wished to read" (14) but he "looked every inch a king" and used to call his second wife "the most empty-headed woman he had known" and "she used to laugh melodiously at such comments".

Kamala Das's *My Story* contains ample evidence of her "awareness of the arrest of feminine development brought about by an economic system, a family structure which produced in women dependency, insecurity, lack of autonomy, and an incomplete sense of who they are even at the level of bodily ego" (Waugh 85). The feminine mystique, she feels, has always been exploited by man who treats woman as his slave. She talks about an oilseller who:

> drove his white cow and the three women of his house round and round his old mill, to extract oil from the copra and the sesame while he rested, leaning against a tree, abusing them in pornographic language which only amused his victims, for he ways always a good provider and they were, by nature, masochistic.
>
> (28)

This is sexual colonialism in its 'most overpowering form'. It does not let women feel that they are being victimized. Kamala Das who craves for a less oppressive climate for women, seems to be drawing the reader's attention to the close link between women's oppression and the material conditions, i.e., control on women through economic force.

Woman, Kamala Das feel, has always belonged to the deprived categories of humans, while men believe that the privileges they enjoy are theirs by right. Disgusted with the kind of gender arrangements which treat woman as a slave and thwart women's desire to seek freedom, to seek a right to exist as an independent human being, Kamala Das writes:

You planned to tame a swallow, to hold her
In the long summer of your love so that she would forget
Not the raw seasons alone, and the homes left behind, but
Also her nature, the urge to fly, and the endless
Pathways of the sky.

(192)

Kamala Das, who right from her childhood wished to subvert the established order which supports the imbalance of power between the sexes, brought all her unconventional views to marriage. "I hate marriage" she declared. "I hate to show myself naked to anyone. . . ." (72) She had a fierce aversion to marriage because for her a married adult was a "clown in bed", "a circus performer". She made fun of the "sexual acrobatics" which "the dignified couples" perform in the dark.

The male manufactured definitions of femininity nauseated her. She detested the male gaze because it situates woman as an object. The sexual politics that prevailed in the relationship between her mother and father and several other couples around her also shaped her views on marriage. The power politics in sex-relationships was repulsive to her. So, she wanted to escape marriage—the bondage. The way she tried to plea the postponement of her marriage, shows her keen desire for "flight from womanhood", "What is the hurry?" she asked her grandmother. Even when her marriage "was fixed" she tried to escape it. "Not yet, I said. Let me go back to Calcutta to finish my exams. . ." (85). She felt very uneasy to realize that her life "had been planned and its course charted by . . . parents and relatives". Her marriage was fixed. She could not escape her destiny but she displayed tremendous courage in flouting the traditional image of 'the perfect woman'. She refused to be a traditional bride and behaved like a "tomboy" on her wedding day. She refused to hide in her room "looking demure and shy". She refused the traditional bridal bath, she refused to wear "a good saree" and dressed up in "a white sari". She detested "the extravagance" of her wedding. In fact, she says: "All this glut made me feel cheap and uncomfortable". She had an uneasy feeling that she was devalued as a person in her own right that "the bride was unimportant and her happiness a minor issue" (90).

Kamala Das who wished for herself 'a place of human dignity' detested the sexual haste of her husband on the wedding night. She associated the sexual relationships with the fantasy of being attacked, subdued and injured! She, who wanted to assert herself as a "free and independent existent" could not accept the status of an Object, a commodity and this perhaps, was responsible for her frigidity to which she makes several references in *My Story*. She confesses: "I was cold and frigid. I did not know what sexual desire meant. . . . Sex was far from my thoughts. . . I had no need at all for rough hands riding up my skirts. . ."(87) and so on. She is intolerant of man's obsession with his erotic needs and writes. "The word mate with its earthy connotations made me uneasy. I felt lost and unhappy" (87). She felt shattered to realize that her husband could be just a sexual companion and not an emotional companion. She refers to her wedding night as "that unhappy night" because she says: "without warning he fell on me, surprising me by the extreme brutality of the attack" (92). She refers to this sexual attack as a "rape"—a rape of her spirit perhaps. She did not let the rape be successful and says:

> I remained a virgin for nearly a fortnight after my marriage. He grew tired of the physical resistance which had nothing to do with my inclinations.
>
> (93)

She who wanted to question the very concept of femininity, to reject the traditional feminine world and to defy the overwhelming "male ego" could not be "just another of his admirers". She could not "submit to his clumsy fondling". She could not reconcile herself with being treated as just an object, a non-entity and not a partner in the game. The one who was seeking "a pure, total freedom" had the agonizing awareness that she was not valued by her husband for her own singular being and this gave a death blow to the feminist utopias she had been cherishing since her childhood days. The one who "wanted to be given an identity that was lovable", soon realised that she was not needed by her husband except as a slave, a prisoner. Her resentment against the way "the ruling sex" tries to control the subordinate sex is visible in expressions like:

> You called me wife,
> I was taught to break saccharine into your tea and
> To offer at the right moment the vitamins. Cowering
> Beneath your monstrous ego I ate the magic loaf and
> Became a dwarf. I lost my will and reason, to all your
> Questions I mumbled incoherent replies.
>
> (192)

She revolts against the fact that the male psyche tends to treat woman as a desirable commodity. It causes her great anguish that men expect total servility from their wives. Her husband too was an egoist, a bit too sure of his conjugal rights and believed in ruthless exploitation of woman as an absolute Other. She narrates:

> During his stay in Malabar, he spent most of his time with his cousins and his sister-in-law, paying me little attention and never bothering to converse with me. At night he was like a chieftain who collected the taxes due to him from his vassal, simply and without exhilaration.
>
> (98)

Kamala Das has also articulated in *My Story* her restlessness with the traditional sex roles according to which a woman is to find her total fulfilment in submissive domesticity. She protested against the division of world into two spheres, a sphere that belongs to men and another that belongs to women, and the one that belongs to woman, she tells, was confined just to the four walls of the house. Kamala Das was expected to:

> Dress in sarees, be girl
> Be wife. . . Be embroiderer, be cook,
> Be a quarreller with servants.
>
> —An Introduction

Though "the categorizers" expected her to "Fit in", to "Belong", "to choose a name, a role", Kamala Das tried to defy the male definitions of femininity. She refused to fit into any schemes, to play the role of a trapped housewife. So,

> My mother-in-law sulked, for she felt that I was spending too much time away from child and my domestic responsibilities. Whenever she said disgruntled things my husband grew angry, and his anger was directed against me and the baby.
>
> (102-103)

Mr. Das could not tolerate her assertion of feminine subjectivity and "stopped me from going upto the terrace for the rehearsals in the evening. You must remember you are a wife and mother, he said" (103). But she, who was struggling to create a new order, a brave new world where women too could be treated as human beings, could not develop a sense of her invisibility. She reacted against the traditional society's definition of womanhood, against the traditional sex-roles and was resolved not to be a stereotype. She writes:

> I kept myself busy with dreary house work while my spirit protested and cried, get out of this trap, escape.
>
> (103)

She tried to view the social set up with a woman's eye and wished to challenge it. She felt that her refusal to assume the socially defined traditional feminine role was one way of transcending her 'femininity' which is associated with passivity and inferiority. So, when marriage stifled for her all possibility of autonomy, and divorce did not seem possible in a traditional orthodox society like hers, she decided to put an end to her life. It is a different matter that she did not succeed at it but the very fact that the suicide was attempted shows her desire for "flight from womanhood".

A woman with an intense desire for sexual revolution, she wants a utopian state of affairs in which the unequal boundaries of gender do not exist. She presents the picture of such a state of affairs when she writes:

When he
And I where one, we were neither
Male nor female.

(136)

No wonder, it is almost impossible to concretize this vision. So this desire for a feminist utopia entered into a conflict with the traditional image of femininity - a conflict which drove her almost to madness. She felt that she was "a misfit everywhere". She says: "I brooded long stifling my sobs. . ." (109). But, in spite of the fact that she had to stifle her sobs, she was not prepared to stifle her need to choose, to act like an authentic being. Literary creativity came to her rescue and helped her return to sanity. It enabled her give an outlet to her unfulfilled desires and provided her an opportunity to establish her identity. So, even though there was no other possibility of going beyond her situation, she could still do so by creative writing. Thus, the sense of selfhood which in the case of Kamala Das was too strong to be annihilated got sublimated in writing. Creative writing served as a therapy and helped her confront and transcend the overwhelming realities of life. It helped her "Cleanse the stuffed bosom of that perilous stuff/Which weighs upon the heart". Her parents, relatives, husband, children all imprisoned her in her femininity, but creative writing enabled her to go beyond the bonds of femininity and to give expression to her revolt against sexual politics. The writing of *My Story* itself was an act of defiance if we situate her in her socio-cultural background. The Nalapat women, as she tells us, were orthodox and puritanical. They showed an unquestioning acceptance of the traditional sex-roles which tend to doom women to immanence. They did not dine along with men and many of them hardly ever stepped out of the house. They lived a life of self-negation and never thought of taking decisions for themselves. Hence, it required exceptional courage to challenge the long established social system and to preach "a new kind of morality" and Kamala Das did display tremendous courage in revolting against the sexual colonialism and providing hope and confidence to young women that they can refuse and reject the victim positions, that they can frustrate the sexist culture's efforts to exploit, passivise and marginalise women.

References

Das, Kamala. *My Story*. New Delhi: Sterling Publishers Pvt. Ltd. 1977.

de Beauvoir, Simone. *The Second Sex* trans. H.M. Parshley. Penguin 1972.

Millet, Kate. *Sexual Politics*. London: Abacus, 1972.

Parshley, H.M. "Translators Preface", *The Second Sex*, by Simone de Beauvoir, Penguin 1972.

Waugh, Patricia. *Feminine Fictions: Revisiting the Postmodern*. London: Routledge, 1989.

23

Rebellion and Escape: Kamala Das's *My Story*

Rama Rani Lall

Kamala Das's autobiography *My Story* reveals her multifaceted personality in all its power and glory. With exemplary courage and conviction she has explored the innermost depths of her consciousness in this work. The unifying principle of her recollections is her overriding feminist concern. She has accepted her womanhood with all its weaknesses and strengths and has thus become a symbol of the liberated new woman for her generation. In *My Story* she attempts to define her identity as a woman and to create a space within her and around her in order to assert the legitimacy of her dreams and fantasies, and to express her hopes and frustrations.

Early in life she realized that the gender difference practised unchallenged in the traditional Indian society is responsible for many unjust customs and beliefs. In an interview given to Iqbal Kaur, Kamala Das was asked about her mature reaction to all that she had written in *My Story* in 1974, and she said:

> I don't regret having written it because there was a need at that time

> for a story like this. I needed to disturb society out of its complacence. I found the complacence in a very ugly state. I wanted to make women of my generation feel that if men could do something wrong they could do it themselves too.
>
> (167)

Elaine Showalter in her essay "Towards a Feminist Poetics" has mentioned three stages in the evolution of a female tradition of writing in English, the Feminine phase, the Feminist phase and the Female phase:

> In the Female phase ongoing since 1920, women reject both imitation and protest—two forms of dependency—and turn instead to female experience as the source of an autonomous art, extending the feminist analysis of culture to the forms and techniques of literature.
>
> (Showalter 405)

Kamala Das in *My Story* has explored the wide range of female experiences from her girlhood to old age. The book can easily be read in three parts. The first part comprises of chapters one to twenty one and describes her early childhood and adolescence. The second section begins from chapter twenty-second and roughtly ends in the forty-third chapter. In this longest section of the book she records with extraordinary frankness her experiences after marriage. Her frustrations and unhappiness led to a nervous breakdown from which she recovered because of the love and care of her grandmother The tension between what she expected from marriage and what it turned out to be in real life gives a special vitality and vigour to this section. It was the period when all her suppressed psychic suffering burst out into the poems which have made her famous and well-known. The third section of the book from the forty-fourth to the fiftieth chapter records her mature insights and reflections on her art and life. Becoming a truth addict she realized that she loved her writing above all filial and familial ties.

To analyze *My Story* critically the most important question one has to answer is of motivation. To write a sincere autobiography is one of the most difficult tasks. A writer has to look back at the accumulated wealth of past experience and to remodel it to suit the needs and expectations of the present. This dual responsibility has its own risks. Kamala Das had to select and interpret some of the most significant moments of her life and to relive them in her imagination to highlight their contribution in shaping her present personality. With great literary skill and innate simplicity she succeeded in giving us a moving account of her personal life in *My Story*.

This autobiography could not have been written earlier. The country's freedom alongwith the rise of modern feminism of the 1960s and 1970s gave a further impetus to her self-expression. She became the spokeswoman for the victimized womanhood of India. A critical illness provided the right opportunity to her to unburden herself freely. Thus the post-colonial scenario and the feminist movement added a new social dimension to her inner fury.

In the Preface to *My Story* Kamala Das tells us that she began writing her autobiography during her first serious encounter with heart disease. "The doctor thought that writing would distract my mind from the fear of a sudden death, and, besides, there were all the hospital bills to be taken care of." This honest admission of the curative as well as monetary incentives to the book reveal her personality. When an editor, who had been requesting her for such a story for a long time was contacted he enthusiastically gave the whole renumeration for the serial as an advance.

Kamala Das admits that he took a risk as she was very ill at that moment and might not have completed her book. In her interview to Iqbal Kaur she again repeated, "I am speaking the truth. *My Story* was written at the bidding of my husband. . . probably he wanted to sell it" (164).

With the active encouragement of her doctor, her editor, and her husband when she started writing her story there was no stopping her. Her memoirs took such a hold on her imagination that she wrote rapidly with all her energy:

> as though it were a motor boat chug-chugging through the inky waters at night. Between short hours of sleep induced by the drugs given to me by the nurses, I wrote continually, not merely to honour my commitment but because I wanted to empty myself of all the secrets so that 1 could depart when the time came, with a scrubbed-out conscience.
>
> (Preface)

My Story had a great cathartic effect on her emotions and quickened her recovery. It "was serialized in *The Current Weekly* (Bombay) from January to December 1974" (Kohli 57). As the serial flooded the book stalls in Kerala, her relatives were embarrassed. "I had disgraced my well-known family by telling my readers that I had fallen in love with a man other than my lawfully wedded husband. Why, I had even confessed that I was chronically falling in love with persons of a flamboyant nature" (Preface). When she received no appreciation and warmth in her home state she escaped back to Bombay and sadly admitted "This book has cost me many things that I held dear, but I do not for a moment regret having written it" (Preface).

She realized that through self analysis and self-exploration she had succeeded in projecting a self-image which was exciting and lovable. She hoped that her frank admissions of her love-life will win for her the admiration and respect of her readers.

The immediate reaction to the book was mostly hostile. Many readers and critics felt that Kamala Das had deliberately made the story much more sensational and shocking than it really was, for monetary gains. Gradually with the passage of time there was a marked change in the attitude of the reading public. Iqbal Kaur was surprised that after twenty years: "The responses of these Malayali readers, much against my expectations, were sympathetic. They did not seem to be hostile towards her" (Prefatory note XII).

My Story is written in a direct, straightforward realistic style. The glimpses of her powerful personality give a unique flavour to it. According to Kohli *My Story* is written in the confessional mode and is brisk in pace. It is "held together more by a narration of incidents rather than by a reflection on them. In a sense, her autobiography is curiously static, and few incidents seem to (or are shown to) contribute to the organic development of her literary personality" (16). Some of the outstanding passages in *My Story* are closely related to her poems and help the reader to understand the poems better. "The ease with which she turns verse into prose (or is it vice versa?) throws some light on the limited range of her creative process" (Kohli 16).

Kamala Das has pointed out in *My Story* that "A poet's raw material is not stone or clay, it is her personality" (157). Being a compulsively autobiographical writer Kamala Das had an intense need to find some outlet for her emotions. Her poems have the lyricism and beauty of unpremeditated art. Even without much formal education Kamala Das has transcended many of her intellectual limitations. Critics like Kohli are of the view, "this conspicuous absence of an overt intellectual and philosophical framework heightens all the more the primitive energy and emotional directiness of her work" (Kohli 21).

Critics have warned the unwary readers to be on their guard and not to be swept away by the elemental force of her utterances. There is a temptation to oversimplify the complexity of her autobiography. In her writing Kamala Das had no intention to search for pretty words "which dilute the truth, but [to] write in haste, of everything perceived, and known and loved. . ." (Kohli 24). She loved the gift of life and found the world a beautiful place to live in. *My Story* chronicles her incessant search for true love and an ideal lover, wherein she asserts her artistic freedom to create an "autobiographical world", by freely mingling facts and fiction.

My Story opens with the image of a little child growing up in Calcutta when the British still ruled India. With her father always busy in his office work and the mother completely engrossed in composing poems in Malayalam, Kamala Das and her brother felt neglected and unloved. In the European school their dark skin brought untold hardships. Her brother in spite of being the cleverest boy in his class was often humiliated and tortured by white boys. One day, when his shirt-front was covered with blood, Kamala Das could not control her anger and "scratched" the face of Williams, the bully, "in a mad rage" (2). This honest anger at unjust discrimination was to become one of the defining qualities of her personality in later life.

She tells us that her parents were very dissimilar to each other and were horribly mismatched. Kamala Das felt that her mother's "timidity helped to create an illusion of domestic harmony which satisfied the relations and friends. Out of such an arid union were born the first two children, my brother and I, bearing the burden of a swarthy skin and ordinary features" (5).

Amongst her childish pleasures was the possession of a large doll's house complete with dainty furniture. Early in life she started writing sentimental poems "about dolls who lost their heads and had to remain headless for eternity. Each poem of mine made me cry" (8). A strong sense of loneliness inhabited her being and even on a school picnic she felt isolated and lonely (5). But there were some compensations. When the horrors of the Second World War threatened peaceful life in Calcutta, her father sent the family to their ancestral house in Malabar, called the Nalapat House. Here Kamala Das spent some of the happiest moments of her life in close proximity to the beauty of nature and the love of her grandmother, where:

> To the east lay lush fields and also to the north. From the west the blue and frothy Arabian Sea roared at night. Near the snake shrine was the rare Nirmatala tree which burst into bloom every summer with large butter-coloured flowers that filled the inner rooms with perfume.
>
> (13)

As Kamala Das grew up she became aware that the conventional orthodox woman of the best Nair families never mentioned sex in their conversation for they associated it with violence and bloodshed. It was customary for the Nair girl to marry when she was hardly out of her childhood, and found that

"It was also customary for her much older husband to give her a rude shock by his sexual haste on the wedding night" (25-26). Fed on mythical tales of Sita and Draupadi in her adolescence Kamala Das realized that:

> the only heroine whose sex-life seemed comparatively untumultous was Radha who waited on the banks of Jumna for her blueskinned lover. But she was another's wife and so an adulteress. In the orbit of licit sex, there seemed to be only crudeness and violence.
>
> (26)

These doubts and insights haunted Kamala in her later life as well. When she was sent to a boarding school run by Roman-Catholic nuns she enjoyed the companionship of her roommates but was soon disgusted with the unnecessary inhibitions imposed on the thoughts and actions of young girls and said:

> The obsession with sin destroyed the mind of several girls who were at the beginning of their adolescence, normal and easy going. If there was a dearth of sin, sin at any cost had to be manufactured, because forgiving the sinner was a therapeutic exercise, popular with the rabidly virtuous.
>
> (48)

This anger at the social and moral hypocrisy of the nuns made Kamala Das a rebel in her life and writing. Like a normal teenager she loved opulence and luxury. In her daydreams she saw herself as a bejewelled empress who controlled the destinies of her countrymen (5), and wanted to marry a rich man and live in comfort in Calcutta. Reading Bengali novels she found that all the heroines were supposed to bear in their eyes a sadness which made them irresistable to their heroes. With the desire to be like them, Das too "tried to look sad", but it was a difficult task, for a young healthy girl who was ready to burst out into laughter on the slightest occasion (62).

The freedom and carefreeness of youth were short-lived. Soon her marriage was fixed. When her fiance visited their family in Calcutta it proved to be a disappointing week for both of them as the reality was far removed from her romantic dreams: "I wanted conversation, companionship and warmth. Sex was far away from my thoughts. I had hoped that he would remove with one sweep of his benign arms, the loneliness of my life" (84). But none of this happened.

Her romantic dreams of love and understanding were rudely shattered on her wedding night. Amidst all the show of a lavish wedding no one seemed to care about the happiness of the fifteen year old bride. After marriage the young couple could not get away for a honeyman for the husband wanted to bask in the love and admiration of all his relatives and wanted her "to become just another of his admirers, one more relative to submit to his clumsy fondling" (90).

What upset her was the traumatic experience of the wedding night. With the physical gaining over the emotional, there was a sense of hurt and injury which could not be easily mollified. Later when she became a mother she again experienced a sense of alienation. When her husband visited her he could not sympathise with her new responsibilities and was often disgusted with the constant interruptions the child caused during his hours at home. Angrily he ordered her to take him away to her grandmother's room. " 'I cannot sleep with all this noise and fussing'. The baby clung to me and I sensed that he too felt the humiliation of our position" (94). This led to further disillusionment on her part and governed her attitude towards sex:

> At night he was like a chieftain who collected the taxes due to him from his vassal, simply and without exhilaration. All the Parijata that I wove in my curly hair was wasted. The taking was brutal and brief. The only topic of conversation that delighted him was sex and I was ignorant in the study of it.
>
> (94)

With a coldness in her heart she realized that "if love was what I had looked for in marriage, I would have to look for it outside its legal orbit, I wanted to be given an identity that was lovable... I made up my mind to be unfaithful to him, at least physically" (95). Disappointed in her husband she sought kindness and love in the arms of many imaginary lovers. She had the mythical ideal of Radha and Mira before her and believed that the society which gave the highest respect to these figures will also understand her predicament.

In her interview with Iqbal Kaur she justified the narration of all her extra-marital affairs as flights of imagination and pleaded for a space for herself and her fellow sisters who have to endure a loveless marriage. If not in real life at least in their imagination the victimized wives can hope to be in the arms of an ideal lover. She tried to universalize her personal tragedy and said:

> Any book will contain passages which are the creation of the writer's imagination. *My Story* is no exception. Whether something happened to me or to another women is immaterial. What really matters is the experience, the incident. It may have happened to another woman who is probably too timid to write about it. I wanted to chronicle the times we lived in and I had to write about the experience.
>
> (165)

Kohli's analysis of *My Story* focuses on the central ambivalence in a woman's situation, security and freedom are not compatible with each other "Independence is consistent with a non-domestic mode of living" (Kohli 27), Das's attack is directed towards loveless marriages.

The sensibility which is central to her work is the writer's sensibility which often eludes the non-writer. With the help of metaphors and symbols she tries to show the difference:

> The non-writers do not normally trust the writers. This is because they are entirely dissimilar, except in appearance. The mind being an invisible limb, is not taken into consideration. Even birds have their own popular heights. The land birds who do not rise far into the lonely sky, often wonder why the eagles fly high, why they go round and round like ballerinas.
>
> (175)

But as the years passed and poetry provided her emotional expression and allowed her to indulge in her intensities, she substituted the real world with a make-belief one. Like Mira and Radha she turned to Krishna, her god who shall come to her in myriad shapes (186). A conventional escape for an unconventional woman!

References

Das, Kamala. *My Story*, (First published 1974). New Delhi: Sterling Publishers, rpt. 1991.

Kaur, Iqbal. ed., *Perspectives on Kamala Das's Poetry*. New Delhi: Intellectual Book Corner, 1995.

Kohli, Devindra. *Kamala Das*. New Delhi: Arnold Heinemann, 1975.

Showalter, Elaine. "Towards a Feminist Poetics". *Contemporary Criticism* ed. V.S. Seturaman. Madras: Macmillan, 1989.

24

Erasing the Margins: Questioning Purdah

Jasbir Jain

The practice of purdah in many Asian countries is not merely a form of dress or custom, but is indicative of a whole social system. Purdah reinforces the idea of female subordination inbuilt in patriarchal societies; it also defines family and political structures and constitutes the basis of gender ideology. In India, very often, purdah is associated with the advent of Islam and is treated as part of Muslim culture. This is not correct.[1] While, in part, the practice of purdah may be attributed to the vulnerability of women and their being taken away as the loot of war, or their abduction by men with political or military power, it does not represent the whole truth. Ordinarily, when the region-wise differences in the observance of purdah are commented upon, the invasions in the north, the relative insecurity of social life are some of the reasons which are put forward as responsible for the practice as compared to the reduced degree of purdah practice in southern parts of the country. This kind of reasoning also finds a parallel example in the life of newly urbanized Bengali women in the nineteenth century. When these women were brought to

Calcutta to keep home for their menfolk, they led extremely restricted social lives on account of the hostile and strange environment. Patterns of behaviour of immigrant families, the increased ghettoism are all examples of similar situations where even if purdah is not manifest in the matter of clothing, it is perceptible in the unequal relationship which exists between different groups, no matter what the basis of the group formation is—money, political power, colour or gender.

Purdah has many subtle forms and dress is the most superficial and the most visible of these. Ideologically, purdah is the oldest form of colonization, of domination and of control. Here it is the female body which acquires the metaphor of land, and it is this body which needs to be controlled. Female bodies become what Foucault calls "docile bodies". Susan Bordo, while commenting on the concept of femininity, points out that it is the female body "whose forces and energies are habituated to external regulation, subjection, transformation, improvement. Through the exacting and normalizing disciplines of diet, make-up, and dress—central organizing principles of time and space in the days of many women—we are rendered less socially oriented and more centripetally focused on self-modification."[2]

Purdah is based on the principle of inequality (not necessarily difference), and establishes itself on the dual strategy of control and exclusion. It defines space, action and relationships. Several varied systems of thought converge into this practice. The myths of creation which project women as secondary,[3] the projections of an after life in some religions where woman is viewed as an attendant upon male sexual appetite,[4] other mythologies which project woman as a source of temptation and a seduction,[5] the linguistic bias against women,[6] and the actual kinship patterns which treat women as objects of exchange and hence equivalent to property, requiring ownership and protection, are all indicators of female subordination. These patterns are not limited to India or to Asian countries but can be found in many societies and underlie other forms of inequality. A daughter in India cannot ask for her share of the paternal property if it is not being divided;

and a victim of a rape could not ask for redress in nineteenth century England, while her father could sue her seducer for the loss of her services and a husband could claim damages from his wife's lover.[7] It is in this context—the subordination of the female, the control over her body, the confinement of her space—that purdah in India has to be viewed; it exists both in Hindu as well as in Muslim society and is both a manifestation and a symbol of power relationships. But it exists in different ways and has different implications in the two religious structures.

Ancient Hindu scriptures, law texts, conduct books demarcate the division between women as wives and women as prostitutes. Women are respected provided they conform to the normative patterns defined by men. Buddhist literature and the Puranas have references to courtesans and sacred prostitutes. There is also the still-existent practice of "devadasis" in Hindu temples.[8] Sudhir Kakar in "Feminine Identity in India" discusses the prevalent idea that it is not wifehood alone which confers a social status on women, what is required is a faithful adherence to the code of behaviour prescribed for her in the law texts. Kakar writes, "To be a good wife is to be a good woman" (56) and goes on to explain by quoting Manu: "Though destitute of virtue or seeking pleasure elsewhere, or devoid of good qualities, yet a husband must be constantly worshipped as a god by a faithful wife", and "by violating her duty towards her husband, a wife is disgraced in this world, after death she enters the womb of a jackal and is tormented by the punishment of her sin" (62).

Prostitution in the Puranas (Matsya Purana) is seen as a punishment for wayward behaviour.[9] And while mistresses and concubines are viewed as the property of one man, prostitutes are viewed as public women. These relationships, like that of the wife, are defined by the relationship to man. And implicit in this is the idea of respectability being synonymous with male control and female submission. The centrality of man in this kind of framework can be seen in the legend of Ambapali (or Amrapali) born of a plantain tree in the mango grove of the Mahanama. When she grew up to be a beautiful girl and her adoptive father began to look for a suitable match for her, the *guna* was summoned. The *guna* informed him that an independent beautiful girl was for the pleasure of the entire guna and not for one man, hence ruling out the possibility of marriage for her (Chandra 25-26). This defines space which is available to women and the rewards and punishments associated with obedience and defiance. Purdah often talked about as modesty, 'izzat', 'laaj', 'sharam', is symbolic of conformity, while the concept of independence, freedom and self are all relegated to a world outside it. Related to this is the chasm in the cultural and educational avenues available to women in the two worlds. Wives are given a name, protection, respectability and children and deprived of access to education; prostitutes and devdasis in the traditional world had access to learning both of language and of dance and music but none to family life.

Manusmriti deals with the different roles of women and the overall picture it presents of woman is as a person naturally soft and docile, irrational and vulnerable, easily distracted from the path of "virtue" and hence greatly in need of male control.[10] This is necessitated by the need to protect her chastity as well as to ensure the purity of lineage. Thus it is the sexual role of woman which is to define her freedom, because for her the separation of sex for pleasure and sex for procreation cannot exist in one body as it does for the male who divides it between two women—the courtesan and the wife.

The origin of purdah amongst the Muslims has had somewhat similar reasons like the safeguarding of female honour and fear of male seduction. Shahida Lateef in *Muslim Women in India* traces the sanction of purdah to the verse from the Quran enjoining modesty: "Say to the believers, that they cast down their eyes... And say to believing women, that they cast down their eyes. . . (77)". But there have been other accounts for it. Sir William Muir in his *Life of Mahomet* (London, 1877) referred to the story about Mohammed's one day surprising Zainab, the wife of his adopted son Zaid, in her house and being startled by her beauty, exclaimed, "Gracious Lord! Good Heavens! How thou dost turn the hearts of men!" When Zaid heard of this from his wife, he promptly offered to divorce her for Mohammed's sake.[11] But Rafiq Zakaria in *Muhammad and the Quran* refutes this version and is of the view that Zainab, who was to become the Prophet's seventh wife, was unhappy in her marriage to Zaid, who was a slave elevated to the rank of an adopted son. The reason for her unhappiness was the difference in status, and divorce was an outcome of this unhappiness (Zakaria 49-50).

Whatever the origins, the truth of the situation is that purdah is based on discrimination and has a long tradition in India irrespective of religious belief. The varieties of degree are more region-based than religion-based and the differences on grounds of religion are more subtle. They are related to culture and aesthetics. The purdah as worn by Muslim women is ordinarily of black colour, but can be white or green, can use different textures and materials, laces, embroidery, shapes and designs. The *burqa*, though used to hide beauty, can in itself be a thing of beauty, or can be baggy and shabby. As it can conveniently disguise the female body, it confers anonymity on it; it also facilitates mobility. It makes it possible for an area of privacy, however limited this may be, and it also makes it possible for a certain position as an observer without being observed.

Contrasted with this, the Hindu way of observing purdah is either the *ghunghat* or the *chaddar*. The *ghunghat* does not confer anonymity to the degree that the *burqa* does; it also limits the role as an observer and does not disguise the body. The *chaddar* can be drab and unromantic, and specially when associated with widowhood, it can be particularly unaesthetic. Purdah in the sense of being confined to domestic space can also be different in the two cultures. The interaction between men and women inside a Muslim household may not be severely limited. Partly this is so because of the less restrictive kinship laws as marriage between cousins is permitted. Shahida Lateef points out that purdah in a Muslim family is observed vis-a-vis outsiders (134). Zarina Bhatty in "Socialising of the Female Muslim Child" adds that when marriages took place between cousins, "the girl had the advantage of knowing her in-laws but not her husband since parda was observed between male and female first cousins also, a male first cousin being a potential husband" (237).

The same may not be true in a Hindu household, specially an upper-caste one, where the observance of purdah falls to the portion of daughters-in-law. In several parts of the country it was and even now is "severe form of cloistering women", in the interests of regulating "social interaction, the maintenance of traditional authority, and the solidarity of the extended family" (Minturn 73). Leigh Minturn in *Sita's Daughters* has analyzed the tradition of purdah in Rajput families and the manner in which it restricts "interaction of wives with their husbands and other members of their husband's household. These restrictions are designed to ensure that the alliance between husband and wife is subordinated to the alliance of men with their consanguineous kinsmen" (45-46). Resorted to within the family it is not only a segregation between men and women, but also symbolic of the hierarchical positions within the family amongst the women. As such the observance of purdah becomes a powerful instrument of controlling the "disruptive intrusions of brides into the extended family" which may undermine the position of the older women, like the mother-in-law or the aunt-in-law, and also prevents interaction with other male members like the father-in-law or brother-in-law. In fact it is a double seclusion for the daughter-in-law, for not only is she disassociated from her parental family and childhood associations but also restrained from forming any new associations—except with the women of her own generation—in her husband's family. Sudhir Kakar analyzing this situation comments:

> Communication with the older men is minimal (if it exists at all) since they, . . . are traditionally expected to maintain a posture of formal restraint in the presence of the newcomer. . . . She represents a potentially pernicious influence. . . . The nature of the danger she personifies can perhaps best be suggested by questions such as will the young wife cause her husband to neglect his duties as a son? As a brother? A nephew? An uncle? Will social tradition and family

pressure be sufficient to keep the husband-wife bond from developing to a point where it threatens the interests of the other family members?

(Kakar 63)

Historically speaking various social conditions and living styles have been modified and changed to accommodate purdah or to alter its practice marginally, to provide some extra space to the female sex. Architecturally traditional houses often have separate living quarters for women referred to as the 'zenanas', with men spending most of their time in the front portion of the house. In Bengal there has been the practice of *antahpuras*, literally meaning the interior of the house. This symbolized domestic space. Partha Chatterjee in his work *The Nation and Its Fragments* points out how the primary dichotomy between material and spiritual was linked with the social reform movements and with nationalist concerns. The British, Indian reformers submitted, had conquered the external world, but not the inner spiritual world. Chatterjee writes "The world is a treacherous terrain of the pursuit of material interests, where practical conditions reign supreme. It is also typically the domain of the male. The home in its essence must remain unaffected by the profane activities of the material world—and woman is its representation" (Chatterjee 120).

The freedom struggle led to the formation of purdah clubs enabling women to get together; there were purdah hospitals and even purdah parks. The Baptist Zenana missionaries were engaged in educational activities in purdah households and then various attempts were made to understand, accommodate or even transcend purdah. Not that all these efforts were successful. Purdah remains a reality in India to this day when the question of issuing identity cards to women with or without photographs has once again come to the forefront.[12]

Ironically enough nineteenth century reform movements worked in two different directions—one where the desire was to liberate women from the injustices and inequalities surrounding them and the other treating them as custodians of traditional values. It is really questionable how successful these reform movements were. For one, they addressed themselves primarily to Hindu society. Widow remarriage and early marriages were specific to it as was the purdah in the extended family. Movements like the Arya Samaj and the Singh Sabha were fairly traditional in their value structures. And these reform movements were in the main spearheaded by men. It was, as Partha Chatterjee points out, in its core "a male discourse" (Chatterjee 136) and the dents it made were within the hegemonic framework confirming the subordination of women with all the paraphernalia of conformity and respectability.

While the enforcement of purdah, and the stress on conventionality of dress and segregation of women or asceticism on their part wherein they acquire asexual virtues have been motivated by ideological reasons, the fallout of the purdah-mentality has been damaging to the development of both men and women. It is a denial of adulthood to women and shows "an appalling lack of faith in the higher and purer nature of men and women. The men seem to think that the sight and companionship of women would tempt them beyond control. . ." (Cousins 46). Within the family, Jaiths and Susurs are viewed as potential seducers (Minturn 76). The practice of purdah and their extreme repression seemed to result in "a heightened consciousness of sex among Hindu women, rather than the culturally approved sexless opposite" (Borthwick 19). A body which was desired to be made invisible actually acquired a certain visibility simply because it was being thought of as a body. It focused attention on it and consequently a heightened romantic and sexual awareness followed this self-focusing on awareness which is reflected in literature and art.

An early example of this romanticisation can be seen in the Urdu *ghazal*. *Ghazal* is an Arabic world which literally means talking to women. In societies where free interaction is not possible between young people, love can only be communicated and expressed through indirections, in "hushed tones, often with the aid of indirection and innuendo" (Kanda 4). *Ghazals* are ordinarily addressed to a male lover even when the actual addressee is a woman. And its natural sadness owes it origin to the frustrations of unrequited love. Films have helped further romanticise this tradition where young love is nurtured on *ghazals* and *mushairas* and the young lover sings "*dil jalta hai to jalne de/ ansoo na baha, faryaad na kar/ Tun purdahnashin ka aashiq heh, yun namae wafa badnaam na kar.*" A parallel trend can be seen in the Hindi bhajans specially Meera Bai's like "*ghunghat ka pat khol tujhe piya mile gain*". Muslim socials use purdah situations to create romance, mystery, and present unrequited love and fidelity for the inaccessible beloved, And because of the mystery of the unknown or the distantly watched beloved a great deal is made of the wedding night, with the eroticism of the *suhaag raat* bordering on the obscene in Hindi films.

In language literatures purdah has had its own centrality so much so that in Krishna Sobti's *Mitro Marjani*, Mitro's refusal to cover her head threatens masculine control. In all this the real threat which is felt is from female sexuality which is acceptable in its maternal aspects but not in the sexual ones. Again and again writers address themselves to this problem in different ways and using different narrative strategies, in different kinds of narratives, defining space in their own terms and locating women in different situations. Purdah and the resistance to/violation of purdah are present in novels like Bankim Chander's *Rajmohan's Wife* and *Indira*, Tagore's *Home and Abroad*, Sharat Chander's *Parineeta* and a host of others. It is a major issue of controversy in Tagore's *Gora*. The romance of the purdah is exploited even by the non-Asian writer and it lingers on in the bridge party in E.M. Forster's *A Passage to India*, and in Aziz's relationship with his dead wife's memory. M.M. Kaye in *Far Pavilions* makes extensive use of purdah in the romance between Ash and the princess and later on uses it for the princess's disguise as an Afghan woman. The plot is hinged on the purdah situation and more visibly on the burqa.

Behind the romance of the purdah is its extreme restrictive lifestyle which is stiffling and self-denying, and the hidden aspect of this life is the exploitative nature of the attitude to sex. It hides behind the double moral standards as applicable to men and women, rape, incest and dependence. The movement away from purdah is a movement towards self-identity and freedom which, though highly desirable and worthy aims in themselves, are equally traumatic in their effects on women. They may often isolate them, lead to social ostracisation, may expose them to extreme poverty or humiliation or necessitate extreme self-denial. Doing away with purdah calls for a total change in the ideas of socializing, in family relationships and in the manner in which women view themselves. These are required to enable the concepts of personhood and responsibility to grow, and for supportive systems to develop so that the joy of growing up female can be truly felt.

Notes

1. Shahida Lateef, *Muslim Women in India: Political and Private Realities 1890s-1980s*, New Delhi: Kali for Women, 1990. Lateef writes: "There has been and continues to be considerble discussion on the origins of the custom of seclusion of women in India. This discussion has varied from those who ascribe it entirely to the advent of Muslim rule in India (Menon, 1944: 4; Ward, 1963: 478; Abhenanda, 1901: 20; Mujeeb, 1972: XI) to conceding that some form of seclusion existed before Muslim rule (Altekar, 1956: 169, 169, 171, 173, 175) to attributing it to social structures which have reinforced the system (Sorabjee, 1908: 84; Fuller, 1900: 36; Shridevi, 1965: 33; Gray, ND: 17; Nehru, ND: X)."
2. Susan R. Bordo, "The Body and the Reproduction of Femininity: A Feminist Appropriation of Foucault", *Gender/Body/Knowledge*, eds. Alison M. Jagger and Susan R. Bordo. New Brunswick: Rutgers University Press, 1989, p. 144.
3. Most creation myths are male-centred. In the Judeo-Christian tradition the creative power is vested in a male God who created Heaven and Earth and all living creatures in six days (Gen., I: 1-31).

Creation myths in the *Rg Veda* are based on sacrifice, incest or dismemberment-creation being viewed as separation: "One who creates a second with whom he unites as a pair" (*Hindu Myths*, ed., Wendy Doniger O'Flaherty, Penguin (1975) 1978). If there is an exception to these theories of male creation, it exists in early Greek mythology. Robert Graves in his Introduction to *The Greek Myths*, Penguin (1950) 1960, Vol. I writes: "Ancient Europe had no gods. The great goddess was regarded as immortal, changeless, and omnipotent; and the concept of fatherhood had not been introduced into religious thought. . . . Men feared, adored, and obeyed the matriarch. . ." The male partner had a limited lifespan. Creation is first vested in Euronome, the goddess of all things (27), but, later, control shifts to Zeus the Father of Heaven.

4. Refer the idea of *Zannat*, the Mohammedan paradise which is projected as a place inhabited by *houris*, celestial nymphs, beautiful and voluptuous.

5. Refer Menaka's seduction of Vishwamitra. The meditation and asceticism of sages was often disrupted by this onslaught on their sexual natures.

6. The Latin origin of the word family, means 'household servant'. Other words in Indian languages which refer to wifely status are words such as 'dasi' (meaning 'slave') and those referring to the husband's status are 'malik', 'khawand', 'sartaj', indicating ownership.

7. Refer Anna K. Clark, "Rape or Seduction? A Controversy over Sexual Violence in the Nineteenth Century', *The Sexual Dynamics of History: Men's Power, Women's Resistance*, London: Pluto Press, 1983.

8. Marcus B. Fuller, *The Wrongs of Indian Womanhood* (1900) rpt. New Delhi, Inter-India Publication, 1984.

9. Moti Chandra, *The World of Courtesans*, Delhi: Vikas Publishing House Pvt. Ltd., 1973.

10. R.M. Das, *Women in Manu's Philosophy*, Jalandhar: ABS Publications, 1993.

11. Quoted in Marcus B. Fuller, op.cit., p. 79.

12. See *Sunday Express*, 23 January 1994, an Express News Service item "Thumb imprint will do for burqa-clad; EC" which expresses that

as "certain sections may be against getting themselves photographed" the Election Commission has taken care to "show relaxation in the case of burqa-clad Muslim women. . . In a recent order, the commission said: In any area where—due to sentimental or other reasons—electors are averse to being photographed, the thumb impression may be affixed to the card instead of the photograph. A similar exception may be made in the case of *paradanashin* women."

References

Bhatty, Zarina. "Socialisation of the Female Child in Uttar Pradesh", *Socialisation, Education and Women: Explorations in Gender Identity*, ed. Karuna Chanana. New Delhi: Orient Longman, 1988.

Bordo, Susan R. "The Body and the Reproduction of Femininity: A Feminist Appropriation of Foucault", *Gender/ Body/Knowledge; Feminist Reconstructions of Being and Knowing*, ed., Alison M. Jagger and Susan R. Bordo. New Brunswick: Rutgers University Press, 1989.

Chandra, Moti. *The World of Courtesans*. Delhi: Vikas Publishing House Pvt. Ltd., 1973.

Chatterjee, Partha. *The Nation and Its Fragments, Colonial and Postcolonial Histories*. Delhi: Oxford University Press, 1994.

Clark, Anna K. "Rape or Seduction? A Controversy over Sexual Violence in the Nineteenth Century", *The Sexual Dynamics of History: Men's Power, Women's Resistance*. London: Pluto Press, 1983.

Cousins, Margaret E. *Indian Womanhood Today*. Allahabad: Kitabistan (1941) Rev. 1947.

Das, R.M. *Women in Manu's Philosophy*. Jalandhar: ABS Publications, 1993.

Fuller, Marcus B. *The Wrongs of Indian Womanhood* (F.P. 1900). reprint, New Delhi: Inter-India Publications 1984.

Graves, Robert. *The Greek Myths*. Harmondsworth: Penguin (1955) 1960, 2 volumes.

Kakar, Sudhir. "Feminine Identity in India", *Women in Indian Society: A Reader*, ed Rehana Ghadially. New Delhi: Sage Publications, 1988.

Kanda, K.C. *Masterpieces of the Urdu Ghazal: From 17th to 20th Century*. New Delhi: Sterling Publishers Pvt. Ltd., 1992.

Lateef, Shahida. *Muslim Women in India: Political and Private Realities 1890s-1980s*. New Delhi: Kali for Women, 1990.

Minturn, Leigh. *Sita's Daughters: Coming out of Purdah*. New York, Oxford University Press, 1993.

O'Flaherty, Wendy Doniger. *Hindu Myths*. Harmondsworth: Penguin, (1975) 1978.

Zakaria, Rafiq. *Muhammad and the Quran*. New Delhi: Penguin (1991) rpt. 1992.

25

Unveiling Womanhood: Dharker's "Purdah"

Rashmi Chaturvedi

In the last few decades there has been an attempt to interrupt the continuity of the western discourse of modernity which has resulted from the concepts of ontology and to dislodge the white western male from his position of the signifying and subjectifying category of culture and a unifying reference to ethical values. The ontology of man with his progressiveness, continuity and invincibility has disintegrated rendering modernity delinquescent and paradoxical. Differences on the basis of class, gender, race and nationality have made inroads into the unified categories. From the standpoint of the long negated and absent blacks/browns, women, the colonized and orientals, the grand narrative with man, truth and history at its centre appears disjunctive and progress enigmatic giving way to a narrative of social contradictions and cultural differences.

The recent culture studies seek to reason out and rationalize the lived and productive pluralities within the communities. Frantz Fanon explodes the myth of progress and "two-time scheme"—one for the white western male and the other for the deprived and the victim rendering him belated in *Black Skin and White Masks*. Homi Bhabha, carrying this idea forward, speaks from the point of the time-lag, a temporal break in the representation which makes the two categories dependent upon and resultant from each other, rather than being two separate streams and develops this at length in *The Location of Culture*. Foucault's interstices—the gaps in the time and space of the cultural and historical narratives are responsible for giving rise to the difference, distance and discrimination. The identification of the interstices consequent of the culture politics brings him to Heterotopia—a perspective from where negotiation for space and empowerment can be resourced as Foucault writing about heterotopias in "Other Spaces" points out. It moves the signifier and subjectifier white male away to the position of the signified and the subjectified and reconstitutes the given categories within the framework of a culture. When horizon and vision turn incommensurate with the social structures and cultural constructs, heterotopia takes one to the place of one's absence, making one estranged unto oneself and brings one back in order to review, revise and reconstruct one's own subjectivity. It becomes a space of intervention in the cultural here and now.

The split of identity in the subject and subjectifying categories brings one to an understanding of how the Self gets defined and limited in the presence of the Other and how it reconstitutes itself. The personae in Imtiaz Dharker's "Purdah" have arrived at this decentered understanding of the Self.

The poem comprising of two parts—"Purdah" I & II opens with a journalistic nonchallance on the myth that Purdah is both shame and safety for women. It becomes a sign of culture and in bilateral trading sustains man's position as the signifier in the power pyramid of patriarchy. A structure constituted by these power paradigms tightens on the female personae of the poem by making them learn shame to be a part of their growing up. They find 'it came quite naturally' (3). Purdah provides them safety like the "earth that falls/on the coffin after they put the dead man in" (3). Claustrophobic structures close on their life.

In the dead world of the doomed the poet tries to create breathing space for woman. In a sudden shift of stances, the subject takes the position of the subjectifier and constitutes the identity of the other 'they' or men. 'They make different angles/ in the light, their eyes aslant,/a little sly.' (3). She sees and she recognizes them. Through this act of seeing and knowing them, she not only constitutes them from a different perspective but also forms a new identity for herself. She recognizes what she has to be protected from are 'those sly, aslant eyes'. The distinction between the victimizer and protector blurs. The breakdown of these categories is the opening of a search for new possibilities - the little chink from where the expanse of 'beyond' will open up.

Memory forms another structure holding her from the point from where presencing begins. A veiled, unindividuated body is the total space she has been allotted and that too is infested with sin—'between the thighs' (3). She is carefully carrying it forward from the collective conscious of the other women, the mothers, you and me. The individual memories of the torments of womanhood are not transmuted into the collective unconscious or an undifferentiated stream of the culture but remain fragmented, specific and hence conscious and haunting.

The circumspection of patriarchy through the collective unconscious-culture and the conscious-memory by now is complete leaving no space for dream, desire and drive. The present both of time and space is suffocating. Only heterotopia can bring release from this noose. The process of breaking bounds had already begun in her perception and reconstitution of the 'Other and Self'. She breaks the barriers of a definition and stands outside 'inching past herself' (4). She distances from herself to be in all the four corners of the room and scratches for a hold between Adam's first and the second rib (4). Life appears to be coming with a new lease. The expanse is opening up. Doors keep opening/inward and again/inward (4).

Purdah II is set against the backdrop of religion which is termed a "coin of comfort (rattling) against the strangeness of land" (5). Dharker combines in religion both the collective unconscious and conscious of society—"Words unsoiled by sense, pure rhythm on the tongue" (5). From the street to the mosque the scene does not change for women. Sly looks are cast in the street and "hands that had prayed at Mecca/dropped a sly flower on her book" (6). Religion is also a manifestation of man's desire for power and as such a myth sustaining patriarchy. It limits, restricts and intimidates women. "God is justice. Justice could be dread" (7). They must hide themselves. In religion, too, hiding their physicality is essential to their being as they are visible only physically. Their spirituality is neither evidenced nor acknowledged in this myth making which takes place through religion.

From the Quazi to "Evelyn the medium from Brighton", mothers and aunts at home are all traders of flesh in and outside marriage. Experiencing one's own body and through that womanhood, is not permitted to her. Her body is under the proprietorship of society, religion and family. "Night after virtuous night (she) performed for them" (7) had "annual babies" and "sank in the mould/of (their) mothers flesh/and mind, begging approval from the rest" (9).

At this point comes the rejection of mothers and motherhood. Mothers who have become an agency and in turn an agent for power application of patriarchy, by exemplifying what womanhood is all about. They validate the patriarchal customs, beliefs and institutions. They plot at their daughter's wedding and their tear-stained faces burn with shame at the running away of Naseema—typifying a daughter. They ultimately want their daughters to remain here and suffer, efface themselves, and perpetuate and multiply their mould. It is from this mind set of the mothers that their daughters are seeking release.

Release does come. It comes by way of transformation of the coin of comfort into the coin of freedom. She turns a fresh leaf. The act of experiencing the self begins in Saleema "(pouring) out the breast to fill the cup/of his white hands" (9) and Naseema rebelling and running away—"at last a sign, behind the veil/of life." (9). But what it leads them to? Not as yet, to a firm foothold between the ribs. The resultant experience of rebellion is diverse and varied and even frustrating at times, bringing her back to "smile and be accepted/always on her knees" (10). It is, nevertheless, a lived experience. They are no longer an imagined community. The look that sees them with a slant or sly can no longer hold them. They have come out of the "corner of some one else's eye" (4). Freedom, for the personae of Dharker's poem may not bring relief but it does bring the freedom of choices and of will.

References

Bhabha, Homi, K. *The Location of Culture*. London: Routledge, 1994.

Dharker, Imtiaz. *Purdah*. Delhi: Oxford University Press, 1989.

Fanon, Frantz. "The Fact of Blackness", *Black Skin and White Masks*. London: Pluto, 1986.

Foucault, Michel. "Of Other Spaces", *Diacritics*, Spring, 1986.

26

Discreet Rebellion: The Poetry of Imtiaz Dharker

A.K. Tiwari

Born in Lahore, brought up in Britain, Imtiaz Dharker now lives in Bombay, married to Anil Dharker, Editor of the magazine *Debonair*. She has married a non-Muslim, violating a tenet of Islam which forbids a Muslim woman to marry a non-Muslim. This fact shows that she is a person with very independent and unconventional ideas. She has been a rebel against an orthodox aspect of her religion and her community in real life. In some of her poems too, she criticizes certain features of Muslim culture and expresses a discreet rebellion against them.

Two of her major poems have the titles "Purdah I" and "Purdah II". In order to understand and appreciate her views on the purdah it is necessary to have some idea of this tradition in Muslim Society. This community regards, quite strictly, the home to be the proper domain of the woman. She is the mistress of the house. The responsibility of the husband is to earn money for the family, and her job is to make arrangements for the family with the money. She is therefore kept free from all responsibilities which relate to matters outside the house.

The purdah has religious sanction. The Koran carries the following injunction to the Prophet:

> "O Prophet! Tell thy wives and thy daughters and the women of the believers to draw their cloaks close round them (when they go abroad). That will be better, that so they may be recognized and not annoyed. . . ."
>
> (Sur Azhab)

The use of the purdah must have been necessary in the early days of Islam in the Arabic region where there was constant strife and turmoil among the various tribes. The purdah was meant to keep the women safe from harassment. It brought about the segregation of the women, but it also implied high family status.

In many parts of India, between the ages of five and nine years, girls in Muslim families start getting training in adult behaviour and several restrictions are placed on them which are a prelude to much greater segregation from the men folk. This is referred to as *parde me bithana*. In many families, between the ages of 9 years and 16 years, all the girls of the family are sent to the *jenan khana*. Whenever it is necessary for them to go out they have to do so in a *burkha*, *chadar* or in a covered vehicle. There are restrictions on whom girls can meet and talk to, and even on the manner in which they speak.

There seems to be a tendency to associate the presence of women with the baser instincts of men, and great care is taken to seclude them to protect their modesty and honour. The social norms insist on the fidelity of the women. The purdah is an instrument of masculine effort to keep low the spirit of independence in women. In Muslim society, women have been assigned a subordinate role to that of men, and the prevalence of the purdah has ensured the continuation of this subordinate role. The conformance to the norms of the purdah restricts and limits the roles of women, keeping them within the confines of the *jenana* apartments and keeps their status low. The man is the protector and provider in the family. His role carries authority and higher status. The tradition of the purdah has been a major factor in enhancing the superiority of men, as it has prevented women from getting education. Shibani Roy, in a study on *The Status of Muslim Women in North India* states:

> In the male dominated Muslim society purdah is a male imposed symbol of domination and seclusion symbolizing the eclipse of a Muslim Woman's identity and individuality. The woman by wearing it subscribes to male domination and gives up her claim to personal liberty.
>
> (45)

Purdah has the sanction of religion, but the rules of religion which were created for the tribes of Arabia centuries ago are not applicable to present day Muslim society. Social reformers have not been able to bring about the emancipation of women. Some change, however, has occurred as a result of gradual exposure to education, compulsion to seek employment and the urge within women to seek freedom.

The purdah, covering a woman's face and body, had a tremendous influence on a Muslim woman's life. It not only secluded her physically, but also mentally from the rest of the world, reducing her entire world to the *aangan* (courtyard) and *dalaan* of the *jenan khana*. Women of every generation, bound in the constraints of the purdah and subjected to its tyranny have ironically contributed to the perpetration of purdah with its inhibitng effects. In Shibani Roy's view:

> Purdah affects a large area of a woman's life and precludes her from many areas of participation. This vitiates her life and produces a limited perspective and has a dementing influence on her entire personality. These suppressed characters feel protected and safe behind the purdah and consider that they are fortunate to have the means to secure themselves from the vicious world. Thus, a large part of the world remains a mystery to them.
>
> (47)

Imtiaz Dharker's poem "Purdah I" focuses on a very significant turning point in the life of a girl in Muslim society—the threshold of youth. The girl suddenly attracts the attention of people around. In a conservative society with its emphasis on the preservation of modesty and honour, the natural reaction of people is that she should be taught the decorum befitting a young lady. They notice that "She was old enough to learn some shame". This involves teaching her to behave with proper shyness and caution.

The poet refers to the belief that "Purdah is a kind of safety". It is believed to be a protection, at this stage in life particularly. It is a protection against undesirable reactions from people, a way of curbing the possibility of unwanted attention. It is a device to preserve the purity of the person—as it checks the arousing of desire in the minds of those who see the young women.

However, the poetess criticizes the negative effects of the purdah. It can deny a young woman the opportunity to seek learning and enlightenment and result in a deadening of the intellect. It can act as a cover on the intellect just as the earth thrown into a grave effectively covers up the dead person and cuts him off from the outside world of experience.

> The cloth fans out against the skin
> much like the earth that falls
> on coffins after they put the dead men in.

The simile conveys very effectively that the purdah can kill the potential in the mind of the young woman by cutting her off from the outside world. Then it covers a dead mind. The purdah acts as a wall between the woman and the world with the experiences and enlightenment it offers, and even restricts speech.

> A light filters inward
> through our bodies' walls.
> Voices speak inside us,
> echoing in the spaces we have just left.

The young woman has a store of impressions gathered about the experiences of other women. She is acutely conscious of the physical aspect of sex and the potential of sin associated with it—a sense that does not trouble women who have always lived within the bounds of Muslim norms of propriety. The young woman's sense of mystery associated with sex is associated with a sense of guilt. She goes about—

> Carefully carrying what we do not own
> between the thighs, a sense of sin.

The purdah, the poetess conveys, has a very damaging effect on the intellect and the personality of the young woman. Made very self-conscious, she constantly submits herself to her own scrutiny, examining all aspects of herself in all her actions. It seems as though her personality becomes fractured.

> She stands outside herself,
> Sometimes in all four corners of a room.

The poetess brings out the division of a young woman's personality aptly in the simile comparing the woman to a "clod earth." She is a deadened mind and body. At the same time, in her effort to steady herself and seek stability and balance in her personality, within herself, she is compared to the root of a plant trying to get a hold on the clod of earth—between the ribs (the heart) of the deadened person under the purdah.

> Wherever she goes, she is always
> inching past herself,
> as if she were a clod of earth,
> and the roots as well,
> scratching for a hold
> between the first and second rib.

Her actions are not the objects of her own scrutiny alone. They become constantly, the object of the scrutiny of other people who observe her with cunning eyes. All the time, her seclusion grows, cutting her off further from the outside world:

> While doors keep opening
> inward and again
> inward.

The young woman is placed in an environment of seclusion, suggested by the image of doors opening inward, and the seclusion closes in upon her intellect and personality, which are denied the opportunity to develop. The poem does not voice a direct criticism of specific norms drawn from religious books. It carries in it a discreet rebellion against the practice by describing its damaging effect on the psyche of a young woman.

In "Purdah II" the poetess obliquely criticizes several aspects of Muslim society. The setting of the poem is England, and the poem brings out issues relating to Muslim women living in England. At the beginning of the poem she accepts that the faith, represented by 'Allah-u-Akbar'—the call of the *azaan*, offers solace and is reassuring in a foreign land:

> In the tin box of your memory
> a coin of comfort rattles
> against the strangeness of a foreign land.

The image of a coin rattle is apt. The sound of a coin in a box is reassuring. Similarly the call of 'Allah-u-Akbar' is reassuring, providing a sense of security and belonging, even though it evokes routine responses.

In stanzas 2 and 3 the poetess criticizes the traditional kind of education received by Muslim girls, which focuses on religion and does not give them knowledge. In the description the narrator says that words of the Holy Book were repeated mechanically and parrot-like. The children did not worry about the meaning. The rhythm of the words was enough, as their bodies rocked to and fro, giving them a sense of community and belonging.

The rules of decorum which form a part of traditional education fail to curb the surging urges of youth. Rules forbid men to look at and admire a woman's beauty. If a man happens to see a beautiful face, he should turn away his look. Men and women should keep their eyes lowered. Men should not look steadily at a woman's face. The young Haji does not seem to be influenced by such teachings, nor is he purified by his pilgrimage. He, fifteen, looks at the girl with nothing holy in his look and expresses his attraction towards her.

There was nothing holy in his look
Hands that had prayed at Mecca
dropped a sly flower on your Book.

The word 'sly' suggests the intention to seduce. The girl's reaction is a natural one. Her dreams were full of him for days. She responded to the attraction and her physical urges, allowing her thoughts to be impure, burning in the heat of love—unmindful of the punishment that would fall on her on the day of judgement.

You were scorched,
Long before the judgement
by the blaze.

The pronoun 'you' could refer to the poetess herself, or could have a more general meaning—anyone.

The girl has no freedom to have a relationship of her choice. What lies in store for her, as Evelyn, the medium from Brighton tells her is a traditional marriage the nature of which is suggested through the image of the red fabric:

a stretch of brilliant fabric, red.
Yes, crimson red, patterned through
With golden thread.

The purdah system allows girls no expression of individuality, and they are married in the traditional manner, with the promise of a *mehar*, the money assured or given to a girl as a security against divorce or the misfortunes of widowhood. Dharker refers sarcastically to such conventional marriages involving a monetary transaction but no real exercise of individual choice.

They have been sold and bought,
the girls I knew.

The constraints of the purdah and their destruction of the individual's thinking and intelligence are referred to sarcastically:

Unwilling virgins who had been taught,
especially in this stranger's land, to bind

their brightness tightly round,
whatever they might wear,
in the purdah of the mind.

The purdah is literal in the form of a *burkha* or *chadar* but it is also a curtain around the intellect of a person. The girls described by the narrator kept their eyes lowered, and dressed in a manner which concealed their physical charms, according to the dictates of Muslim norms.

They veiled their eyes
with heavy lids.
They hid their breasts,
but not the fulness of their lips.

The girls were able to resist the temptation of 'alien hands'—the young English men around them, because of the dictates of the men in the history of their religion, the religious leaders and the elders in their lives. Guided by the religious teachings they had received, they married within their race, and lived in accordance with the principles laid down by religious leaders. They did not marry to make themselves happy but to please 'them'.

Night after virtuous night.
You performed for them.

They derive solace 'a coin of comfort' from the fact that they have adhered to the norms of their religion, though such a marriage might mean unhappy lives—'years of loss'. The religious books tell the young people of the severe punishments laid down for moral transgressions, of the 'scourge and stones' to save them from impurity. These are particularly severe for women.

In this poem Dharker expresses the futility in the lives of Muslim women in Britain. Even rebellion against the norms of the community is futile. This is brought out through examples like Saleema and Naseem.

Saleema falls in love with an English man, yet since her faith prohibits marriage with a non-Muslim, she marries within her community, and has 'annual babies'. Dharker here refers with irony to the prohibition on the use of contraceptives. Saleema rebels, divorces, marries again and becomes a typical subservient wife like her mother, "begging approval from the rest".

Her life and the life of others like her is a bondage and a burden—and she feels as though she is a prey of the system, never independent, never strong. Dharker suggests this through a simile comparing her to a wounded animal:

> . . . watchful as any creature
> that lifts its head and sniffs the air
> only to scent its own small trail of blood.

The fate of Muslim girls rebelling against the dictates of their society is unhappy. If a Muslim girl, like Naseem, marries an English man, she is given up by her family. The poet says with her characteristic irony:

> The table is laden at Mohurram
> and you are remembered
> among the dead. No going back.
> The prayer's said.

Naseem is completely at the mercy of the English boy who promised her freedom, and ironically she has to be on her knees always to him, "trying to smile and be accepted".

Whether Muslim girls in Britain remain in or out of purdah, that is, whether they abide by the orthodox ways or rebel, their fate is miserable, involving abject surrender because they are not educated enough to be independent.

Another aspect of Muslim society that Dharker criticizes is that women are not allowed to go to a mosque. The Koran considers men and women equal in matters of religion:

> Verily, the Muslim men and Women, and the faithful men and women, and the devout men and women, and the truthful men and women, and the patiently persevering men and women, and the humble men and women, and the charitable men and women, and the fasting men and women, and the men and women who preserve their modesty, and the men and women who remember God much;

God has prepared for them pardon and a great reward.

(Koran S, 33:35)

It is because of the interpretations of the religious books by different *Maulanas* and religious leaders that restrictions were placed on the entry of women into Mosques. Levy says:

> According to one early tradition, Mohammad himself was not averse from allowing women to pray in his company, and declared that they could go to the mosque regularly if their husbands permitted. . . . For the most part, however, the harsh disapproval of the learned has succeeded in driving women out of the mosque, a contributing cause of the restrictions placed upon their attendance at public worship being the extreme sensitiveness of the Mohammad to the opinion of his followers, and the fear of fathers and husbands lest their women folk should by some lapse of conduct disgrace them.
>
> (131)

Raj Pruthi states in his study *Islam and Women* that,

> In the earlier days of Islam, women, it would appear, were free to visit the mosque and pray. This practice was, later, condemned, as good men found it difficult to concentrate their mind on prayers in the presence of women; by the third century of the Muslim era, the practice of letting women attend the mosque generally fell into disuse, though among some sections of Muslims it has continued to the present day.
>
> (232)

Various restrictions are imposed on women going to the mosque. Sushila Jain points out that Muslim women in Rajasthan are not allowed to go to mosques for *namaz* (prayers) except two, Ezha and Tazir, both of which are held after sunset (99). Women believe that their being barred from entering the mosque is in keeping with the rules of religion. Women are barred from entering the mosque even though in the Koran it is mentioned that the foremost duty of a Muslim is to recite the daily prayers (Namaz) without fail and the best way is to pray with the congregation or Jamat in the mosque. This rule applies only to the men because women are instructed to say the prayers in the seclusion of the house.

Certain conditions were to be fulfilled by women while visiting a mosque. These are mentioned by Levy:

> Women should not be dressed up and perfumed while visiting the mosque. In the congregation the women should not stand amidst the men but always seven steps away from them as mentioned earlier. Another restriction was regarding the recitation of prayer. The men are specifically advised to speak out every word of the prayer aloud while the women have been asked not to join in the prayers with a loud voice.
>
> (131)

The restrictions were laid because the presence of women would distract men during the prayers, and the mingling of women and men in the mosque might lead to moral lapses, or endanger the modesty and honour of women.

Also, women were to give up the Namaz during menstruation, and their state would be revealed by their absence in the mosque. Sayed Abdul Ala Maududi defends the practice of prohibiting women's entry into a mosque saying that their being in the state of menstruation, a highly personal and private matter would be revealed to people by their absence in the mosque (234).

In the poem "Grace", Dharker expresses her anguish at women not being allowed into mosques. The mosque is a place which offers peace and security. There it is possible to seek communion with God. A person can assume—

> a bright mantle
> that will fold itself around you.
> God the compassionate, the Merciful.

An old man from whom the narrator would expect words of learning, accuses her harshly of making the Masjid impure by coming inside, hinting at the state of menstruation. Without looking at her as he is a pious Muslim, he spits out his words with contempt:

A woman comes
with her eyes concealed.
She trails the month behind her.
We are defiled.

The woman burns in the 'drought' the 'blazing eye of faith' brings about. The image of the blazing eye represents the severe and stern aspect of religion, the drought representing the empty dryness of humiliation that contempt brings about. She resents the conservative attitude and comments with irony on the grounds for considering women impure during menstruation. It is deeply ironical to her that people do not realize that the clots of blood for which women are considered impure are the clots of blood from which God creates man.

God the compassionate, the Merciful,
created man from clots of blood.

The irony in the poem is enhanced by the fact that a woman is humiliated with contempt in the abode of God who is Compassionate and Merciful. The woman reassures herself uttering the words "Allah-u-Akbar"—God is great. She also utters with great irony the word-"Bismillah"-which marks the start of something in the name of God. She uses the word ironically to refer to the creation of the foetus in the womb.

Only the holy words bring about "A clearing of the heart".

In another poem, "Prayer" also Imtiaz expresses resentment at women being denied entry into a mosque. The poetess describes the scene outside a place of worship (perhaps a mosque) where a large number of sandals lie piled outside. The owners' footmarks are imprinted on the soles, the thongs are ragged, mended many times. The narrator, standing outside, barred entry within, feels curious about the prayers inside and asks "What prayer are they whispering?"

She guesses that the prayers voice the hopes of the poor needy people inside. Standing outside, to her the shoes against the walls of the mosque become a symbol of "a thousand prayers/Washing against the walls of God." Outside the mosque, she wonders again: "What are they whispering?"

The contrasting pronouns *you* standing for anyone, including the poetess, the *they* standing for the men praying inside, emphasize the segregation the narrator feels standing outside the mosque. Her quiet resentment at being unable to enter the mosque is expressed through the repeated question, "What prayer are they whispering?"

In these poems, Imtiaz Dharker expresses with a pervasive irony her resentment against the discrimination with which women are treated in the male-dominated Muslim society, and the damaging effects on their psyche of the social norms that are observed with continued severity. They carry an underlying oblique hope that the lot of women in society will change in future times.

References

Dharker, Imtiaz. *Purdah*. Delhi: Oxford University Press, (1989).

Jain, Sushila. *Muslims and Modernization*. Jaipur: Rawat Publications, 1986.

Levy, R. *The Social Structure of Islam*. Cambridge: Cambridge University Press, 1957.

Maududi, Sayed Abdul Ala. *Purdah*. New Delhi: Markari Maktaba Islam, 1988.

Pruthi, Raj and B.R. Sharma. (Eds.) *Islam and Women*. New Delhi: Anmol Publications Pvt. Ltd., (1995).

Roy, Shibani. *Status of Muslim Women in North India*. New Delhi: B.R. Publishing Corporation, 1979.

27

Feminist Drama: The Politics of the Self: Churchill and Keatley

Jasbir Jain

Waiting for someone to pick me up
Waiting for someone to hold me. . .
Waiting to be somebody.
Waiting to wear make-up
Waiting for my pimples to go away . . .
Waiting for my children to come home from school
Waiting for them to grow up, to leave home
Waiting to be myself
Waiting for excitement
Waiting for my flesh to sag
Waiting for the pain to go away
Waiting for the struggle to end
Waiting for release

The above lines from Faith Wilding's play *Waiting* (1972) express an average woman's life where she is always at the receiving end and the conventions of polite behaviour teach her to be patient, withdrawn and cultivate the habit of not drawing attention to herself, where the time never comes to be just one's ownself but one inhabits roles. Others have control over the female life either through dependence or through power. The history of the theatre projects a varied tale. While Aristotle condemned women (along with slaves) to subordinate positions, Greek drama projects powerful heroines through the figures of Medea and Antigone. And though Shakespearian tragedy gives women secondary roles, Shakespearian comedy projects them as strong, intelligent women. Later writers like Ibsen and Shaw were to adopt strongly pro-feminist stances. Yet even when they attacked the inequalities and exposed the double standards, they did not question the concept of femininity. Women were still dominantly viewed as the fulfillers of the male desire, as the personification of their dreams even when they pursued men as in *Man and Superman*. The acknowledgment of a woman's instinct for survival and the presence of the Life Force in her did not subtract from her role as a woman, the appendage of man. Women had to don a mask—it could be of masculinity (through disguise), of falsity (through pretence), or of seductive roles (as a voluptuous temptress).

Feminist theatre is a recent phenomenon and its objectives are overtly political. The tradition of playwrighting where women are concerned is a broken and discontinuous one. In English literature, it was only with the reopening of the theatres in 1660 that women actresses were allowed the stage. And it is at this time that female playwrights emerged. (Remember that Virginia Woolf in a *A Room of One's Own* weaves a narrative around Shakespeare's sister and the difficulties she would have experienced if she had turned to playwrighting). Paddy Lyons and Fidelis Morgan have recently brought out a collection of plays, *Female Playwrights of the Restoration: Five Comedies* (1991). The editors in their Introduction to the volume point out that, "Women first gained significant access to the English stage as theatre-managers, as performers and as playwrights during the half-century following the Restoration of the monarchy in 1660" (vii). During the period 1660-1710 mere that fifty plays in print were credited to women (xi) several more may have been written or performed.

Playwrighting for women became possible because social inequalities were not so marked in the workplace. It was accepted for "widows and unmarried daughters to run businesses independently;" and "female shopkeepers and tradespeople, bakers and printers were taken for granted" (ix). It was only with the rise of industrialization which provided increaded leisure that gender discrimination and class inequality became more marked.

The majority of the women playwrights of the seventeenth and early eighteenth century were those who came from theatrical families or were actresses themselves. Some, who belonged to aristocratic families, wrote for private performances at home or at Court. But the fact that the work of many of these women has now to be retrieved from the past is itself a comment on literary history and the formation of the canon.[1]

In turning to the theatre, women violate the convention of being invisible. Michelene Wandor in *Carry On, Understudies* and Lynda Hart in *Making a Spectacle* stress this aspect of women's plays. Wandor views the playwright as a person in control and Hart emphasizes the public nature of the theatrical act which renders the women playwright "anomalistic" and "deviant" for she becomes visible (Hart 2). The theatre is more than a space; it is *theatron*, a plaçe of viewing which renders the invisible visible. The theatre is also an heterotopia as Foucault has defined it in his essay "Of Other Spaces". The term is the opposite of utopia which is 'nowhere'. Heterotopia is a counter-site like a resting place, a sanatorium, a prison or a theatre. It is a counter-site where "all the other real sites that can be fond within a culture are simultaneously represented, contested and inverted" and where a juxtaposition of the otherwise incompatible can take place (Foucault 24-25).

Space is not merely the backdrop, the stage or the set. It is also an environment created by the presence of the actors in Chaikin's world, created by the interrelationships between characters and defined both through inclusion and exclusion. It is the performing space, "the immediate physical circumstance in which it is embedded" (Beckerman 18). And it is also body language, for the body occupies space and through the language of gesture, approach, sight and touch defines private space, its preservation, defence or violation (See Julius Fast, *Body Language*). When private space is threatened, violence or aggression ensue for when you don't get off somebody's toe then resentment and rebellion will take place (Jain 92). Social space is directly connected with the control over the body and its sexuality. In fact, the issues problematised in the plays are related to marriage and the task of bearing children. Bodily movements enact rape scenes or scenes of sexual surrender.

Caryl Churchill's *Top Girls* (1983) and Charlotte Keatley's *My Mother Said I Never Should* (1987) are plays with an all women cast. Men, though present in the stories, are absent from the stage. They occupy emotional space but not physical space. At the very outset there is a defining of space, a creation of a feminist world. Keatley deliberately kept the men offstage to provide a space for the women to interact among themselves, "to show the way women use language, silence and subtext when alone together" (Keatley lxxi); Churchill apparently does it for the purposes of sharing, for as Adrienne Rich has pointed out that unless women are prepared to share their "private and sometimes painful personal experience" it may not be possible to create a "collective description" of what is truly a woman's world (Rich 16). In both plays women from different generations and backgrounds meet together to share and to interact but with two major differences. Keatley's characters in the child-scenes are child characters and represent the same lineage whereas Churchill's characters represent several centuries, from the ninth to the present and have altogether different backgrounds.

The moment women are placed centre-stage they begin to interact and introspect, to analyze and to criticize; they cease to look at themselves through the male gaze, instead they begin to problematize their conflicts and the involuntary processes of their bodies. By defining space in female terms, women are transformed from objects into subjects and their passive acceptance of gendered roles is turned into an analysis of socially imposed codes of behaviour.

Plays by women need not be feminist, just as plays about women are not always so. But plays which concern themselves with women as subjects and explore their emotional realities acquire a feminist perspective. The sixties and the seventies witnessed the rise of women's theatre groups and collectives and a consciousness about women's roles.[2] This was the beginning of a feminist theatre with, as already stated, overtly political aims. Women through exploring and talking about their experiences opened out their role confines, created female traditions and entered areas hitherto forbidden to them. Several all-women plays were also written. Megan Terry's *Calm Down, Mother* (1965) was a transformation exercise for women and hailed by Helene Keyssar as the first real feminist play, while her later *Babes in the Bighouse* (1974) was about women prisoners and closed spaces where violence became a natural inhabitant. Eve Merriam's *Out of Our Fathers' House* (1975) was a projection of the struggles of exceptional women, while Wendy Wasserstein's *Uncommon Women and Others* (1977) examined the role conflicts in a lighter vein. Maria Irene Fornes's *Fefu and Her Friends* (1977) is located in the thirties and is a powerful statement about the violence implicit in heterosexual relationships; it is as Schuler has pointed out "impossible to ignore that explicit critique of patriarchy" (226) present in the play. Marsha Norman's *'night , Mother*, coming out the same year as *Top Girls* (1983), is a tense kitchen drama about a mother and a daughter with the daughter at the end committing suicide behind a locked door.

Plays with an all-women cast make a specific statement even before they put this female space to different and individual use. They discard supportive roles for women and provide them with the freedom to relate directly to each other rather than through sons and husbands, "Language, space and the body are loci for the woman playwright to dramatically challenge the images of women determined in dominant discourse" (Hart 13), Memory, history, the past are evoked for different reasons. Time too becomes an important factor, often being projected non-chronologically.

Both *Top Girls* and *My Mother* create hypothetical situations which are historically not possible but are rendered so spatially and proceed to become emotional questionings. Both are 3-act plays but while Churchill after an initial juxtaposition of the past and the present moves on, Keatley keeps on coming back to the childhood scene which is a conjunction of 1905, 1941, 1961 and 1979.

Top Girls in the first act evokes the past, somewhat like Eve Merriam's *Out of Our Fathers' House* where six women are presented together in a "hypothetical conversation". They act out both for themselves and each other the stories of their lives (Merriam 508). It is a journey into selfhood, and at each step they need reassurance from their own selves. They belong to the 18th, 19th and 20th centuries, Caryl Churchill, however, builds on a wider canvas and the dramatic purpose of the bringing together of six women from different backgrounds and periods is very different. The first act of *Top Girls* is in the nature of a prologue where Marlene, a top executive in an employment agency is hosting a dinner for five other women, three of whom are from the pages of history, and two from the world of male imagination. Pope Joan, a ninth century Pope who achieved this through cross-gendering, Lady Nijo an emperor's concubine and later a Buddhist nun, and Isabella Bird, a nineteenth century explorer are the three 'real' women. Dull Gret, a woman from Breughel's 16th century painting and Patient Griselda from the pages of Petrarch, Boccaccio and Chaucer are the two others (Note the words 'dull" and "patient").

Each one of them—except Griselda—has in some way violated the social code as imposed upon them. Joan learnt Latin, ran away from home disguised as a boy and later became a pope. But yielding to passion, she conceives and is detected during childbirth. Male priests have fathered children, but she has never learnt to understand or live with her body, thus alienated from this most fundamental space she might own, she pays for it with death. Lady Nijo on the other hand accepts the code but renders it hollow by creating space for herself. Handed over to the Emperor as his concubine, she takes lovers to fulfill her emotional needs. Out of favour with the Emperor she takes holy orders as directed by her father, but instead of being confined in a convent, she walks the breadth and length of Japan. But she does this at the price of motherhood. Isabella Bird also has to sacrifice marriage and family life in search of adventure. Because she is a woman, she finds it difficult to accept the idea of living for herself alone and therefore occupies herself with good causes.

As contrasted with these women from real life, who have individually made space for themselves, questioned patriarchal structures like religion, ownership, love and motherhood, the two women from the world of imagination are limited in their projections. Griselda's life reads like a fairytale—a peasant woman married into the aristocracy, and children whom she had given up for dead restored to her later. The price of her marriage is unquestioning obedience to her husband's command which is first the taking away of her son and her daughter and later being turned out of her house. Griselda does not question her husband's right over her, nor does she resist his orders. Her case, like Nijo's, is one where motherhood has been reduced to an "institution" under male control (Rich 13-14). Dull Gret is also single minded like Griselda. If for Griselda it is surrender, for Gret it is anger.

These five women have got together to celebrate Marlene's success and as they share experiences they question patriarchal structures either directly like Joan and Isabelle, or obliquely like Nijo, or silently through victimization like Griselda. Travel is a major theme for Joan, Nijo and Isabelle. They travel in their different dresses, Joan in her papal robes, Nijo in her silkgowns and later her nun's habit, and Isabella in her full blue trousers and great brass spurs. (Dress also specifies space. Masculine dress does not constrain the women's private space, though, in the long run, there is no social recognition of that space.) Travel opens out new worlds and spaces. Their coming together in the first act provides "a dramatic genealogy of Marlene's historical community" (Keyssar 97).

The second act is the in-between act with 3 scenes. The first and the third are located in Marlene's office, the second in Joyce, her sister's, backyard. The office scenes have two interviews inbuilt into them, one with Jeanine and the other with Louise, Marlene's two clients; a competitive scene between Nell and Win and Marlene's interactions with Angie and with Mrs. Kidd. The themes of these two scenes are a replay of the themes introduced in Act One—Jeanine who is torn between marriage and a career, Louise who at the end of twenty years finds herself sidetracked by younger men, Nell and Win who wish to go places both literally and figuratively but Marlene has occupied the place at the top and Mrs. Kidd who has come to plead for her husband who has been superseded by Marlene. Mrs. Kidd tells Marlene:

> "What's it going to do to him working for a woman? I think if it was a man he'd get over it as something normal. . . . . It's me that bears the brunt. . . . . I put him first every inch of the way. . . . . It had crossed my mind if you were unavailable after all for some reason, he would be the natural second choice I think, don't you?"
>
> (58-59)

In her view Marlene is abnormal in her determination to be at the top and she'll end up lonely and miserable.

The backdrop of the office room is confined and provides limited space where competition and aggression and violation of territorial rights go hand in hand. The middle scene sandwiched between these two office scenes is in a backyard in a "shelter made of junk" by children. It is a hiding place, away from the taboos and restrictions of the adult world. Kit and Angie talk about running away from home, they talk about travel, about the reality of their menstrual blood which flows from hidden spaces and their love-hate relationship to the adult world. Later Kit seeks shelter from rain within the precincts of her friend's house while Angie herself is left outside with a feeling of rejection.

The third act moves backwards in time. It takes place a year earlier than the second act. It is a confrontation scene between Marlene and her sister Joyce. They open out their past, the

Space and Time in My Mother Said

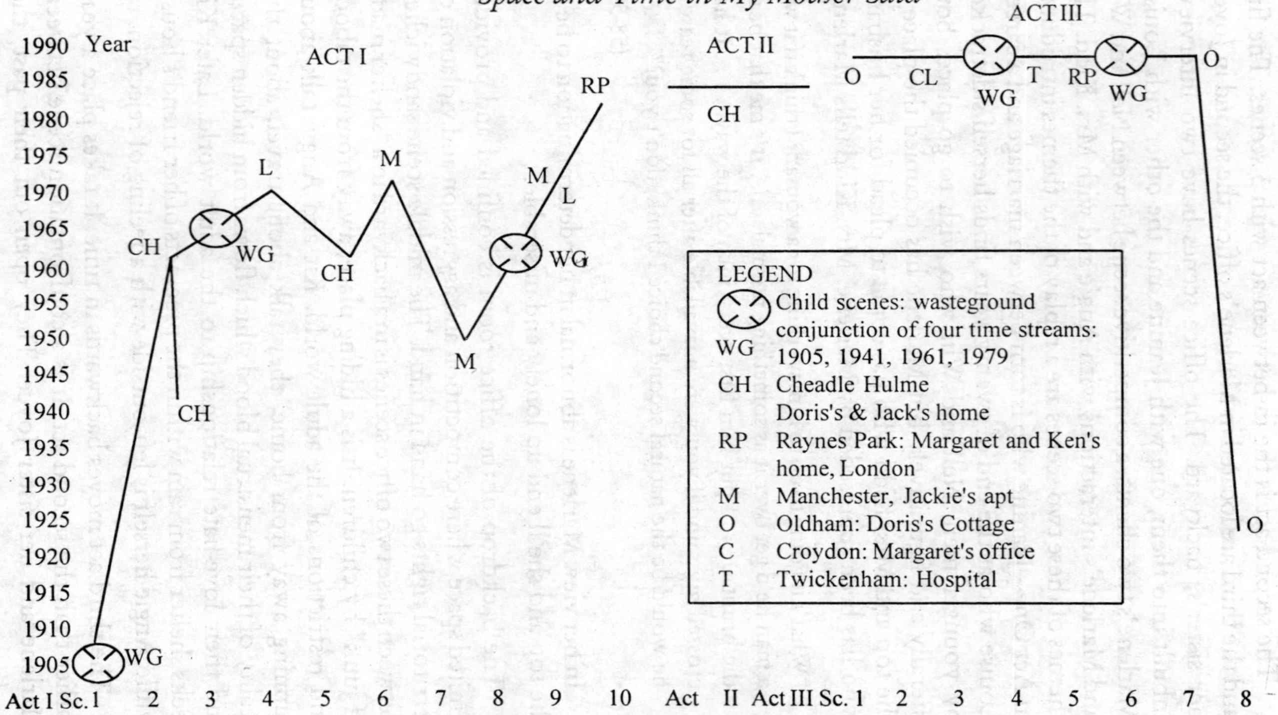

suppressed, sibling rivalry, Marlene's need to escape from her background, Joyce's support, the birth of Marlene's daughter Angie, and her adoption by Joyce, Joyce's miscarriage, and her separation from her husband Frank. Women sacrifice their motherhood for a career; but at times they also have to sacrifice their marriage for their motherhood. Joyce is denied space within her marriage while Marlene is aware that men want her to turn into "the little woman" (83) which she is not prepared to do. In all this it is Angie who feels confused and dispossessed.

Keatley's play is also a three-act play with the first act having ten scenes and moving between 1905 and 1979. The second act is one uninterrupted scene located in 1982, and the third act is placed in 1987 diving back, towards the end, to 1923. There are five child-scenes spread over the play-Act I sc. 1, sc. 3 and sc. 8, Act III sc.3 and sc.6 which act like a conjunction of events, like a voice from the past, like an abandonment of the chronological process. The movement of the play can be seen from the graph. The conjunction scene is shown as a circle with four different time streams flowing together.

Covering four generations, it covers several sets of relationships. Space is used very consciously, and scene shifts are indicated not by sets but with the help of lights as Keatley has stated in her "Introduction" to the Methuen edition of her play. her stage directions specifically mention "no sofas" primarily because it is so easy to slip into comfortable positions once the sofas are there. It is so important to render the women vulnerable, to make them appear "awkward" or uncomfortable" (xxviii). Interestingly enough, it was also a conscious decision not to locate any of the scenes in a kitchen which is considered domestic space; instead the locales are houses, living rooms, gardens, backyards, a hospital room and Margaret's office, places which are gender-neutral or strongly affected by male environment. The recurring child scenes where Doris aged 5, Margaret and Jackie both aged 9, and Rosie aged 8 meet are located in a wasteground, "an uncompromisingly real place" (Keatley iv), beyond the reach of adults and beyond male vision. The wasteground is unpatterned and uncontrolled, closer to nature and reflective of the unconscious; it goes to show that girls are not "born good" and that little girls are not made of sugar and spice and all things nice. They experience rivalry and hatred and harbour murderous intentions, eager to get rid of the goodness of the female tradition.

The five child scenes are played by adult characters dressed up in childhood clothes emphasizing the use of body language. This also underlines the continuity of the unconscious well into adult life. Their attitudes are an indication of the direction their adult lives will take. The child scenes introduce the main themes of the play—"sex, death, gender, courtship, destiny and loneliness" (liv), they also contrast with the world of masks, lies and fibs of the adult world.

Keatley views her play as structured along emotional chronology—the past (Act I), the present (Act II) and the future (Act III). It is possible to view the structure somewhat differently—anxieties of growing up (Act I) widowhood and loss (Act II) loneliness, separation and death (Act III). The lives of the women are narratives of female growth and loss; the men—Jack, Ken, Graham, Simon—remain outside, mowing the lawn, honking the horn, or present at the death bed. Yet the choices women face are centred around men—marriage, family, motherhood. Doris gives up working when she gets married, Margaret decides not to have children because she wants to work. When she wants to better her qualifications, her marriage breaks up. Jackie goes ahead and has a child without marriage, but finding it difficult to cope with the child single-handedly passes her on to her mother. Margaret who has never acknowledged her body dies of stomach cancer and Jackie who takes to art, finds herself trapped in masculine roles and her grandfather's inheritance while Doris who had given her all in marriage ends up with a feeling of having been betrayed. Even the piano she had bought with her own earning is bequeathed to her by her dead husband. Life is a game of solitaire, but one doesn't find the solution to it all by oneself. There are no solutions. There is no space for meeting the conflicting claims.

The central act, Act II, is in many ways a very stark act. The house with its sense of closure, the furniture covered with sheets, the presence of the past in this house of death—they are indicative of Doris's unfulfilled sexuality and Jackie's lost female inheritance which bypasses her to be given to Rosie.

Space is used yet in another way. Suky, the doll which resurfaces as a comforter for three generations is mutilated, rejected, discarded and hidden in dustbins and urns. The background song "Suky Take It Off Again" has sexual implications, the rejection of the doll is the rejection of roles which may appear to be soft. Another song "All You Need is Love" a song escapist in intention contrasts with real life choices where the accent is on facing reality, the hard, cruel choices, and playing solitaire by oneself. Keatley uses the earth as a concrete sense of space:

> Earth is the base element of the play. I think the stage floor the key to the design—grass—a worn rug, a stone backyard. It is only when characters touch earth that they make contact with their true feelings and powers. All child scenes take place on bare earth. On her birthday, Rosie buries Margaret's doll in the soil. When Doris and Margaret finally kneel together with their hands in the soil, planting geranium seedlings, they speak their real feelings. There are key moments of contact with the earth throughout the play.
>
> (xxviii-ix)

Standing barefeet is a literal enactment of "earthing" one self (xxix). Characters in both the plays stress the act of running or walking barefoot whether it be Nijo or Patient Griselda.

Both Churchill and Keatley use an all-women cast to problematize the gender issues, and to project the realistic aspirations of women. Through the use of space, through juxtapositions, closing-ins and opening-outs they also project a need for a new understanding of space, a shifting and loosening of boundaries, of creating more space and moving out of territorial claims. In fact their use of space challenges the very structures of 'reality' that have kept women behind scenes (Hart 2). They move away from naturalistic structures and spaces towards magic and fantasy, mixing history and fiction, in order to fathom the unconscious and realize a woman's self.

Notes

1. Lyons and Morgan write, "Coming from the past, the female playwrights of the Restoration challenge bias from another direction, from history that has been overlooked. From these writers' biographies it is plain, the plays included in this volume were every bit as successful as those by male playwrights of their time" (vii).
2. Amongst the British women writers of the postwar period, Shelagh Delaney's *A Taste of Honey* (1958) broke fresh ground both where the experimental dialogues were concerned and in its focus on mother-dauther relationship. This play about a young adolescent woman is also about the junction between a child-life and an adult-life. Ann Jellicoe's *The Sport of My Mad Mother* produced the same year (1958) is also a play about birth and rejection. But the consciousness of the feminist movement is still not upon them.

References

Beckerman, Bernard. *Theatrical Presentation*. New York and London: Routledge, 1990.

Carlson, Susan L. "Comic Textures and Female Communities 1937 and 1977: Clare Boothe, and Wendy Wasserstein", *Modern American Drama: The Female Canon* ed. June Schulter. Cranbury N.J.: Associated University Press, 1990.

Chaikin, Joseph. *The Presence of An Actor*. New York: Atheneum, 1972.

Churchill, Caryl. *Top Girls*, London: Methuen (1982), 1994.

Delaney, Shelagh, *A Taste of Honey*, London: Methuen, 1959.

Fast, Julius, *Body Language*, London: Pan Book, 1971.

Fornes, Maria Irene. *Fefu and Her Friends, Word Plays.* New York: Performing Arts Journal, 1980.

Foucault, Michel, "Texts/Contexts: Of Other Spaces", *Diacritics*, Spring, 1986, pp. 22-27.

Hart, Lynda. *Making a Spectacle: Feminist Essays on Contemporary Women's Theatre.* Ann Arbor: The University of Michigan Press, 1989.

Jain, Jasbir. "A Meeting with Maria Irene Fornes", *Indian Journal of American Studies*, Vol. 22 No. 1 Winter 1992.

Jellicoe, Ann. *The Sport of My Mad Mother*. London: Faber, 1985.

Keatley, Charlotte. *My Mother Said I Never Should*, London: Methuen Student Edition, (1994), 1995.

Keyssar, Helene. *Feminist Theatre.* New York: Grove Press (1984), 1985.

Lyons, Paddy and Morgan, Fidelis, Ed., *Female Playwrights of the Restoration: Five Comedies.* London: J.M. Dent and Sons 1991.

Merriam, Eve. *Out of Our Fathers' House, The New Women's Theatre* Ed. Honour Moore. New York: Vintage Books, 1977.

Norman, Marsha. *'night, Mother*. London: Faber and Faber 1984.

Rich, Adrienne. *Of Woman Born: Motherhood as Experience and Institution*. New York: Norton, 1976.

Schuler, Catherine A. "Gender Perspective and Violence in the Plays of Maria Irene Fornes and Sam Shepard", *Modern American Drama: The Female Canon* Ed. June Schluter. Cranbury N.J.: Associated University Presses 1990.

Terry, Megan. *Calm Down, Mother*. Indianapolis: Bobbs-Merrill, 1966.

—, Babes in the Bighouse. Acting Edition, Nebraska: Omaha Magic Theatre, 1974.

Wasserstein, Wendy. *Uncommon Women and Others.* New York: Avon Books, 1978.

28

Metaphor of 'Space': Charlotte Keatley's Play *My Mother Said I Never Should*

Tanuja Mathur

Women playwrights, as compared with women novelists, have not had the space and the expression they needed. Women writers were successful in projecting female experiences despite the nineteenth century's closed attitudes towards sexuality and passion. Fiction writing need not be a collaborative effort, even when it depended on authenticity of experience. Play writing being more collaborative was marginalised.

During the seventeenth and eighteenth centuries, women also wrote plays and some of them were very successful. But, it is only since the 1960's that women have been visibly writing plays, which are being staged in different parts of the world. Dale Spender, in her article, "A Vindication of the Writing Women" feels that Joanne Baillie was one "whose achievement should have permanently laid to rest the myth that women could not be dramatists" (6). Charlotte Keatley too, in the late twentieth century, has established herself as a dramatist through her play *My Mother Said I Never Should*, predominantly a play about the life and experiences of women. In her Commentary to the play in Methuen Students' Edition, Keatley says, "When dividing the play, I consciously split the century into the four ages which I felt marked the greatest, most dramatic changes in women's lives. Doris gave all her time to family. . . . Both Margaret and Jackie's generation try to juggle time between work and home. Margaret gives the greater share to home, and although exhausted and finally ill, she wears the mantle of virtuous suffering which women have worn on stage and in life for centuries. Jackie shifts the balance of her time towards her own life and career" (Keatley xxxix).

All the four characters portrayed in the play—Doris, Margaret, Jackie and Rosie—are women. The playwright explains the reasons why she eliminated all the male characters, "In this play, it is women who represent us all, and the massive social changes of the twentieth century. I wanted to show how hugely dramatic the 'ordinary' lives of women have been" (Keatley xxii). In order to highlight this fact Keatley's handling of plot, structure and time are very significant.

The playwright makes use of 'space' at multiple levels. Space in the literal sense of the physical is much talked about. Space is also used as a metaphor in the play. It becomes mental or psychological and emotional too. Language also serves to enrich this idea of space. It is the female language which Charlotte is emphasizing here. The playwright depicts the lack of physical space for the characters in the play. Margaret as well as Jackie create a space for themselves under the piano. This finds a very obvious expression in the description by the playwright where Margaret crouches underneath the baby piano, "hidden from Doris by a pile of bedding also under the piano"(8). There is a repeated reference to the pile of bedding which is folded under the piano. Later in the same scene, Margaret exits taking the bedding with her and Jackie takes her place under the piano.

> Doris: Jackie? (peers under the piano) Jackie! What are you doing under the piano?
>
> Jackie: Seeing what it's like. Mummy says you used to put her bed under the piano here in the Second World War.

And listen to the wireless. . .

(13)

Keatley, through this conversation, is very obviously bringing out the fact that women, through the successive generations have never found a free space to move or even to reside comfortably.

There are ample references to being left alone in the play. Loneliness has a very positive meaning. It is a kind of mental or psychological space which the women in the play need to build for themselves. When left alone, Margaret talks to the doll 'Suky', underneath the piano where she has made a bed for herself, she cuddles and caresses the doll. This is the emotional space which she is creating for herself. She holds the doll tight when she sleeps. The doll becomes a symbolic link for the emotional bond which is lacking between Doris the mother and the daughter. By bathing and nursing the doll, Margaret tries to give vent to her emotional feelings. Doris always insisted on being addressed as 'Mother', never as 'Mummy'.

Later, Jackie plays with Margaret's doll when she lives with her grandmother, Doris. Jackie says, "And your doll. It's like a real baby, its got real curled up toes and fingers. I was practising. I bathed it and put it to sleep, and it shut its eyes." She is creating space for herself by playing with the doll, as Margaret was absent but Margaret understands it otherwise. She feels that Jackie has broken the doll.

Margaret: No! (Gets up)
Jackie: I didn't break her. I didn't break the doll!

(23)

In scene ten of the First Act, Rosie buries the doll 'Suky' because she feels she doesn't need dolls or her 'Mum' any more.

Rosie: It's my birthday today and it's all gone wrong already. I'm going to bury you, Suky. Eight is too old for dolls. . . I'd have buried you ages and ages ago, Suky, if you hadn't been Mum's. I couldn't care less now if Mum sees me doing this.

(38)

She digs a hole in the earth of a garden urn and pushes the doll into it, and says, "shut up crying. There, see, I'm putting you in this urn. People get buried in urns (covering the doll over with earth)" (39). The urn in itself is an enclosure. The burial of the doll is symbolic. It seems that she doesn't need dolls any more as she is grown up. The doll was a kind of an emotional link, now she feels that it is not required. At the end of the scene we see Jackie taking out the doll again. The description runs thus:, "She sees the old spoon and scattered earth, then goes to the cherry tree in its tub, digs out the doll which Rosie buried, brushes it down. . . she raises the doll to her cheek. . ." (43). She takes out the doll because that is the bond between her mother and herself. Her mother played with the same doll. It holds a lot of meaning for her.

There are references to the closed spaces in the play. Inside these women find a space where they can talk on issues relating to themselves—issues which are feminine and therefore hidden from the outside or men's world. These female physical experiences have been dealt with very boldly by the playwright. There is a recurrent conversation about the physical experiences and natural conditions which these women go through. Margaret talks to her daughter, Jackie, on the use of pills by her, hinting at contraceptives. Reading of Jackie's personal diary by Margaret is something which Jackie doesn't like. Diary, is private space where Jackie could keep her personal experiences hidden from others. Diary was used by her to explore and understand many aspects of her personal life. Reading of the diary by Margaret, her mother, is a violation of the space which Jackie has created for herself.

Doris advises Margaret to take 'iron tablets'. This brings forth the fact that she has had a miscarriage and therefore needs tablets to regain the loss of blood or anemia. Issues like child-birth. disposable nappies, sanitary towels, menstruation and menopause are referred to repeatedly. These are ample proofs of the female space which is being created through language. Men are nowhere present here, although there are references to fathers and husbands all the time. There is the sound of a horn of Ken's car, revealing his arrival, mowing of the lawn by Jack, This reveals the fact of his being present offstage. Their presence, it seems, is purposely removed. Keatley has made this point clear and admitted, "I kept men offstage in order to show the way women use language, silence and subtext when alone together" (Commentary 1xxi). There are references to open spaces. The garden or the lawn at the back of Doris and Jack's house where Doris arranges a picnic tea for Margaret's arrival is meaningful. Keatley says, "Outdoors is a potentially freer space for women than that of domestic rooms. . ." (xxviii).

Keatley, in this play, handles the female use of time alongwith space very effectively. In scene seven of the First Act, space and time adjustments go hand in hand. In order to dramatize women's experiences there is the use of non-linear time. Thus a different emotional idea of time from men is highlighted here. Margaret and Doris work while they talk about marriage and children, they are folding, washing, packing up. Many actions, are performed here simultaneously, alongwith the conversation. Keatley explains, "I think the way I use time to structure the play—juxtaposing different times to create urgency and dramatic tension—comes from my own experience of time in everyday life" (xxxv).

Another thing which finds expression in the play is the way this use of mental space is thwarted by the arrival of a man, offstage. The playwright here is probably hinting towards the fact, that it is very difficult for women to ask for personal time and space for their own needs. Traffic noise outside Margaret's office and the blaring red transistor inside Jackie's flat add to the oppressive lack of personal space. The sounds in the play—lawn mower, traffic, an ice-cream van, Ken's car horn, two male radio announcements and four male popular songs seem to represent the offstage world of men, intruding upon the space created by these women characters. So, although men do not figure "in" the play but they are "around" it.

Lorna Sage, in her article, "The Available Space" says, "The place is a very partial account of some women writers. . . from two rather different points of view—first, from the now familiar angle of exclusion and secondly, in relation to notions of writing (as possibly) free space" (15). Keatley has made use of both these points of view in her play, by excluding men and including women who try to make a free space for themselves, although they do not fully succeed in this. The playwright emphasizes the denial of personal time and space for women in the play.

Women's writing was criticized by many critics. Elaine Showalter feels that "rather than protesting against such criticism, women writers reinforced it by playing down the effort behind their writing, and trying to make their work appear as the spontaneous overflow of their womanly emotions" (83). This doesn't hold true of Charlotte Keatley in her play *My Mother Said I Never Should*. She is, here, primarily defining the practical physical experiences which women in their lives have been facing through out the successive generations the world over. This is a representation of reality and poses the recurring nature of the main problem which four generations of women have not been able to solve satisfactorily. When Rosie solves the solitaire game she feels that she does it all by herself—but in reality it is possible because of the support other women have provided and the atmosphere which they have created for her. She has a bit of each one of them in her.

References

Keatley, Charlotte. *My Mother Said I Never Should*. Methuen Students' Edition, 1995.

Sage, Lorna. "The Available Space', *Women's Writing* ed. Lorna

Montieth. Harvester Press. 1986.

Showalter, Elaine. "The Double Critical Standard and the Feminine Novel" in *A Literature of their Own: British Women Novelists from Bronte to Lessing*. Princeton N.J., 1977.

Spender, Dale. *Living by the Pen: Early British Women Writers*. New York: Teachers College Press, 1992.

29

Exploring Female Bonds: Keatley's *My Mother Said I Never Should*

Fatima Sugarwala

Keatley's young career is rooted in poetry and drama. Her first dramatic production was a student production of *Underneath the Arudale*, a play about six characters trapped in a nuclear bunker beneath the city shopping mall centred around a West Indian woman's view of England. Another of her plays, *The Iron Serpent*, is a musical which takes up for its subject the opening of the first railway between Liverpool and Manchester in 1820. The play is symbolic of the Industrial Revolution and the new social order shown through three generations. Her 1985 play *My Mother said I Never* should is a play about four generations with an all-women cast.

It is one of the finest plays reflecting upon the mother-daughter relationship. It is believed that Shakespeare's plays encompass all human experience, but even he has not written a play on mother-daughter relationship. Keatley remarks, "I saw this relationship as a lens through which to look at huge themes which concern all people." My endeavor will be to focus upon several aspects of the play such as the thematic value of the mother-daughter relationship, the similarities and the changes in the four generations. It would be necessary to question whether this is a feminist play or not. I shall like to lay emphasis on the technique and dwell on the role of the men and the significance of the child scenes.

The play doesn't have a consistent plot, but it develops in flashes and images. There is no historical chronology, but instead there is "emotional chronology" (Notes xiii) as Keatley points out. Childhood is important. In our formative years we are fed with bits and pieces of emotional and factual information. We do not store images in a chronological order but according to their sentimental significance. In Coleridge's theory of Esemplastic imagination and Sigmund Freud's psychoanalytic theory, the human mind is said to be operating on two levels of consciousness, the 'Id' and the 'Ego'. The Ego represents the conscious level of behaviour while the Id is where the repressed and frustrated emotions are stored. Keatley has focused on the child scenes to probe into the inner recesses of her characters. The opening scene is a child scene. Four girls enter simultaneously. By showing the characters first as children the playwright stresses upon their having equal potential before they are separated with different status into generations of mothers and daughters The play is a jigsaw puzzle of time and actions, the pace related to different times and places.

The adult scene begins in 1940 when Doris is forty and her daughter Margaret is nine. The time is Christmas during the world war. The unconscious fear of air raids and the rising crescendo of the sirens, the horror and insecurity of war and its influence on the child Margaret is highlighted. The dramatist's focus is on the mother-daughter relationship. Like any other child Margaret is curious and full of questions. Her questions proclaim her insecurity, they are pertinent and baffling; Doris cannot reply to them. Margaret asks Doris, "Where will you and father sleep?" When Doris replies "In the hall", Margaret's response is, "Gillian's mother and father sleep in one bed not two" (I. ii. 11). Doris orders her to sleep, thus repressing her curiosity and questions. The psychological impact of her mother's attitude is seen in Margaret's behaviour with her doll Suky. She lays Suky aside and says, "No, I won't hold you, you ought to go to sleep now, by yourself, You don't need your mummy to kiss you. You're eight years old" (I. ii. 13). In the wake of war, death and destruction, what Margaret needs is warmth, love and understanding, but Doris is too involved in her struggle for existence, inhibitions and social taboos to establish a rapport with her daughter. The title *My Mother Said I Never Should* is highly symbolic and significant. It reflects the common attitude adopted by most mothers. The don'ts they prescribe, not to do this or that and this has an adverse effect. Little Margaret asks, "Will we win the war?" Doris answers authoritatively, "Not, if you don't sleep" (I. ii. 12) Keatley stresses the impact of this negative approach on the child's mind. Also women's lives are always hedged in by rules; they are expected to live within confines of various kinds.

Relationships are repeated and these repetitions emphasize the differences. For instance, Jackie is as curious as Margaret, but Doris who finds time for her, had displayed no patience with her own daughter Margaret. And despite the fact that she is hedged in by domesticity, she finds fault with Margaret for having taken up a tempting job, which she feels is responsible for Margaret's miscarriage. Being insiders and having gone through similar experiences does not make women sympathetic towards each other. They repeat the same advice and the same admonishments. Margaret, like her mother before her, is critical of Jackie's behaviour. She reprimands her for sleeping with her boyfriend. There is, however, a slight change. Margaret's concern is for Jackie's education which she feels should be attended to.

Later on in the play, Jackie conceives and has a daughter. She tries to combine the two—her career and her motherhood. But unable to cope with the stress of single parenthood she agrees to allow Margaret to bring her up. All women—whether married or not—pass through similar choices. Doris's problem has had a slightly different dimension. Marriage had spelt the end of her career. Her tentative entry into motherhood had been because of Jack's desire for a son. Margaret's success has been marginal. She has a job—of a middling kind, an office job, but she also pays for it with a miscarriage. Jackie has had a relationship with a married man and thus she is aware that she cannot hope for a family life. Her daughter thus has to be given up to Margaret. The question which Keatley asks is related to the choices which women have. They are always being asked to choose, to give up something in order to have something else. It doesn't happen with men. Women's decisions are governed like most other decisions—by past experiences and present circumstances.

Rosie grows up and idolizes Jackie. She tells Suky that no one in the school has a sister as old as Jackie. Denied motherhood, Jackie is strangely the only mother who has a congenial relationship with her daughter. Is it because Jackie's identity as a wife and mother is absent? Jackie wants Rosie to live with her, but Margaret cannot bear losing her. Jack dies leaving all his property to Jackie, she feels responsible for all, she sees her grandfather's will as a revenge for her having escaped family responsibilities. When Margaret dies of cancer, Rosie realizes from her birth certificate that she is Jackie's child. This knowledge disrupts the mother-daughter relationship and Rosie decides to live with her grandmother.

The playwright has a profound insight into the mother-daughter relationship. There are visible and vibrant similarities and differences as they move from one generation to the other. There are two vicious games which recur through different generations. One is the questioning combat. The daughter in every generation asks questions which the mother refuses to answer, but the grandmother complies. The generation gap between mother and daughter is bridged by the grandmother. The other game is challenger. Each character attacks and defends the other in an emotional battle. "Women suppress huge battles under small fights", says Keatley, (lxx). But Rosie is too mature and logical, she detaches herself from this game. Jackie severs the chain, by breaking the biggest social taboo of a mother deserting her child. Ironically Rosie who is cut off from this relationship gets the love of three mothers, which enables her to endure the drastic shock of the identity of her parentage during her teenage.

The child scenes are knit into the thematic cycle. The child characters are played by the adults. The speech and the body language of the children is highly evocative. The child scenes explore prohibited boundaries, break barriers and express repressed emotions. Keatley presents the child scenes to delve into the unconscious of the play, that is why they take place on the 'waste ground', a place of fantasy, a world of female magic where emotions are felt, opinions are voiced and attitudes are formed, but everything evaporates into thin air after clashing against the harsh realities of life. There is still a child in everyone. Children have natural simplicity, they are candid, unbiased and not self-conscious.

According to practical psychology a child's behaviour is scrutinized to understand the adult. Each child scene sets up a major theme of the play. In the first child scene all four women enter, each dressed in accordance to her generation singing:

> My mother said I never should,
> Play with gypsies in the wood,
> If I did she would say
> Naughty girl to disobey!
>
> (I.i.5)

This is followed by another nursery rhyme "Sugar and spice and all things nice", by Doris who is just nine. No one wants to conform to this idea of being nice. Jackie suggests a game, "Let's kill our mummies" each one gets enthusiastic about killing their mummies who have endowed them with this emotional inheritance.

The second child scene reflects the fears and taboos about becoming a mother. Doris wants to play babies, Rosie warns her, "You have to get married first" (I, iv. 18). Simultaneously, in the adult scene Margaret is embarrassed by her daughter's sexual pursuit. Jackie is afraid of her future, she is struggling hard with a job and baby. The third child scene is about the betrayal of relationships. Jackie and Rosie play games about secrets, lies and promises broken. In the adult scene there is a secretive air pervading the arrival of baby Rosie. There is the hushed undercurrent argument between Margaret and Jackie about who will keep Rosie and the discussion about female bodily behaviour.

The fourth child scene plunges into the abyss and awareness of mortality. Child Jackie is more astute, she knows what adult Jackie cannot figure out. Placing the child scene beside the adult scene heightens Jackie's tragedy. She gives up her child in order to pursue her career, but when Margaret dies, she leaves all her bondages to be with Rosie. But by now the relationship has become strained. Rosie idolized Jackie as a sister, but she cannot accept her as a mother. Their relation is severed, Rosie is no longer able to trust Jackie.

The fifth scene peeps over the edge of death. While dying Margaret's mind poses all the repressed questions of her childhood, "Mother, what happens when you die?" (lll. iv, 81) Margaret dies, the questions remain unanswered. The child scenes are placed at crucial points, boldly expressing adult inhibitions, social fears and taboos. They reveal horrifying realities of life. The sexual anxieties and needs are freely expressed. The characters of the child scenes are the core material of the adults. Their ages correspond to the amount of obligation each carried.

The themes of massive social changes and the mother-daughter relationship are entwined and amalgamated in the child scenes. In every generation women face psychological pressure and emotional turmoil. The basic problems remain the same, but the manner in which each one extricates herself, reveals the changing social outlook and attitude. Women are accepted as symbols of virtues. There is so much of expectation from them that at times it becomes difficult to live up to these expectations. Those women who are not self-sacrificing meet with social criticism. Jackie's decision to give up Rosie is prudent, but selfish from the tradition set up by the people. When she gives up Rosie it doesn't mean that she does not love her baby, but having the job and caring for the baby at the same time as a single parent proved to be extremely difficult to face.

In the child play Rosie wants to experiment with sex, death and birth. She is interested in touching blood, bodies and wooden sticks while Jackie anxiously hovers around the voodoo, interested, but hesitant. Margaret is always dependent on Jackie and Doris is not quite sure what is happening around her. Margaret's death releases Jackie. The child scenes and the adult scenes shift the play back and forth recording the enormous social change.

Each woman speaks in a different speech rhythm in accordance to her generation and upbringing. The four articulations in the opening scene where each child addresses her mother as "Mam", (l. i.5) "Mother", "Mummy" and "Mum" specifies the social changes. All the children and Rosie use crisp sentences while all the adults expiate. Each character's rhythm and utterances change as they grow older. They learn to speak in cliches when they discuss sex.

Although the outward appearances, dress, style, language and approach change with time, the deep-rooted yearning to love and be loved remain unchanged. Throughout the play every woman wants her mother to listen to her and express love. The play concludes with Doris addressing her mother, the speech is typical of a daughter asking to be loved and her mother is unable to do so. John Pater in the *Sunday Times* commented that the play is about "the value of real feelings", which make life worth living.

Keatley visualizes life as an endless cycle of feminine struggle and sacrifice carried out from one generation to the other. She has portrayed both men's selfish attitude and women's endurance. When Ken walks out of Margaret's life, Doris remarks, "Your father stopped wanting me years ago" (lll. i. 70). Graham leaves Jackie without qualms, to fend for herself with the baby. There is a denial of their personhood.

Each woman tried to live up to the expectation of society, conform to social standards and comply with the idea of a woman being virtuous and good. It is a great mental stress to attain and sustain that height of expectation. But Rosie is a catalyst who does not fit into any of these roles, she opens a new vista for possible change. She wants to feel free and take life as it comes and lead a very positive existence.

Several critics have remarked that Keatley has deliberately kept men off stage to give a lopsided version of the story. Keatley in her defence states that she kept men away because, "I wanted female language, silence, humour, sexiness and violence to walk on the stage in a way which doesn't happen if men are present" (*My Mother Said I Never Should*, Notes ix). We have very often heard the phrase, "Men's World" where he dominates and dictates. Women since ages have been exploited and subdued, and have accepted docile roles. But the wave of feminism has given women a voice. The epithet "feminist" is used to condemn women who provoke public reaction or question patriarchal structures. The entire play stresses this social change and man's role in it. The male characters are not physically present, but they definitely exist and influence the life and decisions of the women. Keatley highlights the feminine dilemma. A woman plays several different roles, she fights on many fronts; she is a mother, a wife, a daughter, a sister and apart from all these social attachments, she also plays a vital role of financially supporting her family. In these days of inflation the woman works shoulder to shoulder with her man, yet when his needs are satisfied he no longer supports her. All the three men Jack, Ken and Graham leave their women in lurch. Jack dies, but leaves Doris with no financial security, Doris reproaching him says "Sixty one years of housewifery meant nothing to him". Ken wanted a wife, not a working mother and Graham enters into an extra-marital relationship with Jackie leaving her to bear the child, while he is secure within his own marriage.

By keeping men off-stage Keatley has succeeded in portraying women as they really are. A fine blending of their self-sacrificing and virtuous with the jealous, violent and sexy temperament. Keatley has made a detailed study of feminine attitudes and women's way of life. Normally in a male oriented play, the male characters are either smoking drinking, chewing gum or just idling. But one of the most distinct features of this play is that all the female characters are constantly involved in household chores, gardening, sketching, typing and even making kites for charity but never in the kitchen. Keatley wants to give a completely different space to women. Earlier women's duties were limited only to the kitchen, today she keeps herself involved in activities that she desires. Doris is a teacher, Margaret works as a secretary, Jackie is a painter and Rosie at the end of the play is busy making kites for charity.

The play problems deep into the innermost desires, resentment and suppressed anger locked up for years, but today all barriers are lowered and fresh breeze is welcomed. Keatley has successfully created an awareness about the need for love, sharing and caring and the manner in which male detachment from family problems, emotional involvement and male chauvinism may sever the delicate sensitive bonds between man and woman.

Reference

Keatley, Charlotte. *My Mother said I Never Should*. London: Methuen Student Edition, 1995.

30

Image as Meaning in Moore's Poetry

Supriya Agarwal

The literary movement that developed between about 1912 and the end of the 1920's in London had links and parallels with the extraordinary outburst of poetic activity that was taking place in America in the work of poets like William Carlos Williams, Wallace Stevens and Marianne Moore. The poets in their verse moved rapidly from late Romanticism and Decadence to Modernism. Ezra Pound and T.S. Eliot's critical evolution show their "cosmopolitanism", based as Henry James had said, on the American gift for assimilating other cultures. Eliot argued in his essay, "Tradition and the Individual Talent"(1919) that tradition was not simply inherited, it had to be earned and possessed by great moments and meanings not just of the European but of the classical and oriental civilizations (23). Thus, the poets of the time can be viewed as agents of culture and the measuring edge of language.

Marianne Moore is a crucial explorer who gave American poetry a sense of coherent endeavour towards imagism. Her one major subject was the nature of poetry and the complex relation of- reality and artifice, a subject to which she attended with careful wit and a great capacity for meditation in verse. She was born in St. Louis in 1887, like T.S. Eliot who identified her as "one of those few who have done the language some service in my lifetime"(60) and like him she became one of the important modern editors, editing the revived *Dial* from 1925 to 1929. Her early poems appeared both in *Poetry* and the London *Egoist*. Her volume, *Poems* was published without her knowledge or approval in London in 1921 and her first American volume *Observations* appeared in 1924. Her *Selected Poems* were published in 1935 with an introduction by T.S. Eliot. In 1951 her *Collected Poems* received the Pulitzer Prize for poetry and Bollingen Prize in 1953. Marianne Moore continued her literary pursuits till she passed away in 1972.

Moore's interest in poetry recalls Emily Dickinson's, although Moore was in her twenties before her forerunner's work was widely known or appreciated. Both poets worked the spaces they identified as belonging to them as women and both are known for their verbal precision and formal experiment. Like Dickinson, Moore never married and though she led a quiet life in New York, she knew many of the writers and artists of her time and pursued diligently her career as an innovative poet. There is a development in her art which reflects the social and literary movements of the period. She sought to adopt imagist methods to American conditions, her early poem *England* both celebrates and questions her own "languageless country" where letters are written "in plain American which cats and dogs can read".

At her time of growing up and early writing the Imagist poets were active in London. Though she denies that their work influenced her directly, she believed as they did in precision and impersonality of expression. Her later work is different in technique and intensity from the early poems with their precise logic of detail. Her mind, trained to accuracy is directed towards an examination of objects and scenes. Multiple levels of experience and meaning are suggested by her pattern of line endings, intricate rhymes, vocabulary and exquisitely developed syntax, and the juxtaposition of odd fact and ideas.

One of Marianne Moore's chief skills is in her management of the reader's attention, the way she surprises, creating at once fascination and uncertainty. Each line that follows takes the syntax, suspended in the line before, in an unexpected direction, so that the poem is never arrested at a statement, it evolves as a process, an evocation, as in an early poem *A Grave*(1924):

> Man looking into the sea,
> taking the view from those who have as much right to
> it as you have to it yourself,
> it is human nature to stand in the middle of a thing,
> but you cannot stand in the middle of this; the sea has
> nothing to give but a well excavated grave.

The stanza is carefully integrated through interval rhyme and a dominant image of the sea as a grave is presented. The right of the man and of the other creatures of the sea is marked as same. Through images a connection has been established between human life and nature. Man, fish, tree and birds—all are the observers of the sea which has "nothing to give but a well excavated grave". The silence of death and the activity of life both have been juxtaposed and linked with the central image of the sea. Marianne Moore proceeds from one image to another, crossing all gaps but at the same time keeping all in the mind. The images establish a relation between the external and the internal, the visible and the invisible very intricately. Accuracy of perception and clarity of expression can make the humblest and the vilest object a source of poetry and also bring home to us the purest spiritual truth in the manner of the poem *A Grave*. The poem depends on these nicely measured effects, subtle and engaging. We applaud an enjambment she draws our attention to. A curiously comparable picture is given as she describes a ship's boat on the water:

> the blades of the oars

moving together like the feet of water spiders.....
The wrinkles progress upon themselves in a phalanx
beautiful under networks of foam,
and fade breathlessly while the sea rustles in and out
the seaweed;

In this passage we find direct sense impressions and pictured comparisons. It is through images that the threefold nature of poetic experience and expression reveals itself as the accurate and intense perception of objects, the stimulation of feeling and the operation of the mind. Her imagism has a sensuous, an emotional and an intellectual source and it communicates on all three of these levels. In the poem, Moore uses perceived details but soon we find images mixing with each other. She seems to believe in the existence of a spiritual world. She illustrates and proves her convictions by careful selection of exact details to realize the particularities of an object and thus succeeds in making her presentation convincing to the reader. While discussing her poem *A Grave*, John Crowe Ransom in his essay "On Being Modern with Distinction" remarks:

> The energy of movement in this poem does not flag. If it seems to take us in too many directions, I venture to suggest that so far as I am concerned the poet is observing how life is lived as it were over the abyss, and is to be contemplated "sub specie mortalitatis", but not fearfully unless by the fearful, nor brashly except by the brash. (*Critical Essays* 104)

In modern poetry we often find richly suggestive, visual figures that appeal to an intellectual as well as a sensuous and emotional understanding. Such imagery has contributed to the difficulty and complexity that face the reader but has also contributed much that is rewarding in the subtlety and accuracy with which complex strata of experience can be rendered and examined. Unexpected as the images of the poem are, in themselves and in relation to one another, their clarity and rightness can hardly be questioned, for what they finally portray is the way the sharply alert mind of the poet assimilates and regroups through the impressions conveyed by imagery and the technique is therefore subtle and complex. By the end of the poem one realizes that it is not the ocean alone that is being described, it is an impression that is being conveyed, an impression of a life that moves on:

> and the ocean, under the pulsation of lighthouses and noise of
> bell-buoys,
> advances as usual, looking as if it were not that ocean in
> which dropped things are bound to sink
> in which if they turn and twist, it is neither with volition
> nor consciousness, ("A Grave")

Marianne Moore is extraordinarily perceptive and her words convey an ambiguity that makes them refer both to sensation and intelligence. The poem *What Are Years*? is a brilliant exercise in rhetoric where she allows herself the liberty of meditation. There is the sentiment of great glory in sheer mortality and she argues this by comparisons of life with "sea in a chasm" and with a bird who sings, "though he is a captive". There are also contradictory juxtapositions like "resolute doubt", "dumbly calling", "deafly listening". The boldness and originality of these images is characteristic of a conceit—a favorite device of the seventeenth century Metaphysical poets and their modern followers. The principle behind the conceit is that the greater the gap between the two things compared in a simile or identified in a metaphor—the greater is the imaginative leap the poet's mind achieves and the greater is the satisfaction and sharper the conviction. Many successful images are therefore paradoxical, they seem fanciful until the reader's own mind makes the leap. The little poem *What Are Years*? states or rather illustrates a paradox of mortality and eternity:

> And whence
> is courage: the unanswered question,
> the resolute doubt,
> dumbly calling, deafly listening-that
> in misfortune, even death,
> encourages others
> and in its defeat, stirs

the soul to be strong?

An effective figure of speech is both a perception of reality and a projection of imagination and provides a sudden insight into a meaningful relationship between things not often taken to be similar. The poem might be classified as descriptive where the poet goes on to describe the connection between life, death and happiness through juxtaposition of ideas and images. Besides this metaphorical structure, we notice the simplicity and unaffected rightness of the diction and then the easy, natural, exact and colloquial structure of the phrases. The poem expresses an experience which culminates for poet and reader alike in the intuitive flash at the close;

satisfaction is a lowly
thing, how pure a thing is joy.
This is mortality,
this is eternity.

Thus the poem which begins with a question "what is our innocence, what is our guilt?" ends with an answer. Many details in the poem seem to get there purely out of Marianne Moore's attempt to report and judge of a thing's intrinsic qualities, to make us feel its properties as accurately as possible. The poem is witty and playful but it also creates a profound impression. Whatever is experienced through the senses or projected by the imagination constitutes the subject of the poem. Through incongruities of structure and wording, she expresses successfully the paradoxes of existence with grace and candour. This quality of Moore's writing has been summed up aptly by Denis Donoghue in his essay "The Proper Plenitude of Fact":

> The function of a poem, when Miss Moore writes it, is to provide for distinctive energy of mind a sufficient occasion; a direction. The mind moves from its presumed rest; ranges abroad through materials congenial to its nature; comes to rest again. This is the figure the poems make; a sequence, a curve, the trajectory of a mind well aimed. (169)

The intermixture of line lengths is typical of Moore's syllabic verse, as in the poem *A Grave.* There are certain matters closely related to metering which should probably be investigated at this point. Most frequently she uses syllabic form—one of the most mechanical and restrictive of verse techniques. The length of the lines in each stanza is governed by a pre-determined number of syllables rather than stresses, metrical feet or free cadence. The visual pattern of the stanza is established by indenting the shorter lines to a pre-determined degree. For instance she may open a poem with a line which is rhythmically end stopped but unpunctuated as in *The Steeple Jack*:

Durer would have seen a reason for living
in a town like this. with eight stranded whales
to look at; with the sweet sea air coming into your house
on a fine day, from water etched
with waves as formal as the scales
on a fish.

On the surface it appears merely arbitrary to choose such a technique. But in the case of Marianne Moore it was the technique that chose the poet. The style is not only natural to her, after reading even a few of her poems, it is difficult to imagine her writing in any other way. The brilliant ease with which she deploys her measured lines often achieve dramatic effect, especially when deliberately she departs from her prescriptive norm to convey a change of mood or tone.

She does not always use rhyme, but when she does, it appears only sporadically and informally in her free verse poems but is handled in quite a distinctive way in the syllabic poems. Syllabics offer the poet a rhythmic freedom but an altogether new set of disciplines and problems to resolve. The syllabics lend a precision and impose a logic on each line, stanza and poem. The figurative language in her poems, functions as a controlling similitude, like an after thought which reinforces its substantial concern. The elegance of Miss Moore's style suggests manner rather than tone, for the manner remains constant while the tone, images and moods vary. In an interview to Howard Nemerov published in *Contemporary American Poetry*, she suggested that for her, the stanza rather than the line was the poetic unit (16). One of her admirers, Randall Jarrell, described her in an essay:

> She not only can but must, make poetry out of everything and anything, she is like Midas or like Mozart choosing unpromising themes for the fun of it, or like one of those princesses whom wizards force to manufacture sheets out of nettles. (Jones 164)

References

Donoghue, Denis. "The Proper Plenitude of Facts", *Marianne Moore: A Collection of Critical Essays*, edited by Charles Tomlinson. New Jersey: Prentice Hall, 1969.

Eliot, T.S. "Tradition and the Individual Talent", *Selected Prose*, edited by John Hayward. Harmondsworth: Penguin Books, 1953.

— "Introduction to Selected Poems", *Marianne Moore: A Collection of Critical Essays*, edited by Charles Tomlinson. New Jersey: Prentice Hall 1969.

Jones,Peter. *A Reader's Guide to Fifty American Poets*. New York: Heinemann Educational Books, 1980.

Nemerov, Howard. Ed., *Contemporary American Poetry*. New York: Voice of America Forum Lectures, 1985.

Moore, Marianne. "A Grave", *American Literature: The Twentieth Century*. Delhi: Light and Life Publications, 1975.

—, "What Are Years?," *American Poetry*, edited by Karl Shapiro, New York: Thomas Y. Cromwell 1960.

—, "The Steeple Jack", *The Faber Book of Modern Verse* edited by Michael Roberts. London: Faber and Faber, 1951.

Ransom, John Crowe, "On Being Modern with Distinction", *Marianne Moore: A Collection of Critical Essays*, edited by Charles Tomlinson. New Jersey: Prentice Hall,1969.

31

Narrative Strategies in *A Room of One's Own*

N.K. Jain

For *A Room of One's Own*, Virginia Woolf required a strategy that would permit several narratives to coexist in a single test. The author takes a comprehensive look at gender relations, using a perspective wide enough to include the reality of the past, her perception of the present, and also her vision of the future. Each aspect of this composite view exerts a different kind extent of pressure on the narrative strategy, thus pulling each narrative in a different direction. Besides this, the delicate handling which the sensitiveness of the theme required, coupled with the consciousness of two completely different kinds of audience dividing on the basis of gender, made it necessary for the author to communicate part of her meanings through the use of sub-narratives. This essay is an attempt to analyze the different narrative strands and also consider the extent to which they influence each other.

The text of the book, though ostensibly conceived of as "a paper read by a woman to women" (*Room* 167), aims at the male audience too since Woolf knew that the readership of the book would undoubtedly include people belonging to the other gender as well. In *Room*, the author persuasively argues for the creation of female space in the realm of creative writing; for, as she comments "it is perennial puzzle why no woman wrote a word of that extraordinary literature (of the Elizabethan period) when every other man, it seemed, was capable of song or sonnet" (62). In her survey of the literary works produced by women in England in the seventeenth, eighteenth, and nineteenth centuries too, Woolf finds little to celebrate. Her analysis of the causes points to economic, sociological, and psycho-social factors: woman's relation to the patriarchal establishment, patriarchal ideology, and its rhetoric. She provides sufficient testimony to prove that, notwithstanding certain tangible improvement in the areas of educational and professional opportunities for and legal rights to women, even now "England is under the rule of a patriarchy" (50).

Woolf asserts that patriarchal culture was responsible for the economic, intellectual, and artistic impoverishment of women. During the course of her discussion of *Room* in her essay "Virginia Woolf and the Flight Into Androgyny," Elaine Showalter remarks: "Woolf was extremely sensitive to the ways in which female experience had made women weak, but she was much less sensitive to the ways in which it had made them strong" (285). The charge levelled against Woolf may be true, but it overlooks an important fact about her purpose in *Room*. Any discussion of the positive gains of the female experience would have blurred the focus of the essay, which was the debilitating effects of patriarchy on women's creative potential. And that would have weakened the argument of the book.

Woolf argues that the patriarchal system meant that women were without any money. The author tells us that "Mrs. Seton had no money to leave us" (36), and so women's institutions always suffered from "poverty and insecurity" (37). A woman had no *Room* of her own either. As Woolf points out, "If a woman wrote, she would have to write in the common sitting-room" (99-100). Since the general sitting-room was the only place where women could engage in the use of their creative talent, the title of the book seems to have had a literal origin. But the poetic genius of the author turns the expression into a rich metaphor. In *Room* itself, working in the general sitting-room does not merely mean lack of private space in a literal sense. With "all kinds of casual interruptions it also meant that they had no time that they can call their own" (100).

Not only this. In a talk given in 1931 to an audience comprising women from "I know not how many different professions," Woolf fell back on her favourite metaphor:

> You have won rooms of your own in the house hitherto exclusively owned by men. You are able, though not without labor and effort, to pay the rent. You are earning your five hundred pounds a year. But this freedom is only a beginning; the room is your own, but it is still bare. It has to be furnished; it has to be decorated; it has to be shared. How are you going to furnish it, how are you going to decorate it? With whom are you going to share it, and upon what terms? ("Professions" 297)

The expression "a room of one's own" here becomes an extended metaphor and refers to the creation of space for oneself in different walks of life.

Continuing her critical look at patriarchal society, Woolf finds that men enjoy complete domination over women. She remarks: "His was the power and the money and the influence" (50). What intrigues Woolf is that despite such a total domination, when men write about women, the emotion that they display is one of anger: "With the exception of the fog he seemed to control everything. Yet he was angry" (51). Men display the same indignation when they come across an uncomplimentary remark about themselves if it comes from a woman: "Z, most humane, most modest of men, taking up some book by Rebecca West and reading a passage in it, exclaimed, 'The arrant feminist!, She says that men are snobs!' " (53). Woolf argues that a man's insistence upon the inferiority of women "must indeed be one of the chief sources of his power" (53). If A woman does or says something that will shake or shatter a man's self-confidence, he is bound to "protest against some infringement of his power to believe in himself" (53).

At the same time, any woman who believes in herself will find this male attitude of superiority unjustifiable and the male conduct that stems from this attitude indefensible. Anger thus becomes an important theme in *Room*: anger in men at the perception of threat from women and anger in women at the treatment meted out to them by men. Besides the devices of distancing and impersonalization, it is the manner in which Woolf handles female anger in the book that accounts for her remarkably disarming strategy. There are three points worth noting in this contexts. First, with ample evidence from several male writers, Woolf establishes men's anger against women which, as she points out, has no justifiable grounds. Second, alongside the above, she provides proof of the presence of anger in women writers against men, but this time there are very valid grounds for its existence. Woolf leaves it to the reader to ask for himself/herself the question implied by this juxtaposition: if men have a right to be angry without cause, what is wrong with women's anger when that is the only natural and justifiable response in a given situation?

The book describes two incidents which effectively portray the gender bias so characteristic of patriarchy. In the first incident, Woolf has been walking on the precious grass belonging to a men's college. The Beadle's arms instantly go up and she is ordered off it: "Only the Fellows and Scholars are allowed here; the gravel is the place for (women)" (9). The second incident took place when the author was about to enter the college library to look at a manuscript. She was immediately stopped by

> a deprecating, silvery, kindly gentleman, who regretted in a low voice as he waved me back that ladies are only admitted to the library if accompanied by a Fellow of the College or furnished with a letter of introduction. (12)

Like the earlier incident, this one too is bound to evoke indignation in any sympathetic reader. But this time the author's own strong resentment is duly registered, though kept under complete check: "Never will I wake those echoes, never will I ask for that hospitality again, I vowed as I descended the steps in anger" (12-13).

However, Woolf is careful enough to switch quickly to a playful tone: "it was amusing enough to watch the congregation assembling, coming in and going out again, busying themselves at the door of the Chapel like bees at the mouth of a hive" (13). The point regarding the system's injustice to women has been made, but the fact has not been allowed to detract from the general tone of genial charm. One needs to camouflage one's argument "when a subject is highly controversial—-and any question about sex (read gender is that" (7). Woolf does it, to a very large extent, by giving her discourse a lyrical quality, by arguing in prose which is "starred with poetry' (11). This is the third point regarding Woolf's treatment of women's anger against the gender bias which is inherent in patriarchy: anger instantly gives way to either playfulness or the lyrical charm of Woolf's writing. It is extremely important to keep anger out of one's way lest anger should come in the way of one's creative genius. Comparing *Jane Eyre* with *Pride and Prejudice*, Woolf shows how, in the former novel, anger twists and derails the imagination from its proper directions (104).

In *Room* Woolf is not raising a banner of revolt against the opposite gender; she is presenting an argument and that too "with all sorts of disguises to avoid an appearance of an argument" (Bradbrook 25). Lack of an organized argument, however, is not the only noteworthy feature of the text. The writing does not conform to any recognizable model. Woolf announces at the beginning of the book:

> Fiction here is likely to contain more truth than fact. Therefore I propose, making use of all the liberties and licenses of a novelist, to tell you the story of the two days that preceded my comings here... (7)

This statement of intention is soon followed by the description of two incidents already referred to above. Such a beginning could easily lead a reader to believe that he/she should now prepare himself/herself for a novel with a regular plot. However, if we examine the above mentioned "clues" carefully, we notice that none of them actually promises a novel. Making use of "the liberties and licenses of a novelist" does not by itself produce a novel. As regards the word "story," Woolf uses it here not in the sense of a plot comprising a succession of incidents, but in the sense of "a particular person's representation of the facts in a case," one of the meanings listed in the *Oxford English Dictionary*.

As for incidents in the book, besides the two incidents already mentioned, there is only one more incident that occurs in chapter VI—two persons of the opposite sex come down the street, meet at the corner, and get into a cab which takes them away to the destination of their choice. Each of these three incidents is related to the central theme of male-female relations. But taken together they do not constitute a plot each following incident is not the logical outcome of the earlier incident(s), giving us the beginning, the middle, and the end, as Aristotle required of a plot.

Woolf herself describes *Room* as an essay: "This essay is based upon two papers read to the Arts 'society at Newnham and the Odtaa at Girton in October 1928" (5). The narrator's reflections on the place of women in society grow out of particular scenes and events. The writing takes a discursive form. There are frequent changes in the style, as there are rapid, and sometimes abrupt, changes in the direction of thought. The author has already taken a precaution to warn Us: "I give you my thoughts as they came to me" (10). Marcia McClintock Folsom aptly describes these unpredictable shifts: "the slippery, sly, quirky modulations of observations into feelings, thoughts into questions which are only half-articulated, events into indignation" ("Gallant" 255). Despite this looseness of structure, Woolf always keeps a firm grasp on the subject. The essential integrity of the argument is never compromised.

During the course of her extended analysis of the current gender relations, Woolf finds the main cause of women's oppression in the way the male psyche works: "Possibly when the professor (= the patriarch) insisted a little too emphatically upon the inferiority of women, he was concerned not with their inferiority, but with his own superiority" (52). Woolf is, however, careful not to put all the blame on men. Her stance is quite objective. This is clearly brought out in the mirror image the author uses in this context: "Women have served all these centuries as looking-glasses possessing the magic and delicious power of reflecting the figure of man at twice its natural size" (53). The woman too is responsible for the creation of the inflated image of the ruling patriarch, and in this way she has contributed to her own oppression.

Though Woolf finds the root cause of women's oppression in the patriarchal system, she does not ask men to reorder their lives. The most she hopes from men is a proper understanding of the plight of women and an effort on their part to remove obstacles from the path of women. In order to achieve this end, she knows that it is important that she does not point an accusing finger at men more than is absolutely necessary. The argument must be shorn of all abrasiveness. One technique she employs in this context is that of juxtaposition without any elaboration of its negative implications for men. We saw an example of this earlier when we discussed the subject of anger in men and women.

Another fine example of the same technique is the sharp contrast between the two meals: the lunch at Oxbridge and the dinner at Fernham. The Oxbridge lunch consists of soles sunk in a deep dish covered with a counterpane of whitest cream, delicious partridges with their retinue of sauces and salads, exquisite pudding, and sparkling wine, the kind of meal that would provide just the right setting for the rich yellow flame of rational intercourse. As Woolf sums up the atmosphere, "No need to be anybody but oneself" (17). The dinner at Fernham, on the other hand, is the plainest of fares: a plain gravy soup, beef, prunes, custard, biscuits, and cheese. Woolf offers no explicit comment on the glaring contrast, but for the reader it illustrates concretely the difference between the prosperity of men's colleges and the poverty of women's. It is left to the reader to feel the injustice of the system and to sense the indignation it should cause in women. The author merely reiterates her conviction regarding the important role that material things play in fostering intellectual activity: "One cannot think well, love well, sleep well, if one has not dined well" (28).

The social, political, and economic realities of a woman's life impoverished her as a creative artist. For centuries she was excluded from education, power, money, and various facets of life experience. A woman has to accept certain limitations from which men are free, for instance, child bearing and rearing, which takes away a lot of time. A woman artist's reality is that she is likely to be one who happens also to be a mother, though the number of children may come down from "tens and twelves" to "twos and threes" (170). By stressing this aspect of a woman's life, Woolf seems to be implying two things at the same time. One is the need to consider the relation between daily life and creativity. The argument seems to be that while considering a woman's writing, the reader must also take into account all those factors that make up the writer's reality, the limitations under which she lived and worked. On the other hand, Woolf seems to be pointing out that there are certain areas of experience which are accessible only to women and so women's literature held a promise of exploring and communicating some of those physical and emotional experiences which are out of bounds for the male writer, thus privileging the woman artist over her male counterpart.

In real life, however, the insignificant place that is assigned to women in the realm of power and privileges brings to Woolf's mind another paradox: "She pervades poetry from cover to cover; she is all but absent from history" (66). The woman is the highest source of inspiration to a man's creative faculty she can set fire to his imagination, but on the earth, in a society dominated by men, she seems to have an insubstantial existence.

The distinction between fact and fiction is quite vital to Woolf; as quoted earlier also, she remarks, "Fiction here is likely to contain more truth than fact" (7). And she maintains a parallel distinction between reality (what *is*) and vision (what *should be*). When she looks at life around her, besides the fact of patriarchy, she finds that after the war (the First World War) the male-female relationship had undergone some change and that the change was for the worse:

> Before the war at a luncheon party like this people would have said precisely the same things but they would have sounded different, because in those days they were accompanied by a sort of humming noise, not articulate, but musical, exciting, which changed the value of the words themselves. (19)

Woolf wonders: "shall we lay the blame on the war? When the guns fired in August 1914, did the faces of men and women show so plain in each other's eyes that romance was killed?" (23). She observes a distinct note of uneasiness in the relations between men and women. She feels pained since this state of affairs runs contrary to her vision of the ideal state of man-woman relationship: "The normal and comfortable state of being is that when the two live in harmony together, spiritually co-operating" (147).

Instead of looking upon the other gender as an antagonist, Woolf emphasizes the need for men and women to live and move in perfect co-operation. Nature has ordered them in such a way that they complement each other and each is incomplete without the other: as Woolf states, "Perhaps a mind that is purely masculine cannot create, any more than a mind that is purely feminine" (148). Therefore, the new literary sensibility, Woolf argues, should be androgynous. She, however, makes no demands on the other gender. But, in the "peroration," women are enjoined to shoulder a special responsibility: by taking to creative writing, even if it means working in poverty and obscurity, to bring back to life "the dead poet who was Shakespear's sister" (172). This concern with literature is what distinguishes Woolf from most of her feminist successors.

The author's overriding commitment to creativity does not merely require a narrative of its own, it also accounts for the existence of various sub-narratives within narratives. The text's dense realistic matrix demands fidelity to the real, but this emphasis on verisimilitude is opposed by the author's conviction that fact is inimical to art and also that fiction is the superior vehicle for the communication of truth. The demands made by a variety of perspectives and the tension created by conflicting demands make *Room* the rich and complex narrative that it is.

References

Bradbrook, M.C. "Notes on the Style of Mrs. Woolf." In *Critics on Virginia Woolf*. Ed. Jacqueline E.M. Latham. Reprint, Delhi: Universal Book Stall, 1997. 21-25.

Folsom, Marcia McClintock. "Gallant Red Brick and Plain China: Teaching *A Room of One's Own*." *College English* 45:3: 254-262.

Showalter, Elaine. "Virginia Woolf and the Flight into Androgyny." In *A Literature of Their Own*. Princeton, New Jersey: Princeton University Press, 1977. 263-297.

Woolf, Virginia. *A Room of One's Own*. London: Grafton Books, 1989.

— "Professions for Women." In *The Little Brown Reader*. Eds. Marcia Stubbs and Sylvan Barnet. Boston: Little Brown and Company, 1983. 293-298.

32

Interpretation of Literature: A Case for New Strategies

Santosh Gupta

The title of Annette Kolodny's essay "Dancing Through the Minefield: Some Observations on the Theory, Practice and Politics of a Feminist Literary Criticism" brings together unlikely elements—dancing, minefield, politics and literary criticism. She explains within the essay how these contradictory terms come together, as she examines the risks involved in pursuing feminist literary criticism, the hazards which seem to be equivalent to crossing a minefield. Laid with explosives the ground of a minefield presents serious dangers; the feminists' pursuit of literary criticism seems to provoke extreme hostility and resistance, somehow leading to violent reactions from the leading male professional critics. Then why, one may ask, do feminists pursue literary criticism laid over with dangerous political issues ? What are the dangers? Dancing is usually an act of pleasure and skill; dancing through such grounds would call for extreme dedication and determination and the purpose of such devotion would certainly be of great significance. The issues that Annette Kolodny raises in this essay a call for serious consideration as they are woven within culture and social relationships.

As one reads other critics dealing with these issues in feminist literary criticism violent imagery recurs more frequently than one would expect it to. Kolodny's essay was written in 1979 (Notes 164). Sandra M. Gilbert's "What Do Feminist Critics Want : *A Postcard From the Volcano*", in 1980. Gilbert's essay echoes the danger of volcanic disturbance as being inherent in women's writing and criticism; Gilbert discusses at some length the theme of violence associated with poetry as well.

Both Emily Dickinson and Wallace Stevens who are eminent American poets, belonging to the nineteenth and twentieth centuries have used in their poems 'volcano' as an image to suggest some forms of violent eruptions. In his poem titled 'A Postcard from a Volcano' Wallace Stevens has, Gilbert observes, talked about the continued tradition of poetry, western and American, his place within it and the legacy for the future. Dickinson, a woman, has used the trope of volcano to indicate suppressed anger for being placed at the margins of society and in literary writing. The different symbolic implications in the poems by the two poets draw out the different relations of the male and female poets with their society, culture and history. American feminist critics have tried to read these literary texts from perspectives that recognise these tensions and meanings which have so for been more or less ignored and neglected. The great western culture that male professors proudly refer to (Gilbert 33) have so far been happy to ignore a great deal of its own creative and intellectual inheritance, by leaving out of literary histories, cultural records, the achievements of fine female writers and thinkers. It is the feminists scholars—both in literary and philosophical spheres—who try to discover, the hidden, marginalised and silenced women writers, their works, the themes, styles, narrative techniques contained therein as they question prevailing male-dominated critical works, ideas and theoretical formulations. By talking of the 'volcanic interiorty' (Gilbert 33) these critics draw attention to the suppressed emotions of anger, frustration and destructions, urges the women have repressed, trying to maintain a deceptive calm, submissive and reconciliatory stand. Susan M. Gilbert, Annette Kolodny are some of the foremost feminist literary critics who have examined the several issues related to the western civilization's persistent neglect of women's writing and talent and looked for ways in which this intellectual blindness can be removed.

Kolodny's essay examines the existing literary histories and the significance of the missing female writers from them. These absences indicate the patriarchal intellectual traditions of erasing the female creative presence simply by not ackowledgeing it. Kolodny and the other feminist literary critics' main endeavour is focused on foregrounding women's continued literary production within such an atmosphere and commenting on the several fine women writers who are there and the role feminist critics have played in building up the tradition of women's writing. In the first part of her well-researched and argued paper she talks about the driving spirit of the feminist critics of the 1960s and 70s. Most American feminist literary critics, she points out, argued about the persistent 'sexism' i.e. sex based discrimination, in the literature that was highly regarded by critics. Not only were most of the writers and critics men, they also, in an unstated, undeclared manner, treated women's writing—whether poetry, fiction or criticism, as unintelligible and inferior. These critics, usually declared women's work to be far below men's work, and then proceeded to reject them as being unfit to be included within the 'canon' ; the result has been a long neglect of much of women's good writing often rejected without careful analysis.

One of the implications of such a persistent de-valuation of women's work is the realisation which most feminist critics hold to, that literature is one of the most formative and normative of the social institutions we live with. Reading, and even listening to, narratives about how men and women live in society, we as readers acquire most of our social codes of conduct, sense of values and the awareness about reality. What is being read and how the texts are read, becomes extremely important. If men's writings alone are read, and if only male critical views inform our critical opinions then it is extremely important to examine the reasons why women's writing is systematically, carefully turned down as 'badly written' or lacking in significance. Reviewing the sexual politics within literary critical practices itself that women/feminists have talked about in the last half a century has led to new insights, regarding how this practice has led to the exclusion of women's writing from the 'canon'—the list of great literary work agreed upon by a society. This practice has had serious consequences, as it has led to the women writers and their work being constantly kept out of literary histories, courses taught to new generations of students, and forever being left out of public knowledge. How will writers like Elizabeth Barrett Browning, Charlotte Perkins Gilman, Kate Chopin, Susan Glaspell (some of the writers Kolodny mentions in her discussion) be known, if they are never included in literary selections, anthologies, discussed in classrooms, conferences and other related fora? The canon is one of the influential modes of giving life to an author's books. If left out of the list of good literature the texts quietly fall out of public knowledge/memory.

Kolodny presents the view that this neglect of women's writing is the result of a deep-rooted male prejudice against women—both in social life and in literature—in the construction of knowledge. She strongly recommends the need to change the prevailing reading habits of men, who have learnt, and now teach others, to value male writers with their interest in the so called public domains, the political and economic pursuits which so far have been exclusively male concerns; interest in the higher values of abstract philosophical, political theories are also considered to be the male intellectual concerns. Kolodny, as a feminist, questions the male criteria of disregard for female work which according to them is mostly confined to domestic spaces and their long devotion to the care of their family. The importance of reading correctly—i.e. to pay attention to the depiction of the lives of women, the women writers' preoccupation with these activities is emphasised by Kolodny as she realises how the male readers' minds would resist the suggestion about changing their habits of reading. The destabilising impact of this shift of attention is perhaps the cause of the suggested violence and dangerous encounters that have been refered to. The suggested plan to create a non-sexist view of women's works may lead to a rewriting and revision of the prevailing evaluations. The view that criticism itself is arrived at through the predominant social and cultural values, which change with time, is an attempt to adopt a historical view of literary canon and criticism. Elaine Showalter, Sydney Janet Kaplan and other American feminists mentioned in Kolodny's essay have established through careful research and scholarship the existence of a continued female literature and even "female imagination" (Patricia Mayer Spacks) which has been studiously ignored by male scholars. The experiences and perceptions contained in women's work have been disregarded as it was found to be about the "trivial" concerns of women within family spaces and relationships. These feminist scholars have unearthed not only existing women's works but also an equally consistent male prejudice. It is clear from these studies that the claims of universal value or objectivity in evaluations of literary texts are basically governed by many gender related prejudices. (Kolodny 152–54)

This scholarship has resulted in one of the major feminist ideas that Kolodny now discusses—she says that the sexual politics, i.e. the power struggle inbuilt within men women relationship in the existing patriarchal systems, is reflected in an equally strong form in the literary works, their structures and reading habits. Feminists find close inter-connections between social practices in which we live and the literary constructions, forms, and, even the language used to depict human life. She clearly critiques the way we read, for she says what we read "are not texts but paradigms'" (153), and the social value imputed to the readings by one social group, neglecting almost one half of the population (161). These mental habits of readers are reflected in literary criticism, and, their selection of 'great' works. Thus, feminist critics argue, they face the imperative need of "finding new critical directions" (157). It is important to get into the problems of reading correctly.

Kolodny discusses in some details why men are unable to 'read' women's writing; why is it that when men read women's work they cannot either understand or treat it with any degree of seriousness, the concerns of women : their lives in the "lying-in room, the children's room, the parlor, the nursery, the kitchen, the laundry and so on" (Kolodny 155).These parts of family space constitute the contexts to women's lives—the many dramatic situations that they experience, living there.

Men's distance from women's domestic sphere is, in itself, the outcome of a social ideology that has put women on a lower level in the social hierarchy. It reflects the male view that the world of economic, political pursuits has more social value than the lifelong work of women; that child rearing, family care and dedication to the well-being of the family are insignificant and socially inferior. If the literary evaluation is based on such a patriarchal value system, it has led to the peculiar condition where half of the population is believed to be incapable of creating good imaginative or evocative work, in literature as in other art forms and intellectual pursuits.

For feminist critics the inter connections between male prejudices against women as writer's and as social beings are very deep lying. As women's suffering is borne silently in life, so are they put under silence within the literary spheres. Even within literary texts, for example, Kolodny asks the readers/audience to pay some attention to the suffering of the women characters. She refers to the character of Ophelia in Shakespeare's well-known tragedy *Hamlet,* for a change; she suggests that some shift of significance and of meaning would definitely take place if the tragic suffering of *Ophelia* is recognised. So far all the critical attention, all the audience's sympathy focuses only on the character of the hero, Hamlet. In recognising how Ophelia is ill-treated by the hero, which causes her untimely death, the response to the play would also gain a new shade of meaning. Recognition for women's lives, work and creative talent is one of the factors that can change literary understanding also. These reversals and shifts, the feminist critic thinks, would have far reaching results; when literary texts are evaluated differently, the feminist critic hopes for changes in the rating and evaluation of these works as well.

When women's writing is read with more attention many texts will be rated differently. Gilbert says, like Kolodny, "we must redo our history ... review, reimagine, rethink, rewrite, revise and reinterpret the events and documents that constitute it" (Gilbert 32). These are the tasks for all literary critics, as the impact of rewriting will concern every reader. When new interpretations come forth, there would be subsequent changes in perceptions.

Introducing new reading skills, as many other recent theories have done, invariably leads to change in the evaluation of existing texts. Canon is somehow readjusted when texts that were so far treated as mere thrillers or popular work, begin to be seen with a new appreciation for new reasons. It has been recognised by a large section of literary scholars that literary canons do not remain unchanged. Sripad Bhat argues this point in his discussion of the changed status of the eighteenth century popular novel *Moll Flanders* after new readings of it were made in the twentieth century. The emergence of a new awareness of the role played by middle class in England, the prevalence of Calvinistic values and their impact on the country's prosperity in that period, in the shaping of the British empire has led to a significant change of perception of the novel which is seen to contain these values. The novel was seen for almost two hundred years since its publication in 1722 as a pot-boiler, as a story about a criminal-minded and immoral woman, Moll. Her struggle for survival and success in social acceptability in the upper class, has now acquired a new respectability with the appearance of new points of view in the critics in the 1920s and later. Ian Watt's *The Rise of the Novel: Studies in Defoe, Richardson and Fielding* (1975) has been specially influential in casting a new image and status of the writer as well as of the novel. The novel is now rated a 'classic'.

This example of changed critical evaluation is used by Bhat to argue that the emergence of new critical approaches, changed political, economic values have "led to the revaluation of the past texts, rediscovery of hidden meanings in hitherto neglected texts and writers" (Bhat 94). So, he concludes "literary meaning is not a question of unchanging, a historical literary discourse which is, in turn, mediated in a specific ideological and historical contexts" (Bhat 95). Literary texts can reveal different and many meanings, an idea that post-structuralists and Marxist theoretical studies have established so far. If feminist perspective does something similar, ask the feminist critics, why does it disturb the male readers/critics and scholars so violently ? That there is a constant interconnection between literary texts, criticism and ideology is not such a new idea, by the 1970s and 80s. Then why is the presence of feminist criticism so disturbing? Literary histories and criticism keep changing their selections and values, for these intellectual exercises take place in social and political situations, and contexts.

What most men fear about the prevalence of feminist theory is that this theory will lead either to a chaos or anarchy; that there will be no recognisable canon or continuity in it. The male professors claim to have formed the principles of literary criticism on the basis of serious learning and; the feminist insistence upon upsetting this order will, they fear, lead to a lowering of standard and indiscriminate choices (Kolodny 161).

Kolodny comes to the last part of her essay as she takes up the problems that new feminist approaches seemingly present. What will emerge, she argues, is a variety of choices and selections, leading to a 'pluralism' (Kolodny 161). Rather than sticking to "A single reading method" (not even feminist) she says "our task is to initiate nothing less than a playful pluralism, responding to the possibilities of multiple critical schools and methods ...." (161). No one method alone can suffice, and all of them will contribute. These plural methods well help in realising the richness and complexity of the texts we have. Here again Kolodny assures the critics (of feminist theory) that there is no desire to claim that feminist theory alone is needed or correct. With this acceptance of being one of the many valid approaches there can be a constructive critical deliberation. Ideology governs and guides our thinking and life, and no one ideology can explain everything. If the male fear of feminist ideology can be exposed and accepted for what it is: a prejudice, the "minefield" where feminist were pushed into, is also laid bare. In changed intellectual atmosphere feminist can 'dance' through such fields, and perform their intellectual inquiry more freely and peacefully. The pleasures of literary criticism will make such actions more enjoyable, and of course, devoid of violence.

Building up a dialogic relationship between the male and female critics is, perhaps, one of the ways of destroying the prejudices, and the unacknowledged fears among men. The women treated as a hostile 'other' could become part of the mainstream when accepted without any gender bias. Kolodny lays bare some of the issues underlying the anger with in women, the male hostility towards women's efforts to build up women's literary tradition and why does it matter to do so.

Kolodny raises important questions about the hindrances faced by women writers and critics. In foregrounding the role of the reader—how one reads—the responses to literary texts are shown to emerge from existing mental approaches. Kolodny's persistent arguments lead to the point where she shows that literary critical principles are often subjective and guided by some psychological fears; they are not neutral, objective and, universally acceptable, as it is claimed.

Through her logical and argumentative analysis she shows how the close relation between the "primarily male structures of power" (161) in social relationships are "inscribed (or encoded) within our literary inheritance" (162) she endeavours to question the prevalent literary practices and perceptions. Through such arguments Kolodny draws out the 'ethical' significance of the literary matters. These ideas are as much related to how we live and think, as are the actions of real human beings. Moving on from the critical studies of the feminists of the 1960s, Kolodny's essay marks an important stage of literary theory. Her essay deals with the radical importance of the whole of literary critical theory, and how the emergence of a new approach which is making space for itself within the existing knowledge system will enrich our total understanding of human life and literature.

Its references to other feminist critics connects their different ideas, arguments and visions; Kolodny's contribution to feminist theory is important as it also looks forward to a changed intellectual world, changing with the social contexts of our lives. It is a plea for pluralism, tolerance and an open-mended reading.

Notes

1. Annette Kolodny has taught in various universities in the USA. Her struggle against gender discrimination in the academia led her to legal battles and she has been an activist for ecological issues as well. Her major works of criticism include *The Lay of the Land : Metaphor as Experience and History in American Life and Letters.* University of North Carolina Press. 1975. (This book is a pioneering study of feminist ecocriticism), *The Land Before Her : Fantasy and Experience of the American Frontiers. 1630–1860.* University of North Carolina Press, 1984. The essay 'Dancing Through the Minefield ...' is considered to be one of the most reprinted essays of American feminist literary criticism.

References

Bhat, K. Sripad, "The Politics of Reading and the Birth of a Classic : Juxtaposing *Moll Flanders* with *If Tomorrow Comes" Indian Journal of American Studies.* Vol. 23, No. I, Winter 1993, 93–95.

Gilbert, Sandra M., 'What Do Feminist Critics Want? *A Postcard From the Volcano'. The New Feminist Criticism: Essays on Women, Literatures & Theory,* Ed. Elaine Showalter, New York: Pantheon Books. 1985, 29–45.

Kolodny, Annette, "Dancing Through the Minefield: Some Observations on the Theory, Practice and Politics of a Feminist Literary Criticism". *The New Feminist Criticism : Essays on Women, Literature and Theory.* Ed. Elaine Showalter, New York: Pantheon Books. 1985, 144–167.

33

Whose Story is *Mary Barton*? A Study of Emotional and Moral Conflict

Jasbir Jain

Elizabeth Gaskell's first novel *Mary Barton* (1848) not only appeared the same year as Marx's *The Communist Manifesto* and, across the Atlantic, Hawthorne's *The Scarlet Letter* but was also contemporary to the serialisation of Dickens' *Dombey and Sons* which reached completion in 1848. Each one of these writings harbingered a different trend. Marx's *Manifesto* theorised about class and economic differences which also form the basis of Gaskell's novel. But the others spread out into different directions—in Hawthorne romance, adultery and morality, the conflict between the body and soul; in Thackeray's *Vanity Fair* the story of Amelia and Becky, placed against England's two major engagements—India and the Napoleonic war. At another level *Vanity Fair* was a story of courtship and marriage. Thackeray's *Book of Snobs* also appeared the same year.

Amidst all this cluster of themes, it is natural to ask: is *Mary Barton* a woman-centred narrative? One hastens to point towards its economic and moral concerns. And despite the fact that Mary's life is torn between her two lovers—Carson who is rich and is merely flirting with her, and Jem, her childhood friend, who is protective enough to stand between her father's guilt and the law—it is not a courtship novel. Mary is not really going husband-hunting, on the other hand, she is a working woman. Can one treat the novel as a tale of growing up, a *bildungsroman*? Mary is introduced to us as a sixteen-year-old girl and through the narrative she faces several losses—her mother's death, the haunting memory of her aunt Esther's elopement, the love affair with the mill-owner's son Carson, her job in the confines of a seamstress's establishment and her father's frustration at the rebuttal that the Chartists suffer. He keeps this wound alive. To top it all Carson Junior is murdered and Jem is held guilty. For the first time in her life Mary moves out of Manchester in search of Jem's cousin, a sailor who may soon sail away, as his alibi alone may be able to save Jem. The realisation, at this moment of Jem's possible death, leads to her own moment of knowledge that it is Jem she has loved all along, Carson has held an attraction merely because of the high life, which a possible marriage to him had held for her.

From the above point of view, *Mary Barton* is a tale of growing up, both in years and maturity, a maturity in moral values and personal realisation, gained through a series of crises. But its involvement with industrial England and the class problem sets it apart, both from the earlier women writers as well as the male writers. She presents a very different world from that of the genteel classes or the underground world of crime and violence one comes across in Dickens' novels—a world of abductors, criminals and money extractors who hold children and the helpless to ransom. Raymond Williams in *Culture and Society*, recognises it as the beginning of the industrial novel and describes it as 'the most moving response in literature to the industrial suffering of the 1840's. Continuing in this vein, he writes:

> The really impressive thing about the book is the intensity of the effort to record, in its own terms, the feel of everyday life in the working-class homes. The method, in part, is that of a documentary record, as may be seen in such details as the carefully annotated re-

> production of dialect, the carefully included details of food prices in the account of the tea-party, the itemized description of the furniture of the Barton's living-room, and the writing-out the ballad (again annotated) of *The Oldham Weaver*. (99)

Prior to this, Elizabeth Gaskell had already published a collection of short stories titled *Life in Manchester* (1848) originally published in Howitt's *Journal of Literature and Popular Progress* (1–3, 1847–1848) under the pseudonym of Cotton Mather Mills, a work which was a preparation for *Mary Barton*. The atmosphere of the working-class homes is reproduced here through a combination of observation and a 'genuine imagination re-creation' (Williams 99).

The opening pages present an idyllic rural scene of a day in the fields, a village a short distant away, the lowing of the cattle, the sounds of the milkmaids before transferring the reader to the Barton's home and an evening of shared happiness. The home is warm with hospitality and goodwill, even if mugs have to be borrowed. Guests are summoned and a congenial atmosphere prevails. Later in George Eliot's *Adam Bede* (1859) and Thomas Hardy's *Tess of D'Urbervilles* (1891) such scenes were to recur but these were in connection with rural homes and agriculture. In *Mary Barton* these give way gradually to loss and deprivation. Even in this scene of hospitality, the absence of her mother's younger sister Esther, who has run away, casts a shadow. Then a childbirth goes wrong; Mary's mother dies leaving her husband grieving. Other deaths follow—Wilson's is one of them. Sorrows descend on the two families and the struggle of the industrial workers is under way. The Chartist Movement has begun. John Barton is chosen as a spokesman and makes a trip to London where their endless wait yields no negotiations, bears no result except for a degree of frustration and continued unemployment and poverty. The reader, while placing it against other nineteenth century novels, will recall Charlotte Bronte's *Shirley* (1849), where Robert Moore feels compelled to get workers from outside in order to teach his striking workers a lesson and Gaskell's own *North and South* (1855), finds Margaret Hale opening the door to the resisting strikers. Except, in both *Shirley* and *North and South*, the industrialists' perspective is presented, first through Shirley's courage and the collective foresight, and in the second through Margaret's sympathy and negotiations. In *Mary Barton* it is the working class which finds a representation and the consequences of their struggle as these affect their everyday lives.

It is this strong engagement with the working-class and the foregrounding of the class struggle, with scenes of the masters conferring with each other and deciding to recruit new weavers, in order to meet their foreign orders on time, that provides a double perspective—one on the worker, who is being rendered dispensable, the other on trade relations and state policies. Both Imperial concerns and Communist theorisation lurk behind this struggle. Two entirely different worlds are portrayed side by side but not in equal balance. The mill-owners are on the periphery, despite the power they wield; it is the working-class which is at the centre. At one point, John Barton says: "I tell you, it's the poor, and the poor only, as does things for the poor. Don't think to come over me with the old tale, that the rich know nothing of the trials of the poor. I say, if they don't know, they ought to know." (9) It takes a murder and a death to get the mill-owner to know them in the end—his son is murdered and Barton confesses to the act before his death. What a heavy price to pay for understanding the 'other'!

From this perspective, the subtitle which does not feature on the title page but shares a parallel header on every alternate page, "A Tale of Manchester Life", claims its share and leads to the query: is *Mary Barton* more a study of Manchester-based working-class, its problems and the impact on the individuals than of Mary Barton? Spatially the novel is, for a large part, confined to Manchester. People from outside come into it through marriage or in search of employment; people travel out in search of employment, escape or a fortune. Mary Barton bears her mother's name Mary. Esther, the mother's sister, pretty, fashion conscious and independent, first moves out of the Barton home, then out of Manchester but she makes an appearance at several critical junctures, mostly at night. Herself desolate and lonely, she wants to act as a guardian to Mary. It is she who informs Jem of Mary's affair with Carson Junior. She also comes home to die towards the end.

The moral debates are carried out at several levels, not necessarily through speeches or dialogues, but often through behavioural acts—the way people behave whether it be Margaret Wilson, who is slowly losing her vision, or Job Legh who is well-read, a scholar and an undeclared councillor, who finally acts as advisor to Mary and an escort to Mrs. Wilson, when they journey to Liverpool. Moral conflicts are also depicted through events, soliloquies and facial expressions and at times by authorial comment through some other eye witness. As for instance, the narrator describes Mary at the trial:

> I was not there myself; but one who was, told me that her look, and indeed her whole face, was more like the well-known engraving from Guido's picture of "Beatrice Cenci" than anything else he could give me an idea of. He added, that her countenance haunted him, like the remembrance of some wild sad melody heard in childhood; that it would perpetually recur with its mute imploring agency. (305)

Such narratorial interventions, without any acknowledgement of an omniscient narrator, make the narrator a participant in the happenings as observer, witness, sympathiser and narrator. And these interventions occur only on rare occasions allowing the reader to forget them. *Mary Barton* does follow a realistic framework without painting the 'real' only in dark shades. The unfolding of the story which revolves around the two families—Bartons and Wilsons—and some of their neighbours, truly becomes "A Tale of Manchester Life" : Another overseeing narrative function is performed by the epigraphs that introduce each chapter. Songs, poems, ditties, ballads and a hymn or two strike just the right opening note and in themselves present varied aspects of cultural range. As for instance, when early in the novel, we have the hospitality scene in the Barton's house, the introducing ditty is "Polly go and put the kettle on". The epigraphs go on getting weightier and weightier as the seriousness of the novel grows and scenes of conflict, struggle and sorrow are foregrounded. These narratorial aids build an atmosphere but do not intervene in the act of narration as the interplay of the different strands continues.

There is yet a third strand which emerges in the reading—the moral conflict and message presented through John Barton and his history, his growing bitterness, frustration and silence and then the act of violence. At one point, Gaskell had considered the title *John Barton* and has written in this connection, "Round the character of John Barton all the others formed themselves; he was my hero, the person with whom all my sympathies went ..." She was familiar with people of this kind, poor but sterling in character qualities and knew the language and the dialects they used. But in the publication, the title was changed, perhaps at the insistence of the publisher. Inevitably, some changes would also have been made, reducing Barton's presence to three main slots—the beginning, the Chartist march and the war with his own conscience. Who and what is he? Barton has all the courage and the conviction of his views. He is chosen to be part of the delegation to the Parliament in 1839, one of the "Life-worn, gaunt, anxious, hunger-stamped men ..." (80). But the delegation fails to get an audience. John Barton returns a sad man and he tells Mary, "we must speak to our God to hear us, for man will not hearken; no not now, when we weep tears O' blood!" (92)

John Barton's silence and hunger lead him to excessive brooding, a brooding which nurtures hatred and revenge, and finally breaking out of it bounds kills Harry Carson. This results in a self-exile from his home, his daughter, his past and the act of the murder. The last, however, is a burden he has to carry and live with. From Barton's point of view, *Mary Barton* is a tragedy as one by one he fails in all the trials of his life. Except, at the end, he rises out of the low depths of guilt, self-pity and remorse, to rise above them and make his confession to the bereaved father. In this he creates a tradition of grief and repentance which can raise a man to great heights, a tradition which later characters like Henchard in Hardy's *The Mayor of Casterbridge*, were to follow. Despite his grim, shadowy presence, the final confession renders him worthy of being the hero—had it so transpired but apparently the centrality was pushed on to Mary. Barton's final confrontation is not only with his own conscience but also with the senior Mr. Carson, Mary and Jem. Mary enters upon a scene where her father and Carson are face to face—one stern with his gaunt looks, the other bent upon punishing the guilty. (343) Barton neither asks nor expects mercy, he only wants forgiveness in Christian terms. The grief of the father touches John Barton: "The eyes of John Barton grew dim with tears. Rich and poor, masters and men, were then brothers in the deep suffering of the heart; for was not this very anguish he had felt for little Tom, in years so long gone by that they seemed another life!" (345)

Barton's moral schooling has been in the world of life, suffering and frustrations, "No one learned me and no one telled me ... only I heard the Bible was a good book" but others do not live by the Bible. His deathbed confession is not in search of a reprieve from punishment but for human forgiveness, which would necessitate a going across in empathy on part of the wronged father, despite the personal loss caused by the sinner. It is at this moment that Mr. Carson comes to their dwelling for the second time. Moved by the dying man's anguish, freshly having read the Bible, he can only repeat what he had read a short while ago, "Forgive us our trespasses as we forgive them that trespass against us". Thus ends John Barton's earthly life. There is nothing in this aspiring, caring human being, one who has travelled through loss, loneliness and despair, through crime, repentance, confession and humility that does not raise him to heroic levels. Elizabeth Gaskell avoids extreme sentimentality. Job Legh's presence, his essential goodness, his sobriety and considered sympathy contribute towards balancing the emotions of grief and repentance.

Everyday morality was still not governed by utilitarian values, especially at this mid-point of the nineteenth century. And even though church-going may not have been very common among the working people, their life-belief was still governed by the words of the Bible and personal ties of affection. Raymond Williams in his essay "David Hume" writes "Hume seeks to embody two principles: the communication of feeling, which is sympathy, and the engagement of feeling which is the necessary involvement of man with mankind". In this there is not only a dependence on convention, on what is thought to be correct and upheld as axiomatic moral law but also "a practical equivalent between humanity and society" (139).

The question still remains to be addressed that over and above being an industrial novel, a tale of Manchester life, of the class issues which are foregrounded, and John Barton's moral stature, why is the novel still titled *Mary Barton*? Is it because she is a woman and woman heroines were of importance? Mary, additionally, marks a new break in feminist thought as the novel does not foreground the genteel class. She is far removed from all kinds of earlier representations such as the picaro Moll Flanders, in and out of prison, the educated heroines of Burney, Austen and Edgeworth who stand at the periphery of working/professional life, governesses who seek independence, heiresses who find it difficult to shake off male relatives, economically independent women who are still dependent on male mentoring or real life women like Mary Hay or Mary Wollstonecraft, who are strong in their convictions of their ideological positions.

In contrast to all of them, Mary Barton is not educated, she only earns her meal at the seamstress's establishment and is not in the true sense economically independent. With her mother's death and Esther's elopement there is no other woman in the house to guide her. On the other hand the world of temptation is wide open and with her beauty she is further exposed to both temptation and seduction, which the advances of the rich Harry Carson open out to her. There is also the constant coaxing by her co-worker Sally that she should continue the affair with Harry. On the plus side are Mary's decisions not to meet Harry Carson during her father's absence. She learns through observation, through Margaret whose endurance and patience is exemplary even as darkness, through loss of vision, looms ahead of her. She learns from Job Legh, who is a constant guide and also from the Bible. Her greatest teaching comes from personal suffering and the silence and withdrawal of her father. Then there is her own moment of recognition that she loves Jem, not Harry Carson. As the truth dawns on her, she realises she already stands accused amongst all the people she loves and values—Mrs. Wilson, Margaret, Job and Esther. There are not one but at least three different trials—one is the legal one of Jem, second, the moral one of John Barton and third, the double trial for Mary—one of her love and the second of her knowledge that her father is the real murderer. But she cannot betray him; the only other course open to her is to go in search of Will, Jem's sailor cousin, who was with him on that crucial night and can provide an alibi. It is this decision that stirs her into action.

Harry Carson's death takes place almost at mid-point of the novel. And this acts as a catalyst on the events both of the past and the present. The murder is, on the face of it, centred on Mary's relationship with Harry Carson and this causes a lining up of Mrs. Wilson, Margaret and the others against her, bringing her to a low point in her moral life. The journey to Liverpool is an act of expiation as much as for her love of Jem as her loyalty to her father. Her public confession of her love for Jem at his trial drains her both emotionally and physically and when Jem's release is announced she breaks down and lapses into a delirious fever.

Though Jem is freed, her father is a guilty fugitive. There is no release from this knowledge. The reader, perhaps by this time, so taken in by the mounting pressure of events and sudden happenings, may not recall that Barton had been appointed the murderer by destiny itself. At a meeting in the Weavers' Club, when grievances against the masters were being aired, the workers' resentment, grief and anger, at the ruthlessness of the masters and their insensitive response to their deprivation, had mounted (176–180) leading to the formation of a retaliatory plan. Collecting a piece of paper, they cut it into small chits, which all looked alike but one was marked. In the darkness each picked up a paper, and then when they lit the gas, each picked up his hat and went his way. Who had picked up the marked paper and was the appointed assassin? (180) It is only much later that we realise that it was Barton. The whole action is a reflection of the growing restlessness of the working class.

Working her way gradually to recovery, Mary has still much to endure. The scene of confession and guilt in the court of 'conscience', finally allows her to rehabilitate her moral being. Whether innocent or guilty, they possibly cannot continue here. Jem is no longer employable. Hence the ending, it is at this moment that one realises that Mary is indeed the central character. The political issues are a period study and capture individual lives as they get caught in the socio-political issues. Gaskell's *North and South* (1855) explores the middle class's dilemma, placing it against a similar background, as does Bronte's *Shirley* (1849). The woman question has many angles to it over and above independence, freedom and equality.

A couple of decades later, Matthew Arnold in *Culture and Anarchy* (1869), explored the class problem crediting the middle classes with vitality but yet holding back his approval of the working class. Gaskell in 1848 is sharper than Arnold in attributing moral goodness to the working class. Mary Barton is a working class heroine, who opens up fresh ground for the Victorian women. And yet, unlike several of the others who lose their moral balance in the face of glamour or temptation, Mary does not. The reader wonders as to what is it that holds her back? Is it her instinctive understanding of the class difference? Or is it the influence of her home atmosphere, one full of care, and of sharing and warmth? There is also the fear of wrongdoing. The sorrow that Esther has caused to the family to which Mary has been a witness, most of all it is Margaret who, even if she does not share her attraction for Harry Carson, provides support and Job who is like a wise father figure, who has absorbed all the cares of the world. They, unknowingly to herself as well as to them, protect her by merely being there.

Gaskell weaves the different strands of her narrative together into a configuration of event and meaning. Esther's appearance is one of the punctuation marks that knits different sections together; the Barton home, with its centrality to the story is the next. It is the place which witnessed happiness, loss, fleeing away and return, loneliness and desolation, and finally the confession and the resultant forgiveness. In contrast the Wilson home is in shadows and Mrs. Wilson a shadowy character. Her one moment of greatness is when, towards the end, she refrains from chiding Mary about her relationship with Harry Carson.

Like almost all Victorian novels there is an element of mystery and excitement—Esther's disappearance, Harry's murder, Mary's pursuit of Will, his having moved on toward the ship, a second pursuit—partly futile, delay, reprieve, exhaustion and then illness. The little piece of paper which Esther brings supplies Mary with the identity of the actual murderer leading to a conflict in her mind: father or lover? Betrayal or loss? Her moment of confession of love for Jem during the court trial, is another powerful moment. Can one say that the last section contrasts with the peaceful beginning? Both represent collectivies but the nature and purpose of the gatherings is different. The first was hopeful, filled with the hopes of a new child, health and happiness, but when conflict takes over, each member is torn apart. There is suspicion, distrust, a distancing and several moral battles are being fought between good and evil.

Amidst all this turmoil, amidst politics and trade, glamour and temptation, fear of exile, need to go escape and to return, the silence between father and daughter, the unacknowledged lover and the man who plays with her emotions, Mary remains both the cause of action and agent of redemption. And in this course of events, Mary does not remain a passive, inactive subject. She goes on to become an active agency, rising in the reader's estimate and justifying the naming of the book *Mary Barton*.

References

Gaskell, Elizabeth. *Mary Barton* (1848). London: Penguin Books, 1994.

Jain, Jasbir. "Tales of Growing Up: The Novels of Elizabeth Gaskell" in *Women's Writing : Dialogues with* Patriarchy. Eds. Jasbir Jain and Veena Singh. New Delhi : Creative Books, 2005, 188–196.

Williams, Raymond. "The Industrial Novels" *Culture and Society 1780–1950*. Harmondsworth, Middlesex: Penguin (1958), 1984. 99–119.

— "Thomas Carlyle", *Culture and Society 1780–1950*. Harmondsworth, Middlesex: Penguin (1958), 1984, 85–98.

— "David Hume: Reasoning and Experience", *The English Mind : Studies in the English Moralists Presented to Basil Willey*. Eds. Hugh Sykes Davies and George Watson. Cambridge. Cambridge University Press, 1964. 123–145.

34

Spare Parts in a Human Garage: Technology, Global Power and Human Dignity in Padmanabhan's *Harvest*

Urmil Talwar

> The medium, or process, of our time—electronic technology—is reshaping and restructuring patterns of social interdependence and every aspect of our personal life. It is forcing us to reconsider and re-evaluate practically every thought, every action, and every institution formerly taken for granted. Your education, your government, your family, your neighbourhood, your job, your relation to 'the others.' And they're changing dramatically. (6)

The above statement from Marshall McLuhan's (1967) classic *The Medium is the Message* marks the beginning of the social effects of digital and electronic technology and Manjula Padmanabhan's play *Harvest* is a critique of the use of technology to exploit and to treat the human organ as a commodity by the west. With technological advancement in biomedical science in transplanting human organs for the benefit of human beings initially, on humanitarian grounds, the organs from corpses were used. Later, the rich diseased west began exploiting the third world population with a lure of money and material comforts and the poor began selling their body organs to provide subsistence to their families. This paper is a reading of Padmanabhan's play that depicts how advancement in technology, in computer mediated communication and in medical science, has made the west more powerful and rendered the third world jobless, losing their relationships, their interactions with society, and even their bodies for materialistic gains. Padmanabhan suggests that the play is based on the theme "of age cannibalising youth in quest of longevity" (106). It is about an impoverished family living in the slum area in Mumbai. An embittered unemployed youth Om Prakash who cares for his family has lost his job of a clerk. Desperate for money he signs a contract to sell his body organs for the basic amenities of life. The idea for writing the play, writes Padmanabhan, germinated from the sight of men "an odd assortment of strollers, wearing *pajamas*, dressing-gowns and sterile gauze mouth masks ... recovering from kidney transplant surgery", in Chennai and this event was reported in the newspaper, "the way in which sudden wealth distorted the lives of donors, how a man might sell his kidney or his wife's kidney for Rs 20,000, how the money would inspire the man to marry a second time, perhaps selling the second wife's kidney too" (106). Making easy money, living privileged healthy life without an effort to work makes the poor sell their body organs. The amount of money which they will get is that they can never dream of, nor they can ever earn through years of toil and hard labour. This voluntary decision is propelled by the promise of millennial capitalism that promises magical means to overcome poverty. The third world is seduced to sell body organs—a kidney or a cornea, and in this play his whole body—to solve their monetary problems. Technology that should be used in service of society, for its betterment is now being used to exploit the third world. The trade in human organs is taken up by Padmanabhan, to reveal dehumanisation, the disruption of human interaction and loss of human dignity. In her article, "Manjula Padmanabhan's *Har-*

vest: Global Technoscapes and the International Trade in Human Body Organs", Gilbert illustrates that the play focuses on "the global spread of late capitalist technology [and it's] significant risks...Manjula Padmanabhan's *Harvest*, locates these risks as intensely intimate and yet thoroughly social through a chilling drama about transnational flows in two distinct but related areas; biomedical technology and digital technology including virtual reality" (125).

Padmanabhan raised the Indian English drama to an unprecedented level of recognition as she is the first Indian to achieve international fame for her fifth play *Harvest* that won the first prize in the Onassis International Cultural competition for theatrical plays about futuristic society in 1997. Three parallel strands can be discerned in the play. First, the role of technology in the dramatisation of the play and the effect of technology on human life; second is the disruption of family life and values and marital relationships; and third is the relationship of the powerful first world with the poverty-stricken third world. The play is a criticism of the willingness of the third world to be exploited for the newness and glamour of the first world that soon changes into despair and desolation. As the title suggests the third world healthy human body is harvested, like land, for its human organs. The term 'harvest' borrowed from agriculture is indicative of the rich yield of the soil used for feeding human beings. Similarly, the harvest from the third world healthy human body is used for rehabilitating the diseased first world body for financial gains. This later developed into a means of subsistence for the needy sections of the third world countries. The impoverished and disenfranchised population of the third world countries is lured with a promise of healthy food and hygienic conditions along with undreamt amounts of money to sell their organs. This industry gained further impetus with the discovery of immuno-suppressant drugs as cyclosporine which helps all bodies to accept the donor's organs. The drug makes it highly improbable that the organ will be rejected by the buyer.

The twentieth century is a period of technological revolutions in all fields of life. In the nineteen eighties technology began to make its mark in theatre and then one marvelled at the shows which used light, sound and sets that were computer generated. Later with technology at their service, images were conjured by theatre makers and sounds were being fed directly into the ears of the audiences. Multimedia became the buzzword. With the growth of media and digital technologies theatre makers were facing unprecedented new challenges and opportunities. The electronic media gave rise to "virtual reality"—a reality projected by media that is willingly accepted by audiences. The boundary between "fiction and social reality is an optic illusion" (1991:149), writes Donna Haraway. Quinn notes that "We've narrowed the gap between fantasy world and reality [...] the border no longer real" (1993:106).

Writers in the field of critical theory and creative writing have raised questions regarding the effects of science and technology on society, societal institutions and social relationships. In a collection of essays on the relationship between the fields of literature and literary criticism and those of science and technology, Davenport poses certain questions regarding this relationship "Does mechanization affect human values, and if so, how? To what extent and under what conditions should we allow technology to shape our definition of ourselves as a civilization or as a species?" (227). Several contemporary writers, one of whom is Manjula Padmanabhan, have focussed on the deterministic aspects of technology and its role in dehumanising interactions and individuals. For basic amenities and healthy living Om Prakash, the unemployed youth, signs a Faustian contract with Mephistopheles, the Interplanta Services to sell his body organs. Om Prakash and his family do not realise that signing this contract will shove them towards their own destruction.

This three-act play is set in Bombay 2010 to look at the greedy soulless world. Using many technological props for depicting the futuristic setting of the stage, Padmanabhan has employed scientific gadgets for seducing and policing the third world donor. Om Prakash, the donor and his family receive a "contact module" from the Interplanta Services to be in touch with his beneficiary. The module hangs from the ceiling "a white, faceted globe, at least three feet in diameter. It looks like a Japanese lantern, unlit" (I. i. 18). Ginni, an irresistible gorgeous a young blonde in California appears on the screen. She is "beautiful, in a clear eyed, unequivocal manner, exuding a youthful innocence and radiant purity" (I. ii. 24), never physically present on stage, yet controls every aspect of their lives—who they meet? What and when they eat? Who comes to their house? Who uses their toilet? To whom they sell water? There is a sinister control over each and every action of the donor and his family. It is later reported that the contact module recorded each and every happening and communication in the house "even when the Module was off" (III. ii. 94). The remoteness and severe surveillance of the controller Ginni fill the audience and the reader with fear for she is a monster whom the third world donor cannot fight. Through this remoteness of the receiver, Padmanabhan demonstrates the tensions underlying the predatory relationship between the donor and receiver. The guards and the agents are like the robots that channelise resources from donors to receivers and violate human dignity. It is the human dignity, the human soul, the self that is predicated. The mechanical existence of characters revealed through their ruthless precision and efficiency is a mark of total dehumanisation.

The contact module aids to intervene in the third world, which is supposedly only squalor and dirt, without setting foot on the geographical locale. The organs are purchased and the donor is given healthy food and hygienic conditions without taking the risk to visit their dwellings. When during the first contact Ginni comes to know that Om is sharing toilet facilities with forty other families, she exclaims, "But that's shocking! ... I can't accept that .... It's wrong! It's disgusting! I mean, it's unsanitary!" (I. ii. 28). Interplanta Services is directed to install a toilet in their home the same day. Their kitchen too was transformed and the traditional stove and other things were replaced with a new cooking device and bottles of multi-coloured pellets (I. i. 15). Jaya who is disgusted with all this tells Jeetu, her brother-in-law, that all natural food is replaced with "goat shit pills and some strange powders ... and–its' all measured out you see, I couldn't take a portion without having to explain" (I. iii. 33). In the next scene, two months later, the house is transformed and fitted with all kinds of electrical and electronic gadgets, TV set, a computer terminal, mini-gym, AC, two cubicles containing bathroom and toilet, sofa-cum-bed and a dining table. They have their own remote source electrical connection. Finally the self-sufficient Video Couch in which the mother locks herself to enjoy a thousand TV channels.

The social relationships are also devalued. Madhu Jain in her review describes it "Savage, Swiftian ... play is an allegory about relationships". One finds a complete breakdown of the Prakash family as a social unit. To begin with Om has declared Jaya as his sister to the company employing him to donate his organs just to circumvent the precondition of the company that the donor has to be unmarried. When she comes to know of this she angrily "smears off the red kumkum on her forehead" in her torment and succumbs to tears, saying "My forehead burns, when I say that word, sister'"(I. ii. 22). This gesture, usually associated with widowhood, is useful in making the audience critique the mental anguish of Jaya who does this when her husband is still alive. For Jaya the word 'sister' being used in connection to herself and Om is like a death knell to her marital relationship. Her actions create empathy in the audience as a large part of her identity is based on this relationship which accounts for her presence in that home. The pain that this distortion of relationships causes is reinforced when Ma says "But these aren't words! They are people" (I. i. 20). The word 'sister' negates the very foundation of her life and so this gesture forms a point of enquiry into the circumstances forcing Om to take such a decision. For a person like Om, unemployed and struggling to provide two square meals to his family, calling his wife 'sister' on paper is a small price to pay if it ensures financial security. This problematises the desperate situation in modern day society which forces a man to choose between being cut up and dying one day at a time and abject poverty.

Om's mother presents a different attitude to the same predicament. Being an uneducated lower middle class woman, with no means of earning a livelihood, she represents a large chunk of the female population in India whose life is dependent on men. This gives rise to a dual personality, sycophancy toward the bread winner male holding the purse strings and tyranny toward the other dependents. Ma's words are an evidence of this. While Om is addressed with endearments such as "my only delight", Jaya, her daughter-in-law and Jeetu, her younger unemployed son, are abused. 'ho-you', 'barren dog', 'pimping rascal', 'soul's disgrace' are some of the words she uses for them. She survives by developing a sense of detachment to people and surroundings. By the end of the play Ma is "through caring for or about anybody". Even when the guards drag Jeetu away (mistakenly) for his organs, she is interested only in watching TV. The distaste which she feels for her restricted life is well dramatised in the method that she chooses to escape from this kind life. Ma, who appears a tyrant but is herself a victim of a repressive patriarchal society, chooses to cut herself off mentally and physically from it. She increasingly seeks to escape the reality of her life in the *chawl* through technological devices like TV and Video Couch. She is thrilled at the joys of technological bliss and is awed and amazingly satisfied at the fortunes for she believes that Lady Luck is smiling on her and that they will be rich and rich for ever without doing any physical labour. She orders for a Super Deluxe Video Coach. Once she lies down in it, tubes are attached to a recycling and bio-feeding processor that takes care of all her needs. Total silence is her route of escape.

Om has signed the contact but when it's time to be taken to the hospital, he goes into hiding and lets the guards take his brother Jeetu. Om betrays Jeetu and Jeetu betrays Jaya. Jeetu, lured by Ginni, is willing to give his body even after a bout of depression when his eyes are taken away, he says:

> ... I am in place beyond death. I am in a place worse than death. [...] I see you. And through you ... my brother ..., a blaze of fried nerves and straining bones, his eyes like ping-pong balls jittering in their orbits ... . Ma—a dim bundle of red desires bathed in blue haze of radiation my ... Jaya ... I can see your purple blood, ... I can see your heart twitching like an epileptic kitten ... I can't end this poison-vision. I can't sleep, I can't dream, I can't even cry. (III. i. 75)

A little later when the contact module swivelled around to find Jeetu and Ginni beams her video image straight into his mind and he can see what Ginni wants him to see. Jeetu is awed at seeing the image of Ginni and is willing to go back to the clinic to give some more organs, Jeetu says, "Tell me Ginni, tell me what you want [...] Anything, you want is fine, Ginni –" (III. i. 79).

Condemning the selling of one's body organs as a violation of human dignity, Padmanabhan upholds the Kantian idea of human dignity. The seeds of rebellion flower in a 'checkmate' tactic by Om's wife Jaya. Since the very beginning of the play only Jaya opposes Om's decisions (i) to sell the body organs and (ii) to distort the family relationship. In the final act Jaya is the only one on stage to hear the unfamiliar disembodied voice from the contact module as Om is seeking out Ginni to donate his organs. Jeetu betrayed by Om had first lost his eyes and later lured by Ginni donated his body (all his organs) and the mother oblivious of the outside world is plugged into her self-sufficient Video Couch. From the contact module now ensues the disembodied voice of Virgil who, with Jeetu's body, now offers to make Jaya pregnant and is persuading her for childbearing (III. ii. 95). Only when Jaya realises that Ginni is actually an animated front of an old man called Virgil she strikes the contact module to break it. At this the audience too apprehends that Ginni was a bait to hook the fish, this act forces the acceptance of the module as an intrinsic element of the play and pushes the viewer out of the comfort zone of his own life into thinking about people like Om, living desperate lives, where relationships, ethics and even basic humanity are forgotten in the struggle for survival. This shattering also brings into focus, quite strongly, the strength of Jaya who holds on to her dignity and humaneness in spite of all the trauma and disillusionment that she faces. The loud sound and jagged light forces the audience to ask if Jaya (as her name suggests) is victorious over the forces trying to exploit her. The lighted, flickering globe moving around on the stage creates an eerie but contrived atmosphere and this ambience negates any notions of the play being only a piece of evening entertainment and refuses to absolve the audience of active participation.

When Jaya comes to understand that she has been the actual target of the organ buyer, Virgil, and that after using the bodies of both Om and Jeetu, he now intends to impregnate her with his seed mechanically to propagate his race, irrespective of her wishes. Jaya virulently resists lure of money and the seductive escapism of technology, reclaims the human dignity and negotiates with Virgil whose voice she can hear on the contact module and lays down her conditions. On the realisation that she is the most important factor for the implementation of his plans she tells Virgil that she will agree to conceive his child only if he comes to her and goes through the natural process of conjugation and that she will commit suicide if any other means is forced upon her. Saying, 'This game is over! Either you have to erase me and start again or ... . You must accept a new set of rules' (III. ii. 102), Jaya settles down in front of the TV to wait for him. She warn him that she does not want to be disturbed anymore and that she is going to enjoy herself for the first time in her life, eating for three and taking three baths a day. As she does this, a joyous music fills the stage to signify her moment of empowerment. Everybody in the viewer/reader would have gone through a situation of intense dilemma and the relief that comes with the decision to face the consequences, good or bad, of one's actions and beliefs. This connects the audience to the character and her struggle for control over her body and wishes. Jaya's empowerment comes from the fact that she is ready to win by losing. She is willing to go through the agreement but on her terms. She insists if Virgil wants her body he should leave his safe, disease-free environment and come to her in person:

> I know you are stronger than me, you're richer than me. You'll get me in the end ... . But I want you to risk your skin for me. Even though it's only Jeetu's skin—I want you to risk it for me. (III. ii. 100)

When threatened by Virgil to break into the house she knows she cannot fight the powerful, but in one swift stroke she threatens to kill herself and reclaim her body, she says, "The only thing I have left which is still mine is my death. My death and my pride" (III. ii. 101). Jaya resists Virgil's advances and retains her own dignity. One is reminded of the French feminist Helene Cixous's words about how a female physiology, as a source of expression, can be empowering and enabling, "Women must write through their bodies, they must invent the impregnable language that will wreck partitions, classes and rhetoric, regulations and codes, they must submerge, cut through, get beyond the ultimate reserve-discourse ..." (Marks and Courtivron 256). Jaya certainly uses her own body to write her own fate and thus to voice resistance. She threatens Virgil, "I'm holding a piece of glass against my throat. If you force the door, you will push this glass into my throat." (III. ii. 101), thus embracing mortality that Virgil, the representative of the first world, wishes to evade. She frustrates Virgil's plans saying, "I've discovered a new definition for winning. Winning by losing. I win if you lose" (III. ii. 100). Donna Haraway, in "A Manifesto for Cyborgs" writes about how, in today's world of technological advancement, women can voice resistance through an analysis of their situation in inter-national migrations and the increasing rate of male unemployment. Padmanabhan takes the argument a step further by suggesting that a reaction to commodification of women's body might not necessarily lead to compromised situations like exploitative women-headed households but also to a more assertive control by the women over their body. For, even in the face of her husband's unemployment, and the consequent poverty in the family, Jaya refuses to 'migrate' to a foreign land and asserts her power through her control over her body. Throughout the play, Ginni and Virgil, the foreigners buying Jaya's husband's organs, persist in pronouncing her name as 'zhaya' and Om Prakash as 'Auwm Praycash'. But at the end of the play when Jaya finally realises that it is in her power to decide the further implementation of his plans she refuses to talk until he pronounces her name properly. Jaya's unyielding behaviour forces him to bow to her wishes and he pronounces it correctly. Jaya is an assertive female character in the play who candidly speaks her mind to her husband and her brother-in-law with whom she has illicit relations. To her brother-in-law she says, "What do you care of my needs, my desires? [...] A woman wants more than just satisfaction" (I. iii. 32). Padmanabhan does not portray the ideal Indian human relationships instead subverts[1] the sacrificing and caring mother by an unperturbed and totally indifferent mother sitting in front of TV when her son is being taken away for removal of organs. The man-woman relationship is distorted; the Draupadi, Sita, Sati, Ram–Laxman, myths are shattered. Jaya has illicit relations with her brother-in-law Jeetu, and Jeetu is willing to offer his life to the beautiful phantom in the contact module. The two brothers Jeetu and Om are lurching for each other's throat.

A fictitious atmosphere is created by the presence of the contact module, a white faceted globe which looks like a Japanese lantern that lights up, moves in slow circles and also vertically. Throughout the play the characters on stage are seen talking to the image of a beautiful woman called Ginni, the alleged buyer of Om's organs. The movement of the globe disconnects the realistic aspect of the play by drawing attention of the audience towards the illusory nature of economics which society sees as the basis of success. It is also ironic that the people who have the money to buy organs are dependent on those very sellers for their existence. By breaking the wall of suspension of disbelief, intrinsic to realism, this dramatic technique makes it possible for the audience to question the effects of poverty on man. At the end of the play where images are created out of thin air, the shattering of the globe along with the guards shouting for Jaya to open the door are enough to disturb the complacency of the spectator and provoke them into thinking of some kind of intervention to the chaos on stage. It forces the spectator to imagine themselves in Jaya's shoes and feel her desperation though for a brief moment.

This dystopian play ends on an unresolved note and one is left pondering on the question whether 'winning by losing' was the right choice. Does the act of resistance and victory require the death of the exploited people? Can the supremacy of the west laced with power of money and technology be overcome only by death? Should the third world individuals resist such commodification of their body organs? How should they embrace the human dignity which is the fundamental right of all individuals? Should they promote black market in human organs to relinquish the right to human dignity as they have no other assets to sell. The notion of winning by losing is a very perturbing way to define human predicament for third world countries. The dramatisation of the helplessness creates empathy of shared experience with the third world population in the audience and also for Jaya as a woman.

In this age of globalisation one is struck by the loss of individualism. One realises that today the first world and third world are not so much of political categories as they have become economic zones. Om sells his body to the face of a corporation. When questioned by his mother he replies that he does not know the employer or anything about the package but they will spend on him, he is apathetic to the fact whether the buyer is an Indian or an American. The donors, natives of the third world, Om, Jeetu and Jaya are devalued as depositors but it is also shocking to note that the donors, Om and Jeetu, are enthralled by the prospect of selling themselves and being devoured by the capitalistic cannibalistic west. The organs once removed are irreclaimable and the receiver is hardly bothered. For him, the donor's body is "just a spare parts ... garage–" (I. iii. 34) from where he has purchased a part to prolong his life. There is no prospect of reversal of roles here. The play critiques 'neo-cannibalism'[2] presented through mercantile as well as surgical metaphor where privacy and human dignity is at stake.

Benjamin Mosse, Associate Artistic Director of East Coast Artists who had directed more than thirty plays including *Harvest* wrote that this play quite devastatingly illustrates:

> ... the destruction of not only the proverbial old world, but also psychological axioms of nation, culture, tradition and self. With our conquest by globalization, the postmodern economic colonial project is magnified globally; since the click of a button can alter events on the other side of the world instantaneously. Technology radically re-determines time and space, and the political ramifications are horrifying. A frightening by product of economic aggrandizement is replacement of the tangible human with the notional corporation, which has, in law and society, become the surrogate of the individual. That in the play is Ginni.

Notes

1. S. Robert Gnanamony in his article "Paradigms of Subversive Construction in Manjula Padmanabhan's *Harvest*", looks at the subversive characteristics in the play.
2. Nancy Scheper-Hughes (1998:14) an anthropologist, compares the trade in human organs to capitalism and suggests that 'neocannibalism' is to be understood in context of global capitalism where organs do mirror the flow of capital "from South to North, from Third world to First world, from poor to rich, from black and brown to white" (2002:197)

References

Cixous, Helene. 'The Laugh of the Medusa'. In Elaine Marks and Isabelle de Courtivron. Eds. *New French Feminisms*. Amherst: The University of Massachusetts Press, 1980.

Davenport, F. Garvin. "Machines and Sexual Ambience in James Agee's *A Death in the Family*'. In J. W. Slade, & J. Y. Lee (Eds.), *Beyond the two Cultures: Essays on Science, Technology, and Literature*. Ames, IA: Iowa State University Press, 1990, 227–239.

Gilbert, H. "Introduction to *Harvest*" in H. Gilbert (Ed.) *Postcolonial Plays: An Anthology*. New York: Routledge, 2001, 214–16.

Gilbert, H.M. "Manjula Padmanabhan's *Harvest:* Global Technoscapes and the International Trade in Body Organs". *Contemporary Theatre Review*. Routledge, 16: 1, 2006, 123–130.

Gnanamony, S. Robert, "Paradigms of Subversive Construction in Manjula Padmanabhan's *Harvest*" in *New Writings in English*. New Delhi: Swarup and Sons, 2005.

Haraway, Donna. "A Manifesto for Cyborgs: Science, Technology and Social Feminism in the nineteen eighties", *Socialist Review*, 80, (15), 1990, 65–107.

Jain, Madhu. "Review of *Harvest*", *India Today* April 23, 1998.

Jayashree, K. "Studying Aspects of Technique and Language in the Plays of Manjula Padmanabhan" http://mayurigaya.blogspot.com/2012/04/manjula-padmanabhan-techniques-26.html.

Marks, Elaine and de Courtivron, Isabelle. Eds. *New French Feminisms*. Amherst: The University of Massachusetts Press, 1980.

McLuhan, M. *The Medium is the Message*. New York: Random House, (1967) 1993, 6–10.

Padmanabhan, Manjula. (1997), *Harvest*, New Delhi: Kali for Women, 2000.

Pravinchandra, Shital. "The Third-World Body Commodified: Manjula Padmanabhan's Harvest". Internet reference eSharp, Issue 8, 1–17. www.gla.ac.uk\media\media_41208_en.pdf.

Quinn, M. 'Beyond the Valley of Morphs'. *Wired* Premier Issue 1993, 56–59, 106–107.

Scheper-Hughes, Nancy. "The New Cannibalism: A Report on International Traffic in Human Organs.' *New Internationalist*, 1998, 300-14-17. http:\\www.public anthropology.org\Times Past\Scheper-Hughes.htm. (Accessed on Dec. 10, 2013)

— "The Global Traffic in Human Organs,' *Current Anthropology*, 2000, 41(2), 191-224.

Scheper-Hughes and L. Wacquant. eds *Commodifying Bodies*. London: Sage, 9-31.

Sethi, S. "Of a Future Mephistopheles' in *Outlook* 15 Dec. 1997, 97-101.

Slade, J. W. & J. Y. Lee. eds. *Beyond the two Cultures: Essays on Science, Technology, and Literature*. Ames, IA: Iowa State University Press, 1990.

Walker, Nancy. *Feminist Alternatives*. Mississippi: University Press of Mississippi, 1990.

Contributors

Supriya *Agarwal* teaches English in Khandelwal College for Girls at Jaipur. She has researched on nineteenth century fiction.

Madhuri *Chatterjee* has worked for her doctoral degree on *The Theme of Homecoming in John Updike's Work*. Interested in postcolonial writing, Madhuri has also translated from Hindi into English, Dr. Chatterjee teaches English at Subodh College, Jaipur.

Rashmi *Chaturvedi* is on the faculty of English in Kanodia College, Jaipur. After having worked on *The Plays of Archibald Macleish*, she has moved on to expatriate writing.

Savita *Goel* teaches at Savitri Girls College, Ajmer. Her doctoral work is on American drama. Amongst her current interests are feminist writing and literature in regional languages.

Santosh *Gupta* is Associate Professor in the Department of English, University of Rajasthan. Her major interest is in postmodernist and postcolonial writing. Her doctoral work was on Iris Murdoch.

Ranjana *Harish*, Associate Professor, Gujarat University Ahmedabad has worked on *Indian Women's Autobiographies*, Dr. Harish is also interested in New Literatures.

Jasbir *Jain*, Professor of English, University of Rajasthan has written extensively on a wide range of areas—drama, feminist and postcolonial writings. Amongst her forthcoming books is *Women and the Rise of the Novel.*

N.K. *Jain* is on the faculty of English, University of Rajasthan, Jaipur. Dr. Jain has worked for his doctoral degree on American fiction. He also specialises in Language teaching.

Veena *Jain* has recently joined government service. Prior to this she was teaching at Mittal Girls College, Sardarshahr. She has recently completed her doctoral work on the *Male Presence in the Novels of Jean Rhys.*

Priti *Kapoor*, teaches English at Sant Jai Acharya College, Jaipur and is working on her doctoral project on Muriel Spark.

Iqbal *Kaur* was on the faculty of English, School of Correspondence Studies at Panjabi University, Patiala. Dr. Kaur published work an Sylvia Plath, Kamala Das and *Gender and Literature*. She passed away in 1994.

Viney *Kirpal* is Professor of English at Indian Institute of Technology, Powai, Bombay. She has authored *The Third World Novel of Expatriation* (1989) and edited anthologies on *The Novel of the 80s* and *The Girl Child in 20th Century Indian Literature*.

Rama Rani *Lall*, Associate Professor, Department English, University of Rajasthan is the author of *Satiric Fable*. Her current interest is in Tennessee Williams and Indian Writing in English.

Tanuja *Mathur* teaches English at the University of Rajasthan, she has worked on *The Plays of O'Neill* for her doctoral degree.

Mini *Nanda*, Assistant Professor, University of Rajasthan is currently working for her doctoral degree on *Spatial Metaphors in the Novels of Graham Greene.*

Sarla *Palkar* is senior Reader, M.S. University of Baroda, Vadodara. Dr. Palkar has worked on critical theory and has published extensively area.

Sudha *Rai*, Associate Professor, University of Rajasthan has authored S. *Naipaul* and *Homeless by Choice*. Her doctoral work was on the Expatriate Sensibility. Her main interest is in postcolonial writing.

Neelam *Raisinghani* teaches English at Dungar College, Bikaner. She is engaged in research on the Novels of Fanny Burney. She has also translated from Hindi to English.

Krishna *Rathore,* teaches in M.S. Girls College, Bikaner. She has recently completed her work *The Male Mentor in the Victorian Novel: From Burney to Eliot*.

Sarojini, Associate Professor, University of Rajasthan has worked for her doctoral degree on *Autobiography* with special reference to Bertrand Russell. She has interest in Sindhi language writing.

Veena *Singh* Associate Professor at the University of Rajasthan worked for her doctoral degree on Elizabeth Gaskell. Her main interest is in the novels of the Empire including the work of Paul Scott.

Fatima *Sugarwala* teaches English at Rajkot. Her interests lie in feminist writing and drama. Her doctoral work also reflects this interest.

K.V. *Surendran* teaches English at Government Brennan College, Thalassery, Kerala. His areas of interest are twentieth century British Writing.

Urmil *Talwar* teacher English at Government College, Shahpura. Her areas of interest range from narrative explorations to dramatic analysis.

Ashok K. *Tiwari,* Associate Professor, Department of English, University of Rajasthan has specialised in Applied Linguistics. Mr. Tiwari also has interest in translation from Hindi to English.

C. *Vijayshree* is Associate Professor, Osmania University, Hyderabad. She has published on a number of Commonwealth writers, edited a volume on Browning (1995) and contributed to the Routledge *Encyclopedia of Postcolonial Literatures.*

Index